HAPPINESS E

Khurshed holds an M.Sc in Mathematics from IIT Bombay. He is a Parsi and is fondly called Bawa, a nickname he inherited from his IIT days. More than 20 years ago, he decided he would rather teach people how to meditate and make them happy instead of teaching them math and making them miserable. He became an Art of Living teacher and this allowed him to do exactly that and gave him the freedom to explore many of his varied passions.

Dinesh holds a B.Tech in Metallurgy and Material Sciences from IIT Bombay. He'd always wanted to make a difference to the people around him and the world in general. At the age of 21, he became an Art of Living teacher and has taught the secrets of the mind and meditation in more than 30 countries. He is a fitness enthusiast and thoroughly enjoys his daily workouts. He does awesome Yoga. He has a unique, and often, humourous take on current affairs which he prolifically expresses through his tweets.

They live in a beautiful home surrounded by nature in the Art of Living Bangalore Ashram with their friends who are their family, all of whom contribute in some way or other to everything they are involved in.

HAPPINESS EXPRESS

EXPRESS

A JOURNEY TO EVERYDAY WELL-BEING

Khurshed & **Dinesh**
Batliwala Ghodke

Illustrations by
**Gowrishankar Venkatraman, Gauri Gupta,
Abhiram Viswanathan, Susha, Pinpoint Studios and
Trupti Gawde**

First published by Westland Publications Private Limited in 2018
61, 2nd Floor, Silverline Building, Alapakkam Main Road, Maduravoyal,
Chennai 600095

Westland and the Westland logo are the trademarks of Westland Publications
Private Limited, or its affiliates.

ISBN: 9789387894198

10 9 8 7 6 5 4 3 2 1

Typeset by SÜRYA, New Delhi

Printed at Manipal Technologies Limited, Manipal

CONTENTS

PREFACE

People often ask us how we manage to stay so happy and what our secret is. This book is the answer.

The recipe for happiness involves five major ingredients, and that's how this book is structured. The chapters are quite independent of each other and you could read them in any order.

Do you have trouble resting? Do you feel tired and worn out a lot? The chapters on Sleep and Meditation are for you. One of the best things you can do to get that elusive smile could well be simply closing your eyes. We can almost guarantee that following the steps in these chapters will dramatically improve the quality of your sleep, as well as your life.

Feeling unfit and unwell? Read the chapters on Food and Exercise. Being physically active and eating healthy, tasty meals can make a huge difference to your well-being.

Feeling stagnated? Head to the chapters on the Brain, Learning and Focused Mind Mapping. There's an incomparable joy in understanding and learning something new. Quite a few adults deny themselves this pleasure because they think they cannot learn new things or are afraid of making mistakes. That's where these chapters can come to your rescue.

Do you tend to forget things? Do you wish your memory

could function better? The chapter on Memory unravels the mystery of how our memories work and explores two memory enhancement methods: The Memory Palace and The Spaced Repetition System (SRS).

Keep getting into trouble because of habitually postponing stuff you have to do? The chapter on Procrastination provides insights into the working of your mind and includes an approach we call the S.T.A.R. technique to help you get over this and other infuriating habits.

Want some quick tips on becoming happier? Read Happiness Sutras. This is your go-to chapter whenever you feel low. If you are doing everything right, yet somehow not finding yourself in the best of spirits, perusing this chapter should help you out and restore your smile in a jiffy.

We were recently asked what our dream was. We replied: we are living our dream!

Life is a dream. This book ensures it doesn't turn into a nightmare. Welcome aboard the Happiness Express!

All the very best.

Jai Gurudeva!

Love,

Bawa & Dinesh

ACKNOWLEDGEMENTS

We have the Brobdingnagian fortune of being blessed by our beloved Gurudev Sri Sri Ravi Shankar. We are grateful for the magical, enchanting world of the Art of Living that we are overjoyed to be a part of.

Dinesh is the solidity of the Himalayas and the love of a few saints, rolled into one. Life is absolutely incredible because of him.

My mom passed away while this book was only an idea. There's a little story about her and me in this book. Mom, wherever you are, I love you! Dad, you are in here as well. Thank you for everything. I love you, too.

I thank Dinesh's parents for their love and support, and the car.

Thanks to Abhiram, Salman and Chakri for all the work that you guys so cheerfully do, both online and offline, allowing Dinesh and me the luxury of time.

To Gowrishankar for helping when it was most needed; without him most of the illustrations in this book would not have been possible.

To Lalit for making me enjoy exercise.

To Dr Ankita Dhelia for her osteopathic treatments. This book wouldn't have been possible if she hadn't used her extraordinary skills to get me out of bed after my back injury.

To Devang for being the initial inspiration for us to even think we could write a book.

To Bhanu Didi for her music, love, sweet gentleness with everyone, and the coolest, cutest quote for our cover!

To Arvind and Srivi for ensuring we look as great as we feel.

To Susha for the beautiful suitcase on the cover and her ideas and insights.

To Harish Ramachandran for his laughter and ideas and his wife Bharathy for the timely help.

To Rajesh (Myla) Krishnamurthy for all the pointers we used in the Memory chapter.

To Atin and Pooja for the title of this book.

To Rosy for making us fly!

To Sowmya for ensuring that Rosy could make us fly.

To Manak for guiding us.

To Perviz, my sister, and Carl, her husband, for being there, and Aarman, Ahun and Bhuvana, their children, for all the problems and craziness they create.

To Shiv, Sakshi, JD, Tanu and Anya for all the great food and silly jokes.

To Chakri for the photos in the Memory chapter.

To Mayur and Esha for celebrating their birthdays and anniversaries with us (inside joke, don't bother).

To Hanoz and Rimpy for their supreme generosity.

To Kapil, Puja and darling Aarna for the good times in London.

To Uppi, Manisha, Dhara, Sourav, Rupal, Saleel, Rajesh, Shilpa, Rohit, Shibani and Rashmin for the silent encouragement (I wish they had been more vocal though).

To Esha, Santosh and Kamatchi for reading the book aloud to me, so I could hear how it sounded in order to edit it better.

To Harshal for singing.

To Chirag for dancing and being such a good sport.

As always, thanks to Prama and Ranji Bhandari for sharing their beautiful home with us and for the fantastic food and superb conversations; Shavina for all the pampering; and Abhay Joshi for those little and big things that make our life easier. To Chaital, Milan and their families for all the lovely times.

To Amarja, Raghavan, Anjana and Vivek for the lovely food and all the fun.

To Jai and Pramod Khanna for taking such good care of us in Mumbai. To Nisheeta for being the silent, systematic force in the city, making each visit special.

To Adi Kabra for being our man Friday in Hyderabad. He is actually Monday, Tuesday, Wednesday and Thursday as well. We give him the weekend off.

To Dr Rangana Chaudhary for teaching us EFT and NLP and being such a dear friend.

To Anuraag Agarwal, CEO of Amar Chitra Katha, for stepping in and helping us at the last minute with some of the beautiful illustrations in this book. To Neel from The Amar Chitra Katha Studio for coordinating on many of the illustrations we have used. To Gauri Gupta, Shrungi Panchal, Pankhuree, Jordan and Sakshi who cheerfully gave their time to draw and redraw things just the way I wanted them.

To Nirmal, Poonam, Avinash and Mahika for being a part of so many adventures with us.

To Ram and Sita in Jakarta for sharing their lovely home with us. We finished a huge part of this book while staying with them.

To all my chefs at Café Vishala—Kamesh, PD, Kuldeep, Prasad, Carlotta and a host of others—who provided me with the much-needed food and drink whenever required.

To Bali, all the people who accompanied us for the Vigyan Bhairav course there, and Louisa for graciously allowing our mad bunch to stay at her place. It was highly rejuvenating and so much fun!

To Konstantin and Villa Sonya in Bulgaria for giving me the time and space I needed to put the finishing touches to this book.

To Debasri from Amazon-Westland for saying 'Yes'... again!

A deep gratitude to all those who've read bits and pieces of the book and suggested ideas to make it even better.

And to you, dear reader, thank you for buying this book and reading it. Enjoy the Happiness Express!

Jai Gurudeva!
Love,
Bawa & Dinesh

Chapter 1

BRAIN

The brain is only 2% of the body. Yet our genes accord it great importance. Roughly 50% of the information in our genes is devoted to the brain. The rest is about the remaining 98% of our body.

Many ancient civilisations didn't agree with our genes, though. The ancient Greeks apparently considered the brain a 'secondary' organ, whose only function was to cool the heart. Herophilus and Erasistratus believed otherwise. After studying the brain and a few of its structures, these legendary physicians made a dramatic observation. According to them, human intelligence was possibly linked to the 'convolutions of the neocortex'. We now know that it is these convolutions (folds) that result in the computational power of the brain, owing to their large surface area. Unfortunately, the reigning physicians at the time rejected these findings. If they had bothered to investigate these insights further, it could have changed the history of neuroscience forever.

Cut to the first century AD, when the Europeans believed that the brain was nothing but a cold, moist organ made up of sperms. However, by the time of the Renaissance, the brain was elevated to being the 'seat of the soul'. Leonardo da Vinci dissected many brains in search of this elusive seat. He never found it, though he made a number of detailed diagrams of the brain from different angles.

In 1664 the famous English doctor Thomas Willis published *The Anatomy of the Brain*, by which time terms like cerebrum, cerebellum, medulla were already being used. He used India Ink injections to figure out cerebral circulation of blood, which laid the foundation of neurology as we know it today.

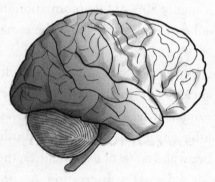

The Brain

Ancient Indians were well aware of the supreme importance of the brain and were performing complicated brain surgeries thousands of years ago. Contrast this with the Egyptians and the Greeks, who would pour milk in both ears if the head (brain) was bleeding.

Even though the brain is only 2% of the mass of the body, it uses a whopping 20% of the blood and oxygen produced in the body. It is 73% water and more than 60% fat (you do the math). In addition, 25% of the cholesterol of the body is found in the brain, where it plays many vital functions. Through its various parts and by receiving information from the rest of the body and the environment, the brain coordinates thought and voluntary action, plus posture, balance, coordination, speech and other movements, to ensure smooth and balanced muscular activities. Most importantly, the brain is involved in regulating and maintaining vital bodily functions such as heart rate, breathing, sleep and digestion.

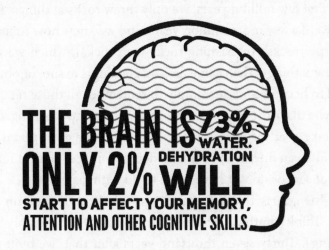

THE BRAIN IS 73% WATER. ONLY 2% DEHYDRATION WILL START TO AFFECT YOUR MEMORY, ATTENTION AND OTHER COGNITIVE SKILLS

More than one lakh chemical reactions take place in the brain every second. Electrical energy like that of a thunderstorm is discharged every few moments on a microscopic scale. The brain guzzles over one thousand litres of blood each day while performing this tumultuous, frenzied activity to maintain what we call life.

There's another role our brain plays. It allows us to think, learn, and remember whatever we've learnt.

Survival?!

As our remote ancestors descended from the trees into the savannah, they had only two survival strategies before them. Get stronger or get smarter. We chose the latter, and we took over the planet.

While other species tried adding muscle to their bodies, we added neurons to our brain. Our progress was super slow. For the first few million years, we only threw rocks at things. Fast forward a few more million years, and we knew how to make sharper rocks (by bashing rocks with rocks), which we still threw at things. Then came fire and cooking. I'm sure our brain had to become smarter simply to remember all those recipes. Maybe that's the reason we chose smart instead of strong. Did we take over the planet just so we could have great pizza? (It could be an interesting topic to debate on: Is evolution really about sex, or does it have more to do with taste?)

Then, forty thousand years ago, we abruptly took up the arts. Think painting, jewellery and sculpture (and possibly fine dining). Thirty seven thousand years after that, we built the Pyramids. Five thousand years later, we landed on the moon. We didn't make too many trips there—after all, there's no food on the moon ☺

We learned and learned and learned. Which brings us to…

How Does Learning Happen?

There's quite an orchestration that goes on in our heads to make all those neurons do what they are supposed to do. Learning happens through a combination of stimuli. When we hear, see, touch, smell, taste, read, write, practise, discuss, teach, or feel emotions, we learn.

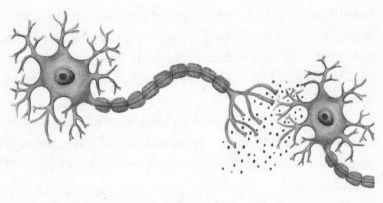

Neurons

Our brain is home to a hundred billion neurons. Each can grow 2,000-10,000 fibrous structures called dendrites. The neurons and dendrites interact with each other and pass information through chemical and electrical signals called synapses. The volume of these interactions surpass the number of elementary particles in the universe! Ancient Indians probably referred to this when they said '*Yatha pinde tatha brahmande*' more than 8,000 years ago. (The proverb means 'Whatever is in the microcosm, i.e. the body, is also in the macrocosm, i.e. the universe.')

यथा पिण्डे तथा ब्रह्माण्डे ॥

yathā pinde thathā brahmānde

For any learning to happen, in the dense, fibrous neural network of the brain, some specific neurons and dendrites would need to communicate with each other through synapses, forming a kind of circuit. This circuit would represent some type of information—it could be your name, where you live, how to bake a cake, how to solve a differential equation, how to say 'I love you' in Tamil, or anything else, depending on the subject. In your lifetime, your brain will process around one quadrillion bytes of information. That's 1 followed by 15 zeroes! That's a lot.

This means that we have an almost infinite capacity to learn. Because learning a particular bit of information is simply the ability to create a neural circuit, we can indeed learn anything!

Even as you read this, masses of neurons and dendrites are swelling, swaying, slithering and splitting within you. The neurons are breaking some connections, moving around, and making new ones. Others are staying put, strengthening their existing connections.

Newly formed synapses are fragile and can dissolve quickly. This is the process of forgetting. The stuff you do again and again is what makes the neurons that are wired together fire together, fortifying their connections. This makes remembering easier and allows you to do certain things without thinking, almost effortlessly.

What's 5 times 5?

See, you didn't even have to think. The moment you read that line, 25 popped up in your head. That's a very strong neural connection.

What did you have for breakfast yesterday?

Unless it was a really memorable meal, you may have to think about this one before you get an answer. The neural connection is there, but you require some effort to get it to fire.

What did you eat for dinner on 21 September last year?

Chances are you have completely forgotten about this.

You may have not even had dinner that day. This is a case of dissolved connections. It's unnecessary information that your brain has decided to delete.

This gives us an insight into how our memories work, and we will explore memory in a later chapter.

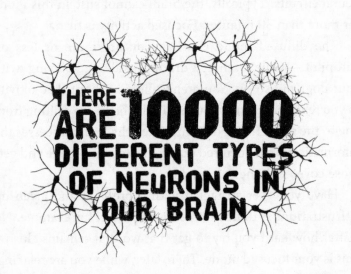

Be Careful About What You Do

Neural connections form for exactly what you do. Watching someone solve a physics problem would create circuits that make you good at exactly that—watching someone else solve the problem. If you want to learn and remember how to solve physics problems, you would have to do them yourself.

Be careful about what you are doing, because you are becoming really good at doing it. Watching TV the whole day will make you really good at watching TV. Not a very interesting life skill to develop. Practise makes one perfect, but wrong practice will make you perfectly wrong.

The Anatomy of Inspiration

According to Dr Barbara Oakley, professor at Oakland University, the brain uses two modes of learning—focused and diffused. The former is when you actively learn things from the external stimuli around you, which results in the creation of neural circuits. Typically, the brain cannot sustain this mode for more than 30 minutes. Focused activity is tiring.

The diffused mode is when you are more or less on autopilot—while bathing, driving, walking, playing with your dog, and so on. You aren't thinking about that activity as you're doing it, and thoughts in the brain are drifting from one to the next. This is the time when the brain processes the information it has acquired during the focused mode and gets those coveted flashes of insight.

Have you ever struggled with a problem and given up in frustration? A difficult crossword puzzle, for example. No matter how hard you try to get that word, it remains elusive. This is your focused mode. Then, later, while you are relaxing, an Aha! moment happens, as the solution suddenly dawns upon you from nowhere. This is your brain in its diffused state. This is when it actually works to solve problems, making the necessary connections, and is at its intelligent best. However, for it to come up with insights and solutions, it needs time.

Be careful not to confuse entertainment with the diffused mode. When you are playing Candy Crush Saga, watching a movie or surfing the net, your focused brain is engaged and you are not in the diffused mode.

To clarify, simply staring out of your window is diffused mode. Looking for something as you stare out of the window is focused mode.

Some of the greatest inventions in history have a certain pattern to them. It's mostly a vision, dream or event that catalyses an insight. Kekulé dreamt of a snake eating its own tail and solved the problem of the benzene ring structure. Archimedes was in the middle of a bath when the Eureka moment happened. Everyone knows about Newton and the apple. We could go on, but you get the drift.

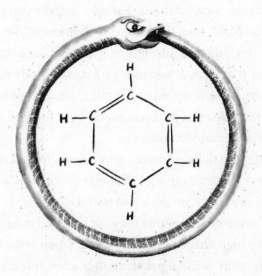

Kekulé's Dream

The anatomy of inspiration is to persevere with a problem until the point of saturation, keeping the focused brain engaged. Then, completely let go and do something relaxing so that the diffused brain can take over. Ninety times out of a hundred, you would end up with a fantastic solution when you return to the problem. This solution, you'd realise, was always out there but you somehow never perceived it.

Meditation is a brilliant practice for encouraging diffused

brain activity. Ancient Indians knew this, and India of yore was possibly the only civilisation where science and spirituality went hand-in-hand. Science was the exploration of the outside, and spirituality the adventure of the inside. All our ancient Indian scientists were saints.

For effortless learning, you need to engage both modes of the brain. This means never study or work on a problem for more than 45 minutes at one go. Decide how long you want to engage your focused mode. I would suggest you start with 20 minutes. Make sure, don't exceed 45 minutes. Set an alarm and turn off all distractions. Work and focus hard on the task at hand for that time. If you use the focused mode for longer, you will usually end up wasting your time as your mind will drift off. Better to relax for a while after your focused work and let your diffused mode take over.

To enter the diffused mode, get up from your desk, stretch and relax for about 20 minutes. This gives your brain some time off. Then return to your work and try tackling something else. This will buy even more time for your diffused mode and you have a very high chance of striking gold when you eventually get back to your original problem after a few more breaks.

For me, a focused effort of 45 minutes, followed by playing the piano, heading out for a walk or listening to music for about half an hour, works best. Rinse and repeat and I can go on for hours.

Don't postpone coming back to the problem for too long. Else, those delicate synapses will dissolve and you'll forget a lot. You will then have to start all over again. It's quite a game, and you will need to figure out the perfect length of the break that's suitable for you. For Dinesh, me, and most people we know, 24-48 hours is optimum. Wait longer than that, and it's like hitting the reset button.

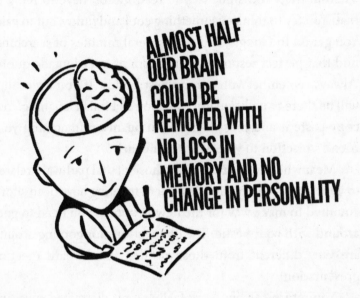

ALMOST HALF OUR BRAIN COULD BE REMOVED WITH NO LOSS IN MEMORY AND NO CHANGE IN PERSONALITY

Do ONE *Thing*

You're sitting at your computer, creating a presentation for an upcoming board meeting. You have to detail the work in progress of a project you are in charge of. You have various spreadsheets open, plus a couple of reports on hand and a slew of related emails from your teammates. You treat this project with paramount importance, considering you have only ten minutes to talk about a year's worth of effort of around thirty people. You are completely involved in your work.

While you're doing this, millions and millions of neural connections are being forged in your brain. Some are gaining strength, while others are breaking off as you chug along with your work. This is your brain in focused mode.

Then a notification pops up. It's a photo from your best friend, captioned, 'I think you're suffering from a lack of Vitamin Me!' You smile as you read it. You have to reply to that. You try to think of something cool and funny, but in vain. You get on to Google, and after several minutes of searching, find that perfect response in the form of a readymade quote: 'Always remember you are my best buddy. If you ever fall, I will be there to pick you up… as soon as I finish laughing.' You copy-paste it and press 'Send'. You beam on imagining your friend's reaction to your witty comeback.

Meanwhile, in your brain, all those neural pathways related to your work, presentation and board meeting have been short-circuited to make way for the new networks you need to goof around with your bestie. The connections for goofing around are very different from those needed for a board meeting presentation.

You return to your work feeling a bit distracted, awaiting a reply from your friend. The goof-around circuits are now being replaced with work circuits. Just as you finish another slide, pop comes another notification. The neurons in your head are going crazy. 'Does he want to work or goof around?' It's a very different environment up there for these two modes.

As your neurons wrestle with themselves, your phone beeps again. This time it's a message from the love interest of your life. Of course, you have to reply to that right away! Your neurons are now forced to enter love mode, and those poor little fellows end up in a tangled mess. Making you end up in a mess.

The bottom line is that there is a very real chemical, electrical and physical change that occurs in the brain when we do a particular task. If we hop to another task, it triggers a full-on change. Our brain cannot and does not know how to jump between these changes effectively. Remember when your mother told you to do *one* thing at a time? She was right. Studies upon studies have shown that people who think they can multitask actually can't and don't. They have poor recall, hazy understanding, slumped productivity, and so on. Their cognitive ability is compromised.

INFORMATION IN THE BRAIN TRAVEL AT SPEEDS FASTER THAN A FORMULA 1 RACE CAR – 431 KMS/HR

While in focused mode, ensure you are shielded from all distractions. One of the biggest things you can do is switch off all notifications on your gadgets. You can check your messages, emails, whatevers after you are done with what is at hand. Those little pop-up windows are the bane of creativity and productivity.

On iOS there is a button with a half moon. It turns off all notifications, phone calls and alerts. Use it while working.

Remember to turn it off when you're done with your work. Android has a slightly more complicated Do Not Disturb feature. Google keeps changing theirs in the different versions of their OS. Read up about it to make sure it works the way you want it to. I hope that in some later iteration of operating systems, there will be a button on the screen that turns off all these pop-ups for a prescribed amount of time. Use this little trick and watch your productivity soar to unbelievable levels.

Your neurons will definitely love you for it.

THE BRAIN'S MEMORY CAPACITY IS AROUND
A QUADRILLION BYTES
THE SAME AMOUNT WOULD BE REQUIRED
TO STORE EVERYTHING ON THE INTERNET TODAY

Chew Gum, Learn Better

Would it be easier to lift 5 kg or 10 kg? Common sense will tell you, the answer is obviously 5 kg. Common sense doesn't quite work when it comes to the brain. It is counter intuitive, but the brain loves to be overloaded with information for it to learn, understand and remember better. The more things sizzle, fizz and sputter up there, the better it functions. The more senses that are involved in the learning process, the more detailed and accurate the comprehension and recall.

Our brain evolved in a very multisensory environment. Survival depended on the keenness of all the five senses. More stimulation and more activity meant better learning.

An interesting experiment required a bunch of students to

chew gum of a particular flavour while studying. These kids were then tested on the material they had worked on. If they chewed gum of that same flavour while writing the exam, they recalled better. The recall was not as good if they didn't chew gum or chewed gum of a different flavour.

Cognitive psychologist Richard Mayer is known for his experiments on multisensory learning. In one of them, he made a group listen to a lecture about a particular subject, made another group watch it, and allowed one more group to both watch as well as listen to it. The third group consistently outperformed the other two in its ability to cognise and recall the subject matter.

Dr John Medina, a teacher of molecular biology, once sprayed perfume on the wall of his classroom before he took a lecture there. He then gave the same lesson to another batch of students but didn't spray the perfume. He later tested both batches on that lecture in a room sprayed with the same perfume. The class who had studied in the perfumed room did significantly better than the other. Every time he repeated this experiment, he got the same results.

When you involve more of your senses in the learning process, you assimilate better and your understanding of the subject matter is superior. You recall more accurately and in greater detail, and you remember things for longer.

In the film *Merry Andrew*, Danny Kaye's character teaches a bunch of kids the basics of geometry in a song-and-dance sequence. While wiggling away, he croons, 'The square of the hypotenuse of a right triangle is equal to the sum of the squares of the two adjacent sides.' Many other geometrical fundas found their way into this little ditty. I watched this movie as a child and still remember the song. It helped sort out the basics of geometry for me. I wish Danny had sung a separate number on trigonometry and organic chemistry as well. My life would have been so much easier.

Vision is our most dominant sense. It takes up more than half of our brain's resources. No wonder visual information is such a powerful learning aid. Pictures, especially moving pictures (animations), are an incredibly powerful media for learning.

Hollywood and Bollywood spend billions creating films that entertain and enthrall. If they'd use some of their creativity and a bit of that money to produce movies that teach physics, math and the like, the learning quotient of the planet would rise dramatically. Who wouldn't want to see Spielberg's Trilogy: *Geometry Wars*, *The Polygon Strikes Back* and *The Return of the Triangle*—a long line ago, in a dimension far, far away…

Think of all the life lessons you've learned and never forgotten. It's likely that a combination of 4-5 senses and a host of strong emotions were involved at the time you learned them. Add in some emotions to as big a mix as possible of the senses, and you can bet that the learning will be cemented into your system.

WORHJKSDFGJKFDS and the Brain

You are walking along in the jungle, admiring the scenery, thanking God that civilisation is far away, praying for some nice pizza. Then there is a sudden movement, out of the ordinary, which you spy from the corner of your eye. There is an immediate change in your entire body-mind system, as your brain gears you up to either fight whatever happens to be there or run away from it.

You start to feel cold in the pit of your stomach, your eyes are suddenly able to see much more detail, your hands and legs begin to get warm as blood gets drained from the stomach to your extremities to prepare for fight or flight. Your heart beats faster to pump more and more blood into the system. If the brain deems the danger intimidating enough, it will release blood even from itself. This is a question of survival. While vital functions are maintained, everything else in the body and brain that could be shut down is shut down. This is what we call fear. It's why a person who is afraid can't think straight. They simply don't have the resources in their system to do so.

You have to understand that fear—feeling cold in the stomach, heart beating faster, sweating as blood moves to your hands and feet, etc.—is simply your brain readying your body for a fight or a sprint.

Three things can happen now.

First, you realise there was nothing to worry about. It was only a big bird. It caws at you and flies off. In a few moments, the fear recedes. You start to think clearly again and relax as blood from the extremities finds its way back to where it was withdrawn from. In a few minutes, the episode is over and you are back to normal, possibly feeling a little drained, and maybe the alertness still lingers until you reach what you believe is a safe area.

Second, there is a threat, but something you can easily deal with. A short scuffle and an animal soul is on its way to the hereafter. Again, the same cool-down period as above. This time, you might feel drained, and strangely energised as you might start cooking up a story to tell your family... 'You know what happened as I was walking through the jungle?!

A worhjksdfgjkfd attacked me and I killed it. This is because I listened to my mother and drank milk and listened to my father and exercised...' and so on.

Third, it's big and dangerous. It's a vpmrieaghlok. And it looks hungry. You run as fast as you can to safety. Either you make it and the usual cool down is initiated again... or you don't. And nothing really matters much anymore.

Did you know that the cool down from the hyper alert state of fear to normalcy happens in a very short time frame? Just a few minutes, that's it. This is how we have evolved over thousands of years. Our brains are wired to handle intense periods of short-term stress.

You must have heard about superhuman feats people are capable of when they or their loved ones are in danger. This is the brain and body doing what they know best, to ensure our continued survival on the planet.

So far, so good. Fast forward to the present.

These days, we feel threatened too. These threats are not from worhjksdfgjkfds or vpmrieaghloks. But it could be from our bosses, mothers-in-law, or a traffic cop. You may be nervous standing on a stage or making a presentation before a bunch of people. You may feel jumpy writing that exam or appearing for a job interview. Unfortunately, our brains cannot distinguish between a worhjksdfgjkfd and a disgruntled boss. All it does is perceive danger. As soon as that feeling of being unsafe is registered, the brain goes about its business. It presses the buttons to drain the stomach of blood and send it to the extremities. And fear takes over.

LOW FAT DIETS CAN FORCE YOUR BRAIN TO EAT ITSELF

When you're at the receiving end of your boss's fury in their cabin, your brain and body insist that you punch them (fight) or run away (flight). Both not very good strategies in this situation.

The brain feels cornered and still thinks vpmrieaghlok and goes about figuring out primitive survival strategies. You are overcome with fear and simply cannot perform. As the situation intensifies, the brain feels even more threat. This means that more of the thinking, coherent brain is shutting down. What happens next is irrational behaviour. You storm off, swear, stop responding... This is really not your fault; it is being created by evolution.

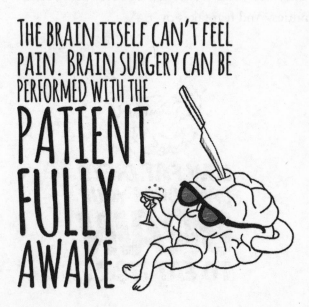

THE BRAIN ITSELF CAN'T FEEL PAIN. BRAIN SURGERY CAN BE PERFORMED WITH THE PATIENT FULLY AWAKE

Here's another scenario. You are in a bit of trouble at work. Nothing serious, just a low-level threat. You then realise you have forgotten your spouse's birthday. Depending on how long you have been married and how your relationship with your spouse is right now, this could be a low- or high-level threat. Plus, you need to finish a report, answer some important emails, pay your bills, see a dentist—all mostly low-level threats. The brain continuously churns out a cocktail of chemicals to keep you on the edge, just getting ready for fight or flight, but not quite. As you can imagine, not enough blood in some places and too much blood in other places for a prolonged period of time is going to hurt you in the long run. This is stress.

The brain and body can easily manage short, intense bursts of danger. But a prolonged feeling of being even a little unsafe has hazardous consequences and ravages our system. The slow boil is what finishes us off.

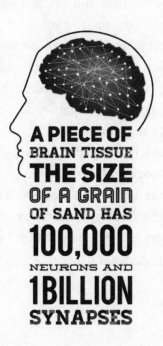

A PIECE OF BRAIN TISSUE THE SIZE OF A GRAIN OF SAND HAS 100,000 NEURONS AND 1 BILLION SYNAPSES

If you observe our places of work and education, you'd agree that almost everyone there is on a slow boil. For most, this continues even at home. Maybe after a few million years, evolution will catch up with technology and our lifestyles, and hopefully, the brain will learn to deal with sustained low-level stress. Meanwhile, it's a real problem that needs to be urgently addressed.

The savage cocktail that the brain releases to combat sustained stress greatly inhibits neural activity and thus our ability to learn. Our neurons detest an atmosphere of stress and simply cannot do their jobs. They don't have enough resources available to make and maintain those delicate synapses. When the environment is safe and you feel happy, your neurons heave a collective sigh of relief and get on with their work—to make a more productive, creative and efficient you. A brain free of stressors translates into a smarter you.

Given that most of us don't live in jungles anymore and are subject to these sustained stressors, the question is whether there is a way to re-programme the brain right now and bypass the dangerous evolutionary response.

The answer is a resounding 'Yes'.

Ancient Indians developed certain techniques for that. They called them yoga and meditation.

Remember, learning is only a process—a matter of growing dendrites and strengthening the connections between them. Here is a summary of the factors that influence stronger connections and enhance learning:

☐ Learn in a multisensory environment. Throw in a few emotions, and you will remember that lesson for a long time.

☐ You grow dendrites for exactly what you do. So, be aware of what you do. These dendrites wire themselves deep within your brain as you do something again and again. Make sure you want them.

☐ After a substantial period of work, taking a break makes learning more natural and easier. You may even get flashes of insight as the dendrites keep forging new connections during this interval.

☐ Do one thing at a time. The brain doesn't know how to multitask.

☐ The brain copes with short-term intense stress remarkably well. It's pathetic at handling prolonged periods of low-level stress that most people are constantly subjected to. Ancient Indians had some solutions to counter this dangerous evolutionary response of the brain. They're called yoga and meditation.

☐ When you're stressed, the chemical cocktail your brain releases inhibits your neurons from firing correctly. When relaxed, endorphins are secreted. Your neurons love being relaxed and calm. They can then get on with their jobs in peace and work towards making a better, smarter you.

☐ The brain cannot distinguish between a vpmrieaghlok and an irritated lover.

☐ Sleeping 7.5 hours each night is one of the simplest, most potent recipes to stay healthy and smart.

Understanding the basics of how the brain works and using those to your advantage will make living life a piece of (truly delicious) cake!

Chapter 2

SLEEP

Sleep is the longest uninterrupted activity that a human being routinely does. Or, should do. If you live to be 90 years old, you would have spent about 32 years sleeping!

It has to be one of the most dangerous things we do. Sleep is an extremely hazardous endeavour. You are blissfully lost to the world when you are asleep. Anything could happen... You could get robbed, kidnapped, even killed. You have no idea

WHEN WHALES AND DOLPHINS SLEEP THEY ARE ALWAYS HALF-ASLEEP. EACH SIDE OF THEIR BRAINS TAKE TURNS SWITCHING OFF SO THAT THEY CAN REGULARLY COME UP FOR AIR

whether you would even wake up. And if you take yourself back a few thousand years and think about it, going to sleep had to be an open invitation to all sorts of nasty predators. Sleep is equivalent to screaming, 'Come, eat me!'

Given the inherent peril of sleep, evolution should have made it vestigial. However, it's the absolute opposite: sleep is critical for the smooth functioning of the body and mind. Everyone needs sleep and, as we shall see, the lack of it can cause major health issues.

I love sleeping, always trying to squeeze in 'a few more minutes'. Back in the day, my mother would do everything she could to wake me up, including switching off the fan or air conditioning and putting our dog, Bobby, in my bed. Yet I'd continue to snooze in delight—even Bobby would snuggle up to me, lick my face, and doze off. When Mom would call me 'lazy' and a 'slacker,' I'd have an irrefutable counter to her accusations. 'All those wars and terrible man-made disasters happen when people are awake. If they only slept more, many of these problems would have been solved.' Mom would laugh and hug me in response, or just whack me to get me out of bed. At the time, I had no idea how true my innocent logic actually was.

Sleep is mysterious, and we have hardly begun to understand why we do it. I guess the biggest reason we sleep is empirical—it allows us to overcome sleepiness. When we aren't drowsy, we are more productive, creative and efficient, and function better. Sleep re-energises the body's cells, clears the brain of toxicity, and plays a huge role in learning and memory. It plays a vital role in regulating our appetite, mood and libido.

Poets and writers, the bards of yore, conjured up beautiful, evocative words to describe sleep.

Shakespeare says:

'Sleep that knits up the ravelled sleeve of care
The death of each day's life, sore labour's bath
Balm of hurt minds, great nature's second course,
Chief nourisher in life's feast.' —Macbeth

'Enjoy the honey heavy dews of slumber.' —Julius Caesar

John Keats makes sleep magical.
'O magic sleep! O comfortable bird,
That broodest over the troubled sea of the mind,
Till it is hush'd and smooth.'

For Robert Leighton, sleep is mystical and beguiling.

'Fair Sleep! mind-soothing, soul-bewitching Sleep!
Come, fair enchantress, I would with thee speak—
O come, and fan this fever from my cheek:
I now with Thought no more communion keep;
Be not afraid, fair spirit, to alight;
Thy breath will soothe me into slumbers deep;
My weary brain hath need of them tonight—
Come Sleep!'

And quite in tune with the science of today, Charles Reade says:

'Sleep is life's nurse, sent from heaven to create us anew day by day.'

In those days, many people had two sleep phases each night separated by an hour or two of chores. The first typically from 8 p.m. to 2 a.m., and the second from 3 or 4 a.m. until daylight.

I remember that my own grandmother used to sleep twice in a night. She would go to bed at around 10 p.m. and be up at around 3.30 a.m. There would be a clanging of pots and pans in the kitchen while she would cook for the day ahead. Once she was done, she would go back to bed until 7 or 8 a.m.

Just about a century ago, people would easily clock in 8-10 hours of sleep every night.

Then 1879 happened.

That was the year Thomas Edison invented the light bulb and vandalised the darkness, magic and mystery of the night.

Very quickly, with the advent of
cheaper electricity, light blazed
forth in our cities percolating
down over time to the smallest
of villages.

Our relationship with
sleep changed. Instead of a 'fair
enchantress' it became a monster
to be conquered and tamed. You
were considered more of a man
(or woman, but through experience it's mostly man… women
typically don't boast about sleeping less) if you got by on less
and less sleep. You were braver and cooler if you skimped on
sleep.

Consider these quotes, the first one from Edison himself:

'Sleep is a criminal waste of time, inherited from our cave days.'

Or,

'Sleep, those little slices of death. How I loathe them.'
—Edgar Allan Poe

Or,

*'It is one of life's bitterest truths, that bedtime so often
arrives just when things are getting really interesting.'*
—Daniel Handler

Finally, from a woman:

'Sleep is for wimps.' —Margaret Thatcher

To be fair, many people from modern times have glorified
sleep too. However, they remain a minority. The hours that
'civilised' society slept started to dwindle. The early 1900s saw
sleep dropping to 9 hours each night. By the 1950s, television

reduced it to 8 hours, and now with 24-hour programming on TV, the internet and all the other distractions of this century, the average human being in 2018 sleeps just 6 and a half hours or less!

Sleep deprivation has become the bane of our 'civilised' society.

Sleep Deprivation Can Kill

Dinesh and I were teaching Art of Living courses in Mumbai and we were scheduled to go back to Bangalore in a few days. Dinesh's parents lived in Pune, which is a quick 3-hour drive from Mumbai at the right time of the day. Dinesh decided to give his parents a surprise visit. Early one morning, he and a few other friends went on a day trip to Pune, planning to come back in the evening to Mumbai.

The night before we had all gone out for dinner and, in true Mumbai style, returned home only by 1 a.m. I was too sleepy to join them that morning and drowsily waved bye to them before going back to bed.

A few hours later, I woke up to the sound of my phone ringing. It was Dinesh. He said they had met with an accident and were in the hospital. He sounded all right. Nobody was hurt too much, he assured me, and they'd soon be in Mumbai. We talked a little more, and he sounded tired so I didn't press him for more details. That could wait for later.

The story unfolded upon their return. It was not a simple accident like he had made it out to be. It was spectacular car crash. Dinesh was driving at over 100 km/hour on the Mumbai-Pune Expressway and had dozed off at the wheel for just a few seconds. The car crashed into the wall of a toll booth, which was fortunately unmanned. The others in the car had been snoozing and slept through the most dramatic car crash they would hopefully ever be in. They woke up woozily in hospital. No one had any serious injuries. The car, however, was completely wrecked. Seeing pictures of it was scary. The fact that they survived, with almost nothing to show for the horrific disaster they had been in, was nothing short of a miracle. All of them had been given a second chance at life.

Many aren't so lucky. An astounding 31% of drivers worldwide fall asleep at the wheel at least once in their lives. When you are speeding at 100+km/hour, your car moves quite a lot in the few seconds that you may nod off. Drowsy driving kills more than 6000 people each year in the US alone.

You start your Friday at around 7 a.m. and work through the day... just your usual routine stuff, looking forward to the evening and a lazy weekend. You head out for a fun evening with a bunch of friends... You are enjoying great food and fabulous company... and suddenly realise it's almost 1 a.m.! You know there is the whole of Saturday and Sunday ahead to catch up on your sleep, so you are not too bothered. In a while, you say your goodbyes and start your drive back home. You have not had any alcohol.

If this has been your Friday, your alertness and reflexes to what's happening on the road while driving will be the same as those of one inebriated beyond the legal limit. This is drowsy driving and, around the world, statistics show that it kills more people than drunk driving.

The Chernobyl disaster could be related to lack of sleep. The engineers involved had been working for at least thirteen hours.

The Challenger space shuttle, which exploded within seconds of its January 1986 lift-off, killed all seven members of the crew. A few of the managers who were part of the launch had slept for only two hours before reporting to work at 1 a.m. The Presidential Commission on the accident admitted the danger of this sleep deprivation in its June 1986 report, saying, 'The willingness of NASA employees in general to work excessive hours, while admirable, raises serious questions when it jeopardises job performance, particularly when critical management decisions are at stake.'

Remember the Exxon Valdez oil spill? The supertanker ran aground in Alaska in 1989, causing catastrophic damage to wildlife and spilling 2,58,000 barrels of crude oil into the sea. The Anchorage Daily News reported that the crew had just put in a 22-hour shift loading oil onto the ship. Third mate Gregory Cousins only had time for a quick 'catnap' in the 16 hours before the crash. Allegedly, he had fallen asleep at the helm and therefore couldn't turn the ship in time to avoid disaster.

Sleep deprived people cannot think clearly. Worse, a person who is sleep deprived may not even feel sleep deprived. An alarming rise in suicides is being attributed to feeling super tired all the time.

Sleep Deprivation Is Expensive

Absenteeism and presenteeism (employees physically at the workplace but mentally elsewhere) cost businesses an estimated $411 billion in the US every year. In the UK, one in every five employees has missed work or arrived late due to fatigue. This dip in productivity amounts to $50 billion per year. Japan loses $138 billion annually; Germany $60 billion. Canada sees a drain of over $21 billion, with one-third of its adult population frequently complaining of exhaustion. This unhealthy trend is fast catching on in India as well.

If Americans who slept under 6 hours a night simply increased their sleep time to between 6 and 7 hours, it would add an estimated $226 billion to the US economy. The amount of money we could add to our country's economy just by sleeping longer is incredible!

Sleep Deprivation Makes You Dumb

Let me quote a poster I spotted in a dorm at an American university where I was teaching an Art of Living course. It said, 'Great Grades, Superb Social Life, Enough Sleep—Choose Two.'

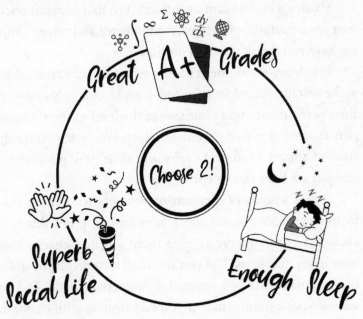

No points for guessing what students all over the world would choose. In our university campuses almost everywhere, young people are horrifically sleep deprived.

We even had a saying in IITB: 'Sleep. What's that?'

Exams and all-nighters usually go hand-in-hand. There was a particularly difficult subject I had to work for and I did what students all over the world would do: slogged through the night, before finally collapsing in bed at around 6 a.m. My exam was at 11 a.m., so I had time for at least 5 hours of sleep. I went to sleep and woke up refreshed and ready—at around 1 p.m. In my super sleepy state, I had forgotten to set my alarm.

Fortunately for me, the professor in charge was an alumnus from IIT and had done something similar in his days as a student so he allowed me a re-exam without any fuss the next week. This is something that can happen in an IIT.

Missing a board exam or entrance test that happens once a year can be catastrophic to your confidence and career, simply because you didn't wake up on time.

The deprivation doesn't just cost you your exams. If you make a straight-A student sleep an hour less for only one week, their performance will plummet to the level of their bottom-rank classmates who clock enough sleep. Worse, it will take that student almost a month to return to their peak performance and pay off their sleep debt.

There's a story of a clutch of students who complained to their professor about the grades he had given them. He created a questionnaire to give them a reality check. There were many questions: Did you attend all lectures? If you didn't, did you make sure you covered the material taught? Did you submit your assignments? If you had trouble with them, did you consult a tutor? Did you discuss your work with your classmates? ... and so on The professor told the students that if they answered 'No' to even two or three of these, they shouldn't be surprised at their bad scores.

The last question in the list was: Did you get enough sleep the night before the exam? If the answer to this question was No, it didn't matter what they answered for all the other questions. They should not be surprised if they got a bad grade.

Sleep deprivation makes you dumb.

Don't believe me yet?

Let's talk a bit about our brain.

The adult human brain weighs about 1400 g. A liquid called the Cerebro Spinal Fluid (CSF) is slowly and continuously secreted in the third and fourth ventricles of the brain. It surrounds the brain and runs all the way down our spinal cord. It mixes with the blood in the upper regions of the skull and is then taken for elimination in a 6 to 7-hour cycle.

And so, the brain floats in our skull and has a net weight of just 200 g! This is great news, because if the CSF was not there, the brain's own weight would cut off blood supply and we wouldn't last very long. The entire assembly of the skull rests on two really small vertebrae, the atlas and the axis, which would never be able to hold the actual weight of the brain along with all the surrounding paraphernalia. We would literally lose our head. It would simply fall off. Nature has cleverly injected that 125 ml or so of CSF into our system so that these niggling problems can be resolved.

The CSF makes our brain float. That's pretty cool. We all have a floating brain! That's not all that the CSF does though. There is one more critical function that the CSF has.

The brain is a bubbling cauldron of chemical reactions that would put an alchemist to shame. As we've seen in the Brain 101 chapter, it generates electrical charges equivalent to a microscopic thunderstorm every few seconds. More than 1,000 litre of blood per day fuel this frenetic activity. And basic thermodynamics tells us that when fuel burns, waste forms. The waste produced in the course of the normal functioning of the brain is known as amyloid beta. I call it brain shit.

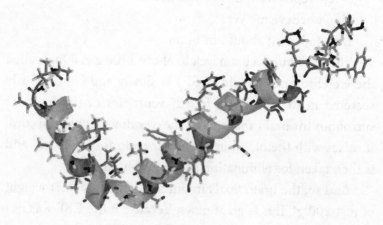

Amyloid Beta

Amyloid beta is a particularly toxic protein implicated in various degenerative brain diseases and needs to be eliminated quickly. Here's where the continuous secretion and elimination of CSF come in. The CSF surrounds the brain, goes into its many folds and flushes out this unwanted substance.

When we are awake, the chemical-electrical storm in our brain doesn't allow the CSF to penetrate into the deeper regions of the brain. There is simply no space.

Make a tight fist and immerse it in water. Very little water will be able to go inside the fist. For the water to get into the fist, the fingers need to loosen. Similarly, for the CSF to reach the deeper parts of the brain, the crazy activity in the brain needs a pause. That pause is sleep.

When we're asleep, the interstitial spaces (spaces between the tissues) in the brain increase by around 60%. The brain loosens up. This allows the CSF to get deep inside and get rid of that molecular trash. That's why when you wake in the morning after a great night's rest, you say, 'I am feeling *fresh*.'

Obviously! The brain shit got flushed. You got a clean brain.

Imagine not flushing and cleaning your toilet and letting everything pile up for a while. It would stink and soon become completely unusable. The same happens to your brain when you don't sleep. If the brain is not cleaned, it's an open invitation to all sorts of terrible diseases to invade your body and mind. The cleaning happens only when you sleep. Please sleep.

This is why, before any critical event, be it an exam, interview or presentation, make sure you get a good night's sleep. Else, you will show up for that all-important occasion with a brain full of shit, and perform accordingly.

In many premier universities and institutions the world over, including IITs and IIMs, surviving on less sleep is almost a holy tradition. It's supposed to prepare you for life. What it does is only prepare you for a premature onset of unpleasant maladies. Have you seen the recent statistics on heart disease, diabetes, hypertension, obesity, depression and anxiety? These illnesses which were the bane of growing older are now affecting people in their early 20s!

Sleep Deprivation Accelerates Ageing

A good eight-hour sleep is far more effective than any cosmetic or medical salve we could massage onto our skin.

Collagen is the most abundant protein in the human body—it forms 30% of the total protein in the body and around 70% of the protein in the skin. It keeps the skin and hair strong and helps the connective tissue hold everything in place. It also guards the skin from bacterial invasions, improves its elasticity, and preserves the youthful, healthy look that everyone craves for. Plus, it is an in-built, natural protection from UV radiation.

Sleep deprivation can not only impair the production of collagen, but also break down its content in the skin. Consequently, your skin will lose its lustre, your eyes will get that tired, puffy look and you will start looking and feeling terrible.

Sleep Deprivation Makes You Fat

Leptin and ghrelin are the hunger hormones. The former is manufactured by fat cells and decreases appetite. The latter makes you feel hungry and is involved with the regulation of body weight.

If we don't sleep enough, the production of ghrelin goes through the roof. We feel the urge to eat way too often and especially crave junk food. Have you noticed how people with hunger pangs in the middle of the night never want a healthy green salad? They desire pizza, with oodles of cheese. That's ghrelin at work. To seal the deal, less sleep equals less leptin. Less leptin means those hunger pangs are magnified even more.

Around the world, the incidence of obesity has doubled and, in some places, tripled within the last few decades. We've already seen that people are sleeping less. There is a direct link.

Sleep Deprivation Makes You Sick

The list of diseases that are associated with lack of sleep is nightmarish and keeps growing.

People who sleep less have greatly increased chances of diabetes, heart diseases, hypertension, mood disorders (depression, anxiety, mental distress), learning disorders, forgetfulness, stroke, compromised immunity and more.

Less sleep reduces life expectancy. Worse, it lowers life quality.

Many people, especially men, feel sleeping less is a symbol of virility. In fact, it's exactly the opposite.

Red alert for all of us who feel lack of sleep cannot touch them: It will make you lose your youth by ageing your skin and will kill your sex drive! There is a reason our nightly rest is called 'beauty sleep'.

Lack of sleep impairs judgement, especially about how much one should sleep. Sleep-deprived people seem to be especially prone to poor judgement when it comes to assessing what lack of sleep is doing to them.

How Much Sleep?

Someone asked Dinesh, how long should one sleep?

He replied, just five more minutes!

Q. HOW LONG
SHOULD ONE SLEEP?
DINESH : JUST
5 MORE MINUTES

Many sleep researchers agree that this chart represents the optimum amount of sleep we should be getting, depending on our age:

New Borns (0-3 months) 14-17 hours

Infants (4-11 months) 12-15 hours

                 Toddlers (1-2 years)   11-14 hours

Preschoolers (3-5 years) 10-13 hours

              Children (6-13 years) 9-11 hours

Teens (14-17 years) 8-10 hours

 Adults (18-65 years) 7-9 hours

Older Adults (65+ years) 7-8 hours

Optimal Sleep Time

The chart doesn't say anywhere that a Type A individual managing a team, eyeing a promotion, frequenting the gym, playing occasional golf, just starting a relationship, or living in 2018 can make do with only four hours of sleep every night.

It's tragic that so many people these days actually boast about how little they sleep.

In a TED talk, Arianna Huffington talks about a dinner date she went on. Her date bragged about how he'd slept for only four hours the previous night. While he droned on and on, she wanted to tell him that if he'd gotten five hours instead, the dinner would have been 'a lot more interesting'. She says the simplest way to lead a more productive, inspired and joyful life is ... to sleep. So, sleep enough. I loved it when she quipped, 'These days we are in the enviable position to literally sleep our way to the top!'

HUMANS ARE THE
ONLY MAMMALS THAT
WILLINGLY DELAY SLEEP

Sleeping less is severely detrimental to our well-being. As we have seen, it is expensive, it makes us dumb and fat, ages us faster, and invites all sorts of diseases. It can even kill.

The Sleeping Brain

Sleep is an enigma and no one quite understands what exactly goes on in our brain when we are asleep. With the advent of technology, scientists are slowly unravelling this mystery. Researchers in thousands of labs all over the world have hooked up subjects to EEG machines to see what's going on in the brain while they sleep.

Some fairly clear patterns have emerged.

A normal human being has mainly two phases of sleep. There is light sleep and then there is deep sleep. Light sleep is

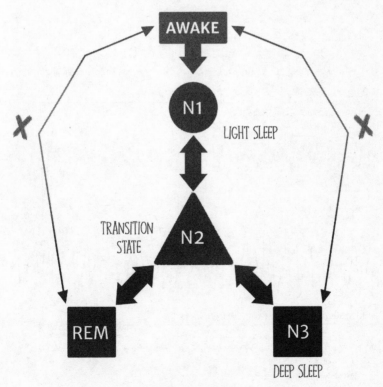

Phases of Sleep

classified into stages N1 and N2. Deep sleep is called N3. And
what I like to call dream sleep which is REM. By the way, the
N stands for Non-REM.

What's important to note is that N2 is the transitioning
phase.

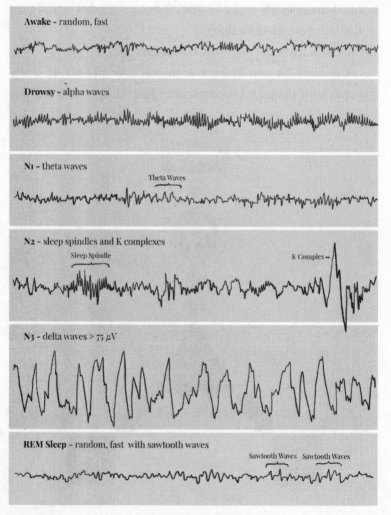

Awake - random, fast

Drowsy - alpha waves

N1 - theta waves

Theta Waves

N2 - sleep spindles and K complexes

Sleep Spindle   K Complex

N3 - delta waves > 75 μV

REM Sleep - random, fast with sawtooth waves

Sawtooth Waves   Sawtooth Waves

Sleeping Brain EEG

When we fall asleep, we first enter N1. We're more or less aware of what's happening around us, but not quite. The brain waves slow down and become more synchronised.

N1 transitions to N2, which sets the stage for deeper levels of sleep. On the EEG, wave patterns called spindles and K-complexes show up. These have been associated with better cognitive ability and the feeling of rejuvenation on waking up.

From N2, you either go into N3 or REM.

In N3, the waves are even slower. This is when the body does maintenance and repair work. Millions of our cells die every day and need replacements. The brain secretes the growth hormone and gets busy printing out our body for the next day. Get more N3 sleep, and your brain maps out a younger, healthier version of you. If N3 and the secretion of the growth hormone are hampered, it leads to an older, not-so-healthy version of you.

The bad news is that as we grow older, the production of this hormone dwindles. Besides, older people have greater difficulty being in N3. This is supposed to be an inevitability and one of the top contributors to the process of ageing. It becomes quite obvious then that not taking advantage of N3 and the nectar of the growth hormone when it is available is going to make us age super fast!

From N2, we may transition into REM sleep. This is a fascinating period. The brain waves in this stage are quite similar to those when we are awake. The brain is busy sorting out the day, creating a chronology of events, learning, making connections, deciding what to remember and what to forget, and so on.

Most importantly, dreams happen during this time. All

those wild fantasies are happening here. So you don't hurt yourself by twitching or thrashing about as all those imageries play out, the brain thoughtfully paralyses the entire body, allowing only the eyeballs any movement. That's the reason it's called REM. Rapid Eye Movement. Flashes of insight are generated during this time. Remember those times you woke up with some sudden brilliant idea?... You got them from REM sleep.

THE IDEA FOR
Google
CAME IN A DREAM

REM or N3 always transitions into N2. From N2, one can return to N3 or wake up. Everyone cycles through these stages multiple times through the span of a night.

Here's a hypnogram depicting a healthy night's sleep:

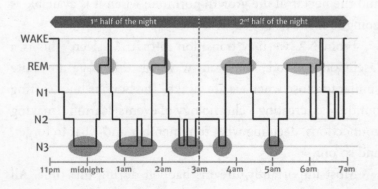

As you can see, the early parts of the night are devoted to N3; as you are getting ready to awaken, you go more into REM. You finally wake up from N2.

We cycle through these stages throughout our sleep time. Each cycle is about an hour and a half long. A good night's sleep constitutes at least five cycles and waking up naturally without the need of an alarm clock.

Before we talk more about sleep, let's talk just a bit about waking up.

A healthy transition into the state of wakefulness is always supposed to be from N2. When we wake up from N2 sleep, we feel amazingly refreshed and energetic. On the other hand, waking up during N3 or REM stages can be disturbing, and will leave us feeling tired, disoriented and groggy until we go back to sleep again.

There are going to be times, though, when you need to be up earlier or, if you are lucky, later than usual. You may have a flight to catch, an interview to prepare for, or any other urgent task.

Say you need to get up at 6 a.m. and you're planning to sleep at 11 p.m. It takes most people between 15-30 thirty minutes to slip into slumber. Your first cycle would start at around 11.30 p.m. Let's divide your sleep into 90-minute chunks.

11.30 p.m. to 1 a.m.

1 a.m. to 2.30 a.m.

2.30 a.m. to 4 a.m.

4 a.m. to 5.30 a.m.

5.30 a.m. to 7 a.m.

Looking at this, it's not a good idea to wake up at 6 a.m. You are going to be in the middle of a sleep cycle and waking up at this time will make you feel terrible throughout the day. Much better to wake up half an hour earlier than you planned—at 5.30 a.m. Amazingly, with half an hour less sleep, you will be far more alert and refreshed than if you forced yourself awake at 6.

A bit of this math before sleeping will ensure a fantastic day ahead.

Certain scientists disagree with this and call it nonsense. They advise on clocking as much sleep as possible. However, I have personally experimented with this, on myself and many others, and found it to be remarkably effective. Maybe it's placebo... but hey, it works!

Given that sleep is such a critical factor for human beings to stay healthy, productive and happy, it is astounding that in 5 years of medical school, most doctors-to-be have a lecture of about 2 hours on sleep, sleep disorders and their treatment!

Although asking about sleep is part of the history-taking

SLEEP   49

protocol, a vast majority of doctors skip this step, mainly because they know so little about it.

A majority of primary health care practitioners just tell their patients to 'take some sleeping pills', not realising the damage that these drugs can cause over time. Except in absolutely exceptional circumstances, sleeping pills don't make you sleep. They sedate you. Meaning you get little to none REM or N3 sleep. Completely avoid these pills. They are no good for you.

Insomnia, sleep apnoea and other sleep disorders can be debilitating for the person suffering from them. If you are suffering from any such disorder, please see a doctor specialising in sleep. In my opinion, ayurveda and homoeopahy normally do a far better job than allopathy in treating sleep dysfunctions. In the bibliography at the end of the book, I have listed a few books on sleep in case you want to delve deeper into this subject.

In the late 1990s, Gurudev Sri Sri Ravishankar was not as busy as He is now and in the evening, after satsang, a few of us would go up to His kutir and sit with Him. We would talk about many, many things, from the mundane to the esoteric. There would be lots of friendly banter, some jokes and always some insights into life.

It would be a magical hour or so after which He would tell us to go and sleep. We would keep telling Him we wanted to sit with Him for just a few minutes more. He would agree. Then, a little later, He would again ask us to go and rest. To which we would say, 'Just a few minutes more, Guruji!' This would go on until He finally managed to get all of us out of His room, so He could get His rest.

During my stay there for more than a month, this would happen every night. On one of these occasions, Guruji made a fine remark. 'Through the ages,' He said, 'the Enlightened Ones would come to the planet and tell people to wake up. And here I am, asking all of you to go to sleep!' We couldn't help but laugh out loud in response.

Guruji finally added in his soft, endearing voice, 'Only when you have slept well can you truly wake up. So, go. Go and sleep.'

The 8 Steps to Absolutely Smashing Sleep

1. Get over the caffeine enchantment.
2. Ban blue and white light after sunset.
3. Transform your bedroom into a sleep haven.
4. Know the three sleep positions. Sleep with your head to the east.
5. Create a bedtime ritual of winding down.
6. Greet the day with joy.
7. Make sure you get at least 1000 lux of light for an hour before noon, preferably in the early morning.
8. Pay off your sleep debt right away. Nap intelligently.

The Caffeine Enchantment

A long time ago, in the highlands of Ethiopia, a goatherd observed his flock developing unusual friskiness and frolic after grazing on the slopes of a certain mountain. The goats had discovered coffee.

Many a yummy treat has caffeine in it. Coffee is packed with it, while chocolate and tea have it in moderate quantities. So do almost all colas, energy drinks and protein bars. These foods and beverages are the pick-me-ups or the get-up-and-go people all over the world turn to, when they need that picking up or getting up and go feeling.

Many a time, finishing off our to-do list requires us to stay awake and alert and function beyond our normal capacities. This is when we reach for that cup of coffee, tea or some chocolate.

But caffeine doesn't boost our energy as we tend to assume. It enchants our bodies into believing that we aren't as tired as we think.

As soon as we wake up, our brain produces a neurotransmitter called adenosine. Our nervous system constantly tracks its quantity in our body. When it reaches a certain level, our system begins to nudge us more and more firmly towards rest by making us feel tired. This is known as the build-up of sleep pressure.

The caffeine molecule is remarkably similar to adenosine and merrily occupies the spaces where adenosine should be sitting. As the body and brain keep getting overworked, more and more adenosine is produced. But this adenosine simply floats around the system because caffeine has occupied its space. So, even though the brain and body are screaming exhaustion, the nervous system is in denial because it cannot feel the sleep pressure building up.

Caffeine has one more trick up its sleeve. It stimulates the production of adrenaline. Adrenaline spikes catapult us into a hyper aroused, super alert state of being. Everything becomes clearer, the brain fog vanishes, and decisions are easier. Even our eyes dilate and we can see much better, like going from 360p to ultra HD. But all this comes at a cost. A dip in adrenaline spike causes a huge crash in our system, leaving us feeling drained and fatigued. Of course, we crave to go back to that superman state and so we reach out for more caffeine. The cycle continues, and we alternate between superhero and zombie modes all day. Thus, our caffeine enchantment quickly turns into an addiction, which compromises the quality of our sleep and our life.

Caffeine has a half-life of 5-8 hours. A cup of coffee has around 200 mg of caffeine. If we consume this cup at around 8 a.m., the caffeine will float in the blood at full power until 4 p.m. Poor adenosine has no chance at this time. The caffeine content will reduce to half in the next 4 hours, i.e., 100 mg till 8 p.m. It will further halve again in 2 hours—50 mg till 10 p.m., and so on. By this time, the adenosine would have found its place and the system would begin to feel naturally tired, paving the way for the real enchantment of great sleep. Note that it takes around 24 hours for all the caffeine to get flushed out of the system.

It is simple and obvious to conclude that for a good night's sleep, you must have a non-negotiable curfew on your caffeine intake. Absolutely no caffeine after 2 p.m.

An interesting thing to note is that people with caffeine in their systems may actually go to sleep, and even sleep for the recommended eight hours. But the quality of their sleep, their ability to go into the deeper stages of sleep are damaged.

To shake off your coffee addiction, choose a week when you don't have too much going on in life to gradually wean yourself off it. Start by replacing coffee with strong tea. Hydrate yourself with water and fruit. The next day, reduce the amount of tea you have. Follow the 2 p.m. rule strictly, and keep reducing the amount of tea you have over the week. Drink water every time you feel the urge to adrenalise your system.

You are going to feel awful for the first couple of days, so be prepared for it and resist the urge to reach for that coffee pot. Surround yourself with things you love to do and people you love to be with. It is tough, but it isn't a very long ordeal. Within a week to ten days, you can overcome years of coffee addiction. You will feel so much more in control of yourself when you are over this, and sleep so much better.

No alcohol or smoking before bed. You may think they help you sleep, but all they do is knock you out. This isn't sleep but sedation. The sleep cycles get deranged, and you always wake up feeling terrible. Actually, stay off the booze and nicotine. They're really no good for you before bed or at any time of the day or night. Pick a cheaper, healthier vice. Try nail biting!

Oh, you want that kick alcohol and nicotine give you? Meditate! You get the kick without the hangover or the lung cancer. Chapters on meditation coming up in a bit...

Ban Blue and White Light After Sunset

Take a young plant and put it in a greenhouse. Ensure all conditions are favourable for its growth. Switch the lights on for 12 hours, then off for 12 hours and keep repeating this cycle. You will see that the plant thrives. Keeping everything else absolutely the same, switch the lights on and off randomly. The plant will shrivel and die in no time.

An entire set of organisms and electrochemical reactions in the brain furiously work to keep us awake. There is another bunch striving equally hard to make us sleep. Each group becomes weaker and weaker as we do more and more of their supporting activity, until it finally gives up. Then the opposing group triumphs, and our state of consciousness changes.

This back and forth-ing between sleep and wakefulness is called the circadian rhythm. This system is independent of the build-up of sleep pressure.

A few hours after sunset, the circadian rhythm winds down and the adenosine-induced sleep pressure builds up. The army responsible for sleep becomes stronger, and the secretion of the sleep hormone, melatonin, begins.

Hold on, though. How does the body know the sun has set?

There are specialised light receptors in our eyes called rods and cones. As daylight fades and darkness comes, these signal to the brain to start letting the sleep army win. For millions of years, human eyes were exposed to the red-orange-yellow glow of fire or the gentle cooling light of the stars and the moon at night. This light ambience would signal the brain about the onset of night and the need to prepare the body for sleep. The mechanism is so fine-tuned that even the white-blue light of a full moon can make people sleep 5 minutes later and wake up 20 minutes earlier than normal.

Can you imagine what full-spectrum light at night does to this delicate system in our brains? Bright night lights completely confuse the brain and fool it into thinking that it's still daytime. The illumination from the screens of your TV, laptop and cell phones isn't that mellow amber that heralds the beginning of sleep. On the contrary, it keeps hammering into

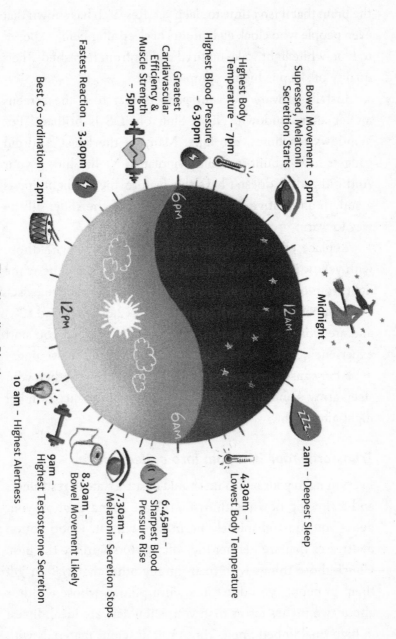

The Circadian Rhythm

Bowel Movement - 9pm
Supressed, Melatonin
Secretion Starts

Highest Blood
Temperature - 7pm

Highest Body
Temperature - 6.30pm

Greatest
Cardiavascular
Efficiency &
Muscle Strength
- 5pm

Fastest Reaction - 3.30pm

Best Co-ordination - 2pm

10 am - Highest Alertness

9am -
Highest Testosterone Secretion

8.30am -
Bowel Movement Likely

7.30am -
Melatonin Secretion Stops

6.45am -
Sharpest Blood
Pressure Rise

4.30am -
Lowest Body Temperature

2am - Deepest Sleep

Midnight

6PM

12AM

12PM

6AM

the brain that it isn't time to sleep yet. Research has shown that even people who clock eight hours of sleep after being exposed to blue-white light wake up tired and far from refreshed. Their quality of sleep is highly compromised.

Install software on your gadgets that turn the screens amber after sundown. Night Shift on iOS is brilliant. For Windows machines, use f.lux. Many of the latest Android gadgets have a built-in facility similar to Night Shift. If your Android gadget doesn't have this feature, the Twilight app is a superb alternative. Make sure you move the slider all the way to warm.

Replace all the light fixtures in your home with those with yellow illumination. If you're still exposed to blue-white light from other sources, a cheap, low-tech alternative exists. Wear amber glasses. They cost less than ₹2,000 (around $27) and are worth every penny for the quality of sleep you start experiencing when you regularly wear them in the evening.

After sunset, ban blue and white light and strengthen your sleep army. You will be drifting off into high-quality slumber night after night.

Transform Your Bedroom into a Sleep Haven

Everything in your bedroom should create a state of restfulness and a slowing down within you. Please spend a *lot* on your bed—you must absolutely be in love with it. Good cotton mattresses that are neither too soft nor too hard are the best. Chuck those things with foam or any other material, or gift them to people you don't like. Firm pillows whose width is about two inches lesser than your shoulders are ideal. Invest in high-quality bed linen. Those soft, luscious materials with

high thread counts (preferably 500-600, definitely at least 400)
are so inviting to lie down on.

Remove all clutter from your bedroom and keep the zone
spotlessly clean. This will utterly transform the quality of your
sleep.

Some slightly esoteric pieces of advice: Do not let anyone
step on your bed if they are not going to sleep in it beside you.
It could create health issues for you. If you are getting too many
thoughts, dreams or nightmares, or you feel your sleep quality
is being compromised, put a few blades of fresh *durva* grass
under your pillow. Your sleep quality will improve.

If you close your eyes and there is light, you will notice
that you can sense it. For almost everyone, even a little bit of
light can disturb sleep. Make sure you black out your bedroom
in the night. Those teeny lights from the air conditioner or a

charging mobile can be a lot of light in the darkness. I keep my mobile on airplane mode and leave it to charge outside my bedroom. I use masking tape on the air-conditioner lights.

If required, get black-out material for your curtains.

Here is a test to figure out if your room is dark enough.

At night, shut the bedroom door, draw the curtains and switch off all lights.

Hold your hands out in front of your face.

Can you see them?

If yes, the room is not dark enough. Find and eliminate light sources.

If you cannot see your hands, congratulate yourself. You have got a fantastic sleep haven. Switch the lights on...

If you put those lights on too easily, there is still too much light!

Sleeping in a truly dark room is magically relaxing.

Another sleep aid is to cool down your bed room to anything between 20-22°C. Imagine a nice pleasant room

**SEA OTTERS HOLD
HANDS WHEN THEY SLEEP**
=== SO THEY DON'T ===
DRIFT AWAY FROM
◤ **EACH OTHER** ◥

and you snuggling into a soft Egyptian cotton comforter on a perfect bed. Most people sleep much better in cooler rooms than warmer ones. Your body temperature falls as you go into deeper sleep and a hot room could awaken you. This doesn't apply much to people from Chennai. They consider 25°C Antarctica cold! ☺

Sleeping Positions

We have all experienced a few aches and pains when we wake up after sleeping awkwardly.

I recently learned at a workshop that if we sleep awkwardly or in an incorrect position, certain parts of the body get blood-deprived while others get too much. This could lead to major imbalances over time, wreaking havoc on our system.

People sleep in a variety of ways, but there are only three optimal positions. You should sleep on a comfortably thin cotton mattress and use a firm cotton pillow with a thickness that is half the size of your shoulder, measured from the neck.

The first: Lie flat on your back, legs a little apart. Hands can be by your side, palms facing up, or on your stomach or chest. Your shoulders should be on your pillow such that your head is on the pillow and your neck is well supported. Around 1.5 inches of your shoulders on the pillow would ensure this. Most people, including me, would use the pillow only to rest the head and leave the neck without support. Try this one, though. It's so comfortable that you'd wonder why you didn't do it all your life!

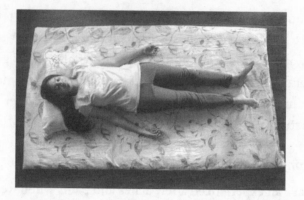

The second: Turn to your right side. Your head should be on the pillow, while your shoulder shouldn't. Your left hand should rest on top of the left side of your body, reaching somewhere near your hip. Your right hand should be bent at the elbow, palm upwards near your face. Your legs should be bent comfortably at the knees so that the heels of both legs are in line with the base of the spine. You may have another pillow between your legs if you wish.

The third: Mirror image of the second, with you turned to your left side.

Do not sleep with your head towards the north or south. Instead, face the east or west. Though there isn't much scientific evidence supporting this, and many claim that it doesn't really matter, I have found that lying in the east-west or west-east direction helps me sleep better and experience pleasant dreams. Moreover, there are many references in our scriptures that say head in the east is the best position.

A friend of mine would complain of nightmares after moving to a new home. Her family did all they could—from ventilation to pujas—but nothing helped. I asked her to note the direction her head was in while sleeping. It turned out to be north. I advised her to move her bed and rearrange her room so that she slept east-west. She grumpily agreed after having tried just about everything else. In a few days, her nightmares stopped and she began to enjoy glorious sleep.

Though it's easy to sleep with our heads in the east, how can one manage to sleep through the night in only those three positions described above?

The answer is simple: by deciding to do it. There was a time I would sleep with three pillows. One under my head, another over it and a third one between my legs. After the workshop, I resolved to change this habit. The effects of a lifetime of incorrect sleeping positions vanished within a few weeks. The body is super intelligent, and when you start doing what's good for it, you would be pleasantly surprised at how wonderfully cooperative it can become.

The Bed-time Ritual

We are creatures of habit and habitat.

Do you notice how, when you enter different parts of your home, you want to do the things they represent? Sit at your workspace, and you start focusing on your tasks. Linger around the dining table, and hunger kicks in. Relax in your favourite armchair, and you feel like watching a movie, reading a book or meditating.

When you step into your bedroom, it should ideally make you want to sleep. These days, though, bedrooms have become multifunctional areas.

Reserve the bedroom and your bed for sleep, *sadhana* (meditation) and sex. I hope by now you are convinced that sleep it vital. If it is important, then it needs to be given importance, right?

When I was ten years old, I would ardently follow a cartoon series that would always end with a man placing a few bottles for collecting milk outside his house and also putting his cat out there, just before heading to bed. The camera would zoom out to show the entire village asleep. What a superb way to depict a bedtime ritual! Even my father would lull us with music before bed. Every night, we would listen to soothing classics as we got ready to sip the honey-heavy dew of slumber.

You need to get ready for sleep, like you would to go on a hot date. An hour before you go to bed, wind down.

Enter your bedroom and do some relaxing activities that signal to your brain that you will soon be sleeping. These vary from person to person, and you can do whatever feels right for you. Here are some examples of winding down that we ourselves do at home.

1. Dinner at least 2-3 hours before bedtime.
2. If you are feeling peckish before bed, sip a glass of water.
3. Or have a cup of chamomile, valerian or kava tea. Just the herbs brewed in steaming hot water. Nothing else.
4. Or a cup of milk, not sweetened please. Make sure you are using the Gir cow A2 milk. I love hot chocolate before bedtime, but chocolate contains caffeine and that compromises sleep quality. I still indulge in it once in a while.
5. No gadgets or TV in the bedroom.
6. Talk about what happened during the day. List out five things you are grateful for. Challenge yourself each night to come up with a new list, so you never repeat what you have already mentioned. Doing this exercise every night for a few months rewires the brain. You will begin to spotlight on things that have gone well, instead of the usual habit most adults have of nitpicking and focusing on all the things that have gone wrong.
7. Play a nice board game. Mumbai Connection highly recommended!
8. Read a printed book. We like to read either a romance

or a comedy. A few shlokas from the Bhagavad Gita or Patanjali's Yoga Sutras are great if you have a more spiritual inclination.

9. Take a nice, hot bath.

10. A couple of light yoga stretches can feel wonderful.

11. Dim the lights.

12. Essential oils like lavender, chamomile, sweet marjoram, clary sage, valerian root or their combinations can lull you to sleep. I like to mix 20-40 drops of each oil if I am doing a combo, and about 50 drops if I am using just one, in a spritzer bottle full of water and spray the room. You may even put a drop or two of the oil directly on your pillow, but I find that overpowering. Lavender is in particular supposed to be sleep inducing.

13. Listen to, or chant some Sanskrit mantras just before bed. I love to listen to the soothing Devi Kavacham as I drift off to sleep. Have you ever suddenly heard a song or a melody from a time long ago that you used to love and have now almost forgotten? Did you notice how it brought a goofy smile on your face as happy, nostalgic memories arose? Sanskrit being an ancient language has the same refreshing effect on the deeper layers of our consciousness. You smile goofily from deep inside and something just feels sublimely right.

14. No work of any sort allowed in the bed room... with one exception. You may think about one, maximum two things, you wish to accomplish the next day just before sleeping. This is like an assignment to the subconscious. You will be pleasantly surprised at the ideas you may get in the morning.

15. You may practise Yoga-Nidra (Yogic Sleep) as you begin to drift off. I get the most amazing slumber when I begin my sleep with this lovely practice. Yoga-Nidra involves effortlessly and gently taking your attention to various parts of the body. You can download a recording we have made of the Yoga-Nidra from www.happinessexpressbook. com/audios/yoganidra.

16. Sometimes, the simple act of changing into comfy loose pyjamas can send a strong signal to your system that you are getting ready to sleep. Please don't sleep in your day attire. I personally know of an astonishing number of people who do that. They often wake up in the middle of the night feeling the need to change into something more comfortable, or rise groggily in the morning with all sorts of itches and pains. Day wear isn't designed for sleep. Slip into something light and easy. Get ready for that date with the 'fair enchantress'.

11:00 PM
LIGHTS OFF.
MAKE SURE THE BEDROOM IS
COMFORTABLE, DARK
AND COOL — SLEEP!

10:45 PM
ALL ELECTRONICS OFF
& BEGIN WINDING
DOWN RITUAL

7:00 PM ONWARDS
MINIMIZE WHITE / BLUE LIGHT.
ORANGE AND RED LIGHT IS OK.
PHONES, TABLETS, COMPUTER
SHOULD START NIGHTSHIFT MODE

6:00 PM DINNER
(PREFERABLY
NO MORE FOOD
AFTER THIS)

TO **9** HRS

z z

7:30 AM – **2:00** PM
GET **1000** LUX OF LIGHT
(APPROX **1** HOUR OF SUNLIGHT)

8:00 AM
FIRST MEAL

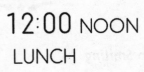

12:00 NOON
LUNCH

00 PM ONWARDS
VOID CAFFEINE

Sleep and wake up at more or less the same time daily. Create a bedtime ritual and follow it every night. Remember 'habit' and 'habitat'.

It's interesting to note that the last thoughts you have while going to sleep are exactly what would be on your mind when you wake up the next day. Be more and more aware of this phenomenon.

GIRAFFES SLEEP JUST *1.9 hours a day*, BROWN BATS CLOCK IN ➤ **19.9 HOURS!**

Wake Up Smiling

Greet the new day with energy and enthusiasm. Be grateful you have been granted yet another day on our beautiful planet. The first few minutes after you wake up lays the foundation of how your day is going to be like.

Make sure you catch at least 20 minutes or so of early morning sunlight. Just as we need to ban white light after sundown to ensure great sleep, morning light is equally important for us. It gives a clear signal to our brain to begin the process of waking up the entire system for the day ahead.

Walk in the shade
9000 - 40,000 lux

Sunny day
10,00,00 lux

Cloudy / Sunny day
2000 - 5000 lux

Sunrise / Sunset
500 - 2200 lux

Driving on a cloudy day
200 - 1000 lux

Bedroom with closed window
7 - 12 lux

Candle
1 lux

Lux Chart

Lux is a unit to measure light illuminance. 1 lux is the light from a candle; 10,000 lux is sunlight in the afternoon on a cloudless day. It is essential for our well-being that we get 1000 lux for an hour each day, preferably before noon. It's important to note that this light should hit our eyes. You could be in direct sunlight for a few hours and still not get enough if you are wearing sunglasses.

This light exposure keeps your awake army functioning well and amazingly even fuels your sleep army so you get better sleep. Many times, people don't sleep too well at night because they have not got enough light during the day.

Sleep Debt and Napping

There are going to be occasions when you have to (or choose to) pull an all-nighter, either to study or prepare a presentation, or write a report. Or binge-watch *Game of Thrones*. Or play World of Warcraft or Albion Online. The next day, you're likely to feel groggy and disoriented. You have accumulated sleep debt.

X hours of sleep debt will take 3X hours of extra sleep to pay it off. These extra hours of sleep must be spread out over the next few days, not done all at once. The caveat is that it must be done right away. If you stay awake for a few nights, it wouldn't harm you much if you clock in a little more sleep within the next fortnight or so. But if you postpone paying off this debt, the damage that lack of sleep would cause to your system is mostly irreversible.

All those night-outs I had in my IIT days must have done some pretty awful things to me... I can't do anything much about that right now. It's something I will have to live with and keep moving ahead.

A little side note: oversleeping isn't good for you either. If you're sleeping more than ten hours a night, you may have a condition called hypersomnia. Pay attention if you're constantly falling asleep even during the day.

A number of people tend to stay in bed on weekends to catch up on their lost sleep. Sleep debt cannot be paid off like this. To settle that sleep debt, you will need to sleep about half an hour more over a few nights. Not four hours more on the weekend. Oversleeping leads to fuzziness in the head, headaches, back pains and lethargy. Chronic oversleeping may heighten the risk of obesity, heart disease and depression.

Psst! There is a cheat code here. It's called meditation. It's not a substitute for sleep, but it can help big time in paying off sleep debt even at a much later date.

How about napping in the day, you ask.

A nap that goes into N3 or REM can ruin your nightly sleep. Stay in N1 and N2, and you feel fresh and ready for the rest of the day. To make sure you don't slip into deeper levels of sleep during your siesta, ensure you don't snooze for more than thirty minutes. Practising Yoga-Nidra is a great way to power nap.

Workplaces around the world are now building nap rooms on their premises. Making intelligent use of these little havens of peace can tremendously boost your performance.

Finally, napping earlier in the day is much better than later.

Sleep is almost always the first thing that is compromised when life begins to get tough. I am reminded of these lines from Robert Frost's legendary poem:

The woods are lovely, dark and deep,
But I have promises to keep,
And miles to go before I sleep,
And miles to go before I sleep.

Explore those woods and keep those promises. But always prioritise sleep. Otherwise, the woods will remain unexplored and those promises will have to be broken. Make it crystal clear to yourself—when sleep is compromised, life gets compromised.

'Great Grades, Superb Social Life, Enough Sleep—Choose Two.' Actually, you need to choose just one: 'Enough Sleep.' Everything else follows.

Goodnight!

Chapter 3

MEDITATION

Snap your fingers please. Good. Once more? Great. This means you are in the first state of consciousness: awake. When you are awake, there is awareness—you know what's going on around you, but being awake means there is no rest. You stay awake for too long and you will start to feel tired. Which brings us to the second state…

Sleep. When you are sleeping, you rest, but there is no awareness. We explored sleep in great detail in an earlier chapter. Sleep is quite enigmatic and scientists and their gadgets have only in very recent times even begun to start to unravel its secrets. They all agree, though, that sleep is crucial. Seven and a half hours of sleep is almost non-negotiable for most adults, with children needing a few hours more. The hours we spend sleeping are an amazing investment—the return is incredible! Enough consistent good-quality sleep keeps us healthy, sane, smart, young, creative, productive and efficient. It improves life expectancy and, most importantly, its quality.

The third state is the dream state. If we are going to have to sleep for seven and a half hours every night, I guess we would need some entertainment to keep us going. Nature provided us with dreams. We dream intermittently through the night, and dreams provide all the spectacle we could wish for, with a small catch: while dreaming, there is neither rest, nor awareness. Too many disturbing thoughts while you sleep—and you wake up complaining that you didn't sleep well. There are treatises on dreams, how to interpret them and what they could mean. I wouldn't bother about them too much. Gurudev once told us about the five types of dreams.

- Dreams about the past: You dream about stuff that has happened to you.
- Dreams about fantasies: Your wishes, desires and fears unfold in your dreams.
- Dreams bought on by the place you are sleeping in: We have all experienced this at some point in our lives. Go to some new city and you might dream of things quite alien to your experiences. These dreams are bought on by the energies of that particular place. A classic example is vicious dreams in certain hotel rooms where violence has happened. We are a very sensitive species and can pick up on these subtle energies, especially when asleep.
- Prophetic dreams: You dream about an event that's going to happen in the future. There are many instances when you wake up with an instinctive knowledge about what's going to happen soon.
- A mix of all of the above.

As dreams don't begin with a drum roll and a label proclaiming which of these types they'd belong to, the safest bet is to ignore them. Otherwise you might mistake something you picked up from the environment or some fantasy as a prophecy and wrongly act on it. Dreams are entertainment. Enjoy your dreams, don't take them seriously.

Then there is something called lucid dreaming. I classify this as state of consciousness 3A. It's when the dreamer is aware that he is dreaming and can influence his dreams to a certain extent a là *Inception*. We'll let that be for now and jump right into that amazing fourth state of consciousness.

Most of us are familiar with being awake, sleeping and dreaming. These three states are more or less automatic and hardwired into our system. The fourth state is the meditative state, one in which you experience deep rest and scintillating awareness. This one is something that needs to be learned and practised. It is my theory that in a few generations, babies will be born with the ability to meditate hardwired into their systems, just like the three other states. Evolution has not yet caught up. Until that happens, meditation is a skill that you will need to acquire.

The Mind

Before we begin our journey into meditation, we need to figure out exactly what meditation is, and for that we need an answer to a question I have been asked very often. What exactly is the mind? Let's take Maharishi Patanjali's help to answer this question.

In his Yoga Sutras, Maharishi Patanjali talks about the five modalities of the mind which could create pleasure or pain within you.

Pramana

The mind looks for proof. It needs constant reassurance that what is going on is indeed going on. I am flying to Mumbai from Bangalore. How do I know I am in an aeroplane? I look outside the window. I see clouds, the wings of the airplane, the jet engines. I hear the throb of the jet... Ahh... I am flying. How do I know I am in Mumbai once I land? I hear the announcement inside the aircraft. I see Chhatrapati Shivaji Maharaj International Airport written on the building. I hear people talking in Marathi. I feel the heat and humidity. Hmmm... Feels like Mumbai. When the mind takes in stuff from the environment and concludes correctly about what's going on, it is in Pramana mode.

Viparyaya

The mind reels in wrong knowledge. It misguides you with wrong perceptions. You see two people you know sitting close together, whispering and giggling. Your mind thinks, they are gossiping about you and laughing at you. It becomes upset.

Someone looks at you and smiles. Your mind assumes they are interested in you. When the mind takes in varied elements from the environment and jumps to very wrong conclusions, it is in Viparyaya.

Smriti

The mind remembers past experiences. It will drag you to your yesterdays and make you re-live certain parts of your life. These could be wistful, happy, neutral or sad memories. Smriti is the mind visiting the past.

Vikalpa

The mind fantasises. It wishes for things. It revels in the joy of how it would be to have some wishes fulfilled. It may

conjure up harrowing and hideous nightmares. It will shudder and feel terrified about something going horribly wrong. All these flights of fancy and reverie happen when the mind is in Vikalpa mode.

Nidra

The mind sleeps.

The mind is involved in one or more of these five activities at all times. There is no sixth thing the mind does.

And what is meditation? When all the five activities cease, you have entered the fourth state of consciousness. You are meditating.

Plastic Brain

It's been established that we are born with approximately 100 billion neurons. Neurons are unique in the human body because they cannot reproduce and multiply. Living fries a few thousand neurons every day. A few thousand from a 100 billion is not much, but over time, this number adds up. (On a side note, drug abuse, alcohol, smoking, etc. are known to add a zero or two to the number of neurons killed each day.)

Earlier it was believed that as we grow older, we would gradually have a lesser number of neurons in our brain. A groundbreaking study on the brain sometime in the 1990s turned this theory on its head. It established that the human brain has the ability to regenerate itself. Many interesting studies that followed showed that the brain can not only regenerate itself, but it can make parts of itself bigger or smaller depending on what activities the person is engaged in. This neuroplasticity of the brain is not a new concept. Way back in 1793, an Italian anatomist Michele Vicenzo Malacarne trained one of a pair of animals extensively for a while. The other he left untrained. When he dissected both the animals and observed their brains, he found that the cerebellums of the trained animals were substantially larger. This finding was largely forgotten for a long time. Two hundred years later, technology developed machines that let us peer into the brain, and neuroplasticity came of age.

London's Black Cab drivers are supposed to pass an incredibly tough exam about the city's roads, so they can take their passengers along the fastest possible route. Scans of the brains of London cabbies revealed that they have a larger hippocampus, an area of the brain associated with learning routes and spatial representations. The size correlated with the time that they had been driving cabs. This meant that being a Black Cab driver in London changed the size of the hippocampus.

All orchestral violinists, for the sake of visual symmetry and orchestral aesthetics, use their left hand and fingers to press down on the strings and find notes and their right hand to bow. The right hand is almost sedentary compared to the left which frenetically moves along the strings. Brain scans of violinists show areas related to the left hand are significantly more developed than the right. Brain scans have established that the volume of grey matter cortex is highest among professional musicians, intermediate in amateurs, and lowest in non-musicians.

In another study, a group of people had their brains scanned and were then asked to learn how to juggle. They built their expertise at juggling over a few months till they could keep three balls up in the air for at least a minute. There was a control group that didn't do any juggling. The brains of the jugglers showed a significant increase in an area of the brain called V5. V5 is associated with the processing of visual movement. The control group, of course, didn't show any significant change. What would happen if these newly acquired skills were allowed to stagnate? The jugglers were then told not to practise their skill for a few months. Their brain scans now showed a decrease in the grey matter in V5 implying that the brain has a use-it-or-lose-it system in place.

The use-it-or-lose-it system was not news to me at all. Before the advent of mobile phones, I knew more than 50 phone numbers by heart. Enter mobile phones, and I didn't need to remember phone numbers any more. Today, I barely remember around five numbers. Use it or lose it. What I didn't know and what these studies have established is that the brain physically changes depending on usage. Our brains are plastic!

The Three Brains

We have three brains. Each sitting on top of the other. As we evolved, so did our brain. At the base of the brain is what I like to call the reptilian brain. It is all about reacting and survival. All the basic life-support systems of the body are governed from here. Heart rate, blood pressure, breathing, digestion are all automatic thanks to the brain stem. Thank God for this, else people would die because they were too busy to remember to breathe. This part of the brain has the ability to override everything for self-protection when faced with an immediate crisis. Have you ever accidentally touched something super hot and recoiled? That recoil is the brain stem at work. Notice that you had no control over that recoil.

The middle brain is the mammalian brain. It creates the fight, flight or freeze response to perceived danger. If the brain senses danger, it presses the buttons to initiate one of these responses. Blood is drained from the stomach and pumped into the extremities. The heart beats faster to get more blood into the system and so on.

Right on top is the human brain. It deals with social engagement. Keep a few babies together and they will play with each other. They engage socially. A bunch of reptile babies will just lie there doing nothing. This is something only humans and higher mammals do. This social engagement, however, only happens when the brain doesn't perceive threat. If there is threat, social engagement stops and flight, flight or freeze is initiated. We have explored this in Brain 101. We noted, too, that the brain is not able to distinguish the danger posed by a 'real' threat, like the attack of a wild animal, from that of an angry boss or a disgruntled girlfriend. It simply feels threatened and goes into fight, flight or freeze.

Most people don't have any control over the fight, flight, freeze evolutionary response to perceived danger. The good news is that meditation allows you to override this crazy response of the brain to stress. The not-so-good news is that you need to learn and practise meditation regularly and over a long period of time for this to work. You are, after all, fighting against the brain's response to danger developed over millions of years of evolution. For you to start seeing the benefits of meditation, you may need to practise for as little as two months. But the important thing to note is that almost anyone can do it. They just need the commitment and the time.

The Meditation Advantage

When I became a teacher of meditation at Art of Living in the early 1990s, many people thought that meditation was primarily for 'old' people. Or weird people. It was airy-fairy, freaky stuff done by those who may not be totally all right in their heads. My own friends couldn't understand what I was doing or why I was doing it. Sitting somewhere with eyes closed seemed such a waste of time… It was definitely not for people who were go-getters and achievers. Successful people didn't have the time to meditate!

Really?!

Imagine a scenario where two people equally qualified and who have studied more or less the same material head to an interview for their dream jobs. The first person walks in and is faced by a very hostile interview panel. A group of people determined to give him a hard time and stress him out. His brain will feel threatened and start pushing the fight, flight, freeze buttons. In this critical time, this person has to appear his best yet his brain is screaming run, run, run or punch them in the face. Both terrible interview strategies. You can imagine this individual's performance in this situation.

The second person meets the same unfriendly group of people. They have the same intention, to overwhelm and stress the interviewee out. However, this guy has been meditating for a long time. Even though his brain feels the danger and wants to press the fight, flight, freeze buttons, he has developed the ability to remain calm and poised. He will be able to shrug off that feeling of doom, and perform at his peak even in that extremely stressful situation.

Guess who is going to get that job?

Guess who is going to rise to the top?

Guess who will be living their dream?

Guess who is going to be truly successful?

Gurudev once remarked: Spending more than half your health to get your wealth and power and then the rest of your life trying to get back your health is not the sign of a successful or intelligent person.

What is the point of becoming the CEO of a multinational in your early forties and having high blood pressure or diabetes or heart problems? All these are stress-related diseases and can be easily avoided if you can figure out a way to deal with the low-level stressors of everyday life.

Through my own personal experience and the experiences of most of my students, if we were to state the benefits of meditation in one sentence, it would be this: 'Meditation enhances life.'

Thousands of studies and research papers support this.

Here are some obvious benefits that anyone who dedicates just half an hour a day to meditation can enjoy:

☐ You feel good about yourself and don't need a reason to be happy. You have truly boarded the Happiness Express!

☐ Fewer things bother you. You experience less stress. You get the ability to effectively deal with pressure.

☐ You get a vastly improved immune system. You don't fall sick so often. Even if you do, you recover quickly.

☐ You focus better and things get done faster.

☐ Your memory improves. At age 50 you can have the memory of a 20-year-old.

☐ Your relationships improve. You feel more empathy.

☐ Meditation can reduce physical and emotional pain. A study concluded that meditation is considerably better than morphine in decreasing the feeling of pain.

☐ Your confidence and creativity go through the roof. You start doing things you never thought you could. Latent talents manifest themselves.

☐ You become more powerful. If you have an addiction, it's much easier to get over it.

☐ You blossom, as the highest ideals and values take root, grow and flower within you.

☐ Pizza tastes soooooo much better after meditation ☺

The Meditating Brain

Remember plastic brains?

If jugglers, London cabbies and musicians manage to physically alter their brain because of what they do, what about the brain structures of people who meditate?

I would like to mention here findings from a series of studies carried out by Sara Lazar of the Neuroimaging Research Program at Massachusetts General Hospital. Sara is an assistant professor of psychology at Harvard Medical School.

The brains of long-term meditators were compared with those who didn't meditate.

It was found that there was increased grey matter in the insula and the sensory and auditory cortices, implying that meditation enhances our senses. Meditation helps us get so much more from the present moment. Sunsets look prettier. Music sounds more melodious. Food is tastier.

The frontal cortex is the area of the brain associated with working memory and executive decision-making. It's well documented that it shrinks as we age, making it increasingly harder for us to remember things and solve problems. Studies have shown that the brains of 50-year-old meditators have the same amount of grey matter in their pre-frontal cortex as normal 20-year-olds do.

Wow!

Playing the devil's advocate, however, maybe these 50-year-old meditators simply had more grey matter to begin with. What then?

A second study took a group of people who had never meditated in their lives and put them through an eight-week program where they learned and practised meditation.

It was quite amazing what their before and after brain scans revealed.

Their brains showed significant 'thickening' in four regions:

☐ The posterior cingulate gyrus, which is associated with mind wandering and self-relevance. Meditation could make you more attentive and feel great about yourself.

☐ The left hippocampus, which assists in learning, cognition, memory and emotional regulation.

☐ The temporal-parietal junction, which is associated with empathy, compassion and perspective. Meditation will make you more compassionate and you will be able to see life from a broader perspective… small things will not bother you as much.

☐ The pons, an area of the brain stem which is involved in the production of regulatory neurotransmitters.

The amygdala, which is associated with the fight or flight response of the brain, and relevant for anxiety, fear and stress, in general actually got smaller. This change in the amygdala was correlated to experiencing a reduction in stress levels.

These were people who had just begun the practice of meditation and did it only for eight weeks, averaging about half an hour each day. As you can see, neuroplasticity verifies the benefits of meditation that my students and I have experienced personally.

Gandhiji and Meditation

If these dramatic changes can happen in just eight weeks, can you even begin to imagine the brain of a long-term meditator? Let me introduce you to Pandit Sudhakar Chaturvedi.

Panditji was Mahatma Gandhi's secretary for a long time. At the time of writing this book, he is still alive, quite active and lives in Bangalore. Panditji was also Gurudev Sri Sri Ravi Shankar's Sanskrit teacher. Thanks to him we know quite a few stories about Gandhiji that have never found their way into history textbooks.

Most people don't know that Gandhiji was a meditator and used to find the time to meditate every day. He once remarked to Panditji, 'I am so busy today, I have so much to do, I don't have the time to do my one hour of meditation. I will have to do two!' Gandhiji was well aware of the benefits of regular meditation.

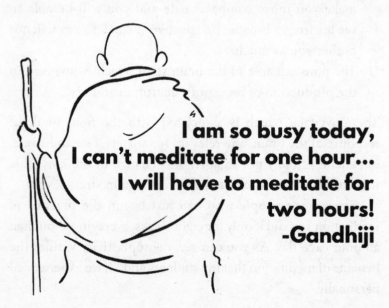

I am so busy today,
I can't meditate for one hour...
I will have to meditate for
two hours!
-Gandhiji

Panditji tells us another story...

'We were travelling to Darjeeling in a toy train. I was sitting next to Gandhiji. There was a sudden jolt as our carriage came unstuck from the rest of the train. It started rolling downwards, slowly gathering speed... There was chaos in the compartment. Screaming, crying, praying...

Gandhiji calmly looked at me and told me to take the dictation of a letter. I couldn't believe my ears. We could die in the next few minutes and you want me to take dictation??!! He looked at me and said, if we die, we die and there is nothing much we can do about it. If we don't die, we are wasting time. Start writing!'

I hope by now you are convinced that you need to learn and practise meditation. There are just too many wonderful things that happen when you meditate for you to continue to ignore this astounding fourth state. The return on investment for just half an hour a day is incredible.

Our Minds: Bug or Feature?

One of the tendencies of the mind is to vacillate between the past and the future. Have you noticed that whenever you are feeling angry, regretful or guilty, it's always about something from the past? You cannot feel anger, regret or guilt about the future. Similarly, all the fear and anxiety we feel is only about the future. There is never any fear about the past. You cannot be afraid of something that's already happened, right? The mind loves to do its pendulum act, whirling you into the past and flinging you into the future, generating a gamut of unhealthy emotions within you.

You may argue that you could go back into the past and

relive those happy times… How many times do you actually do that? You'd notice that you mostly do this when you are feeling miserable in the present.

But I feel great thinking about the wonderful times coming up in the future, you say. Yes, and then, the what-iffing starts. The trouble with building castles in the air is gravity.

The past is gone. You can't do much about it. The future is yet to come. All you really have is this present moment. Happiness is in the present. Right here, right now.

Why does the mind do this then? Why has it been created like this? Why can't it simply stay in the present?

When I was describing the mind and its past-future dance at a talk for a Rotary Club event, a person from the audience asked the same questions as above to me.

Have you ever watched a cow eat grass? I asked him. Do you see how it can keep eating the same grass, day in and day out, 24/7, and not get tired of it? It's because the mind of the cow is in the present. Hence each bite is brand new. Our minds wandering into the past and the future guarantee that we are not cows ☺

Then, a little boy, nine or ten years old, who was listening to all this quite intently, put his hand up. I invited him to the stage and let him address the audience.

'Have you played chess?', he said to the crowd.

'When you have to make a move, you need to look back at all the moves that have been played so far. If you get angry about the moves you made or regret them, you won't be able to make a good move. Merely recalling the earlier moves is not enough either. You have to plan and anticipate what your rival may do. If you get scared, you will not be able to make a good move either. Go into the past to learn from it. Go into the future to plan for it. Make the move in the present!'

This was perhaps the most succinct way of explaining those questions.

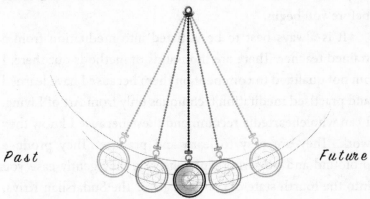

Past   *Future*

Your mind can be a bug or it can be a feature.

Bug: Getting angry, regretful or guilty about the past. Fearful and anxious of the future. Fretting and doing nothing in the present.

Feature: Learning from the past, planning for the future, acting in the present!

Meditation effortlessly brings the mind into the present moment.

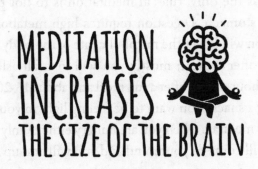

Getting Ready

Please read this section and the next section, The Three Golden Rules, all the way till the end before you start to meditate. You may wish to read and re-read these two sections a few times before you begin.

It is always best to be initiated into meditation from a trained teacher. There are thousands of methods out there. I am not qualified to comment on them because I have learned and practised meditation techniques only from Art of Living. I can wholeheartedly recommend these because I know they work. They are easy to learn and practice. They produce profound and powerful experiences as they gently ease you into the fourth state of consciousness. The Sudarshan Kriya, Sahaj Samadhi Meditation and the processes of the Advanced Course of the Art of Living are, in my opinion, unparalleled in their ability to induce meditation. More details about Art of Living, its founder Sri Sri Ravi Shankar, and its personal development courses can be found at the end of this book.

Having said that, in the rest of the chapter I have outlined a few steps that will at least give you a glimpse into meditation. If nothing else, these guided processes will deeply relax and refresh you.

I guess the only 'rule' in meditation is to not practise it on a full stomach. Digestion requires high metabolism, and meditation will lower the metabolic rate of the body. So never meditate after a meal; mostly you will just fall asleep. Wait about an hour or two after a full meal and about 15-20 minutes following a snack. You want to be feeling light in your tummy.

Don't meditate when you are hungry either. Only thoughts of food will come to your mind and you will end up thinking,

not meditating. If you are hungry, have a small fruit, then sit
in meditation.

In Chapter 6 of the Bhagavad Gita, Lord Krishna tells
Arjuna where and how to sit for meditation.

शुचौ देशे प्रतिष्ठाप्य स्थिरमासनमात्मनः

नात्युच्छ्रितं नातिनीचं चैलाजिनकुशोत्तरम् ॥

*shuchao deshe pratishṭapya sthiramāsanamātmanah
nāthyuchittratam nātineecham chailājinakushottaram*

It means that to practise meditation, make an *asan* (seat)
in a clean, pure place. Put kuśh grass, deer skin and a cloth
one over the other. This seat shouldn't be too high or too low.

Gurudev was giving His commentary on the Gita and
when we came to this shloka, He read it, translated it and
then with a smile said, Krishna is just telling Arjuna to sit
comfortably!

It's great to do a few stretches or light exercises just before
you meditate, even if it's for just 5-10 minutes.

For the first 50-100 times you meditate, find a clean, cool,
quiet and comfortable place to be in. Once you become adept
at it, you will be able to meditate anywhere. In the beginning,
though, where you meditate will matter.

Ensure you sit comfortably with your spine erect, head
facing forward and palms towards the ceiling on your lap. If
you are a beginner, don't become too comfortable. You will
fall asleep.

Do not lie down. Sit.

Eliminate distractions. If there are other people around you, request them not to disturb you for the next half an hour. Pretend you are about to take off on a flight and follow all those things they tell you to do when you fly. Just don't fasten any seat belts. Or worry about oxygen masks.

Don't be in a hurry when you want to meditate. You need to be able to take your time. Find a distraction-free hour or so and settle down.

Once you have settled, read on.

Do a few rounds of alternate nostril breathing or any other pranayama. About five minutes is enough. Ten minutes is great.

The 3 Golden Rules

Have an effortless intention—

Just for a few minutes,

I want nothing.

I will do nothing.

I am nothing.

People find the first two to be easy. Ok, for a few minutes, I will do nothing and want nothing. Just chill and be still. But many, including me, have had problems with the last one. How can I be nothing? I am something. Teacher of meditation, MS in Mathematics, pianist, best-selling author... All these don't amount to nothing for sure. Right?

Once I went to the countryside with a few friends for a night of star-gazing. It was a beautiful, cloudless, moonless night. Perfect for peering into the heavens. One of our friends is an astronomer and he insisted that we spend a night with him, doing what he does. We went along... He had a huge telescope which he took over an hour to set up while the rest of us told each other really bad jokes. It was loud and raucous when he finally announced that the telescope was ready.

As each of us took turns at the telescope, one by one, we went quiet. There was a sudden stillness. We were awed by the immensity and the utter beauty of the skies. We all learned something that night and each of us took unique lessons back home. For me, it was a stunning realisation: I am nothing.

Light travels at the speed of approximately 299,792 km/s. Let me give you a perspective to this number. Clap your hands once. In that instant of a clap, light will go around planet Earth seven and a half times. A light year is the distance light will travel in a year.

The Milky Way is our home galaxy. It is 100,000 light years long and 10,000 light years wide. It is home to between 100-400 billion stars. Our sun is an inconsequential little star in the backwaters of the Milky Way.

99% of the mass of our supremely insignificant solar system is contained in the sun. All the planets, Mercury, Venus, Earth, Mars, Jupiter, Saturn, Uranus, Neptune, Pluto, the asteroids, the moons revolving around various planets, the comets and what-not, constitute just 1% of the mass of our solar system. In that 1% is our Earth inclusive of all its inhabitants. On Earth, there is the country I belong to: India. In India, there is Karnataka. In Karnataka, there is Bangalore. In Bangalore, there is the Art of Living ashram. In that ashram, there is my home. In my home is my room. In my room, there is a chair. I am sitting on that chair and typing this sentence...

Me on my chair on one side. The unimaginable vastness of the Milky Way on the other. And then the knowledge that the Milky Way is just one of billions and billions of galaxies. What am I compared to the Universe. Contemplating this on that starry night so many years ago, it was very easy to say, I am nothing.

If you ever feel you have done something great, just look at the heavens at night.

You too would say, I am indeed nothing.

To reiterate, for meditation, we effortlessly have an intention and simply say to ourselves, just for a few minutes...

I want nothing.

I will do nothing.

I am nothing.

You will say this to yourself as you close your eyes. Repeat it 2-3 times, slowly and deliberately. Keep your eyes closed and your body as still as possible. Relax more and more.

You may feel some sensations in the body. Let them be. There is nothing to do.

Some thoughts and feelings will come up. Accept them, don't try to push them away, don't give importance to them. Just observe. Thoughts are like clouds in the sky. They will come and go. You need to relax and observe the thoughts without getting involved with them.

What does observing the thoughts and not getting involved with them mean?

Ever seen an interesting movie? As you sat among the audience and watched the story unfold before you, did you notice how you began to care for the characters? You rooted for the hero and hooted at the villain. You felt the heroine was a fool for doing what she was doing. You were involved. There was another person watching the exact same things happening on screen. He didn't care at all. The guy in the projector room. He too was right there in the theatre, yet he was totally uninvolved with the drama on screen. Observing thoughts without involvement means easing yourself out of the audience into the projector room of your mind.

Thoughts are just thoughts. They are empty. Our involvement gives them life and impetus. They are waves in the ocean... Just watch...

Once in a while, take a deep breath in, and breathe out slowly and relax. Feel the relaxation slowly dawn within you.

Continue sitting still and let whatever is happening happen... Don't resist anything. Just let it be.

Let time pass.

After a while, when you feel ready to open your eyes, bring a bit of movement to your body. Wiggle your fingers, rotate your shoulders gently, stretch your hands and become aware of your body and the environment. Then slowly, gradually, open your eyes.

Ideally, a session should be for about 20 minutes. More is fine. If it's less, next time have an intention that you will sit for 20 minutes.

Do not set an alarm to remind you that 20 minutes are up. Trust that you would know when to open your eyes.

Relax and enjoy this special time you have created for yourself.

Remember to do some pranayama exercises before you begin.

Fly well!

Peace Meditation

Any prayer or yogic process is always concluded with the *shanti* (peace) mantra: *Om, Shanti, Shanti, Shantihi*. It means peace in the environment around you. Peace in your mind and body. Peace in the subtle realms of the various energies.

Here is a beautiful meditation based on the Shanti Mantra that we created to help you surround yourself with peace. Do this meditation twice a day. If you are feeling stressed out, take out about 15 minutes as soon as you possibly can, and go through this process.

It's best if you record yourself reading out the text below with the appropriate pauses. Speak clearly and slowly in a soothing, soft, gentle voice.

Then, when you want to meditate, sit comfortably, close your eyes and listen to the recording. Don't make any effort to follow the instructions. Just listen and relax and let whatever is happening happen.

We have made a recording of this meditation and you can download it from www.happinessexpressbook.com/audios/ peacemeditation.

Sit easily, comfortably.

Close your eyes and relax.

(Wait 20 seconds.)

Become aware of your breath and watch it as it flows in and out through your nostrils.

Relax more and more as you watch the breath.

(Wait 30 seconds.)

Become aware of the environment around you.

Listen to all the noises: the noise of people talking, noise of traffic, noise in the kitchen.

(Wait 1 minute.)

The sound that your own breath makes as you breathe in... and out...

Breathe in... and out... Relax more and more.

(Wait 1 minute.)

Feel peace descend around you, enveloping your entire surroundings. Even if there are noises, feel in harmony with them as the peace is much greater than the sounds... there is peace around you... Relax more and more... Deeper and deeper.

(Wait 2 minutes.)

Breathe in... and out...

Become aware of the inside of you. The inside of your body...

(Wait 20 seconds.)

The inside of your mind... Your thoughts and feelings...

(Wait 30 seconds.)

There may be some aches and pains in the body. Let them be.

There may be thoughts and feelings, pleasant or unpleasant. Don't change anything. Let them be.

Feel peace come... in waves... through your body and mind... and let everything melt away as you relax more and more... being mindful of the breath, sink in deeper and deeper...

Let peace reign supreme... Like a blanket of light, gentle and soothing, yet profound and powerful. Relax... Relax more and more...

(Wait 2 minutes.)

In the subtle realms of the Devis and Devatas (replace Devis and Devatas with Gods and Goddesses, if you prefer the sound of that), there could be some turmoil. Offer a prayer that the turmoil subsides and all mankind is blessed... Everyone on this planet is blessed with health, happiness, wisdom and prosperity... Let peace win...

Or,

In the world of Subtle Energies, let this same peace wash away all conflict... Let the subtle worlds be at peace... Everyone on this planet is blessed with health, happiness, wisdom and prosperity... Let peace win...

(Wait 2 minutes.)

Take a deep breath in... and out...

Relax more and more... more and more...

Peace in our environment...

(Wait 10 seconds.)

Peace and good health in the body...

(Wait 10 seconds.)

Pleasant feelings in the mind...

(Wait 10 seconds.)

Peace and Blessings from the subtle realms to all humanity...

(Wait 10 seconds.)

Om Shanti...

Shanti...

Shanti... hi...

(Wait 30 seconds.)

Take a deep breath in... and out...

Another deep breath in and smile as you breathe out...

One more breath... Bigger smile, deeper breath... in... and out...

Become aware of your body...

(Wait 10 seconds.)

THE WALT DISNEY CO. IS ONE OF THE FIRST CORPORATES TO INTRODUCE MEDITATION PRACTICES INTO ITS WORK PLACE

Become aware of your environment...

(Wait 5 seconds.)

Slowly bring some movement into the body... Gently move your fingers, slowly rotate your shoulders, stretch your hands...

(Wait 10 seconds.)

When you feel ready, taking your own time, and slowly, gently open your eyes.

Yoga-Nidra

Yoga-Nidra literally translated means Yogic Sleep. It is meditation done lying down. It works fabulously as a power nap. Doing Yoga-Nidra before you sleep at night can greatly enhance the quality of your sleep. Given below are the instructions for Yoga-Nidra. Read through them a few times before practising. You can even record these yourself and play them when you are ready to do it. If you are recording these instructions, use a soft, gentle voice. Be slow and deliberate. Pause for a few seconds in-between each line.

We have recorded Yoga-Nidra and it is available as a free download from our website www.happinessexpressbook.com/audios/yoganidra.

Lie down on your back, legs apart, hands by your sides, palms open. Your hands can be on your chest if that feels more comfortable. You may have a thin pillow under your head. Remember to slide it all the way in, so that your shoulders are resting on it.

Close your eyes.

Become aware of the environment. Listen to all the sounds in the environment. Be in harmony with these sounds.

Take a deep breath in... and breathe out.

Become aware of your body. Your body is a wondrous gift given to you in love by God, by Nature.

Effortlessly become aware of your right big toe. Let your awareness linger there...

Become aware of all the toes on your right foot. Shift your awareness to the rest of the foot.

Become aware of the right ankle...

Right calf...

Right knee...

Right thigh...

Right hip...

Become aware of the entire right leg...

Take a deep breath in... and let go. Another deep breath in... and breathe out.

Relax more and more... Relax more and more...

Become aware of your left foot... all the toes on your left foot...

Left ankle...

Left calf...

Left knee...

Left thigh... and hip...

Become aware of the entire left leg...

Take a deep breath in... and let go. Another deep breath in... and breathe out.

Relax more and more... Relax more and more...

Take your attention to your genitals...

The abdomen...

Stomach...

Liver...

Diaphragm...

Gentle awareness in the chest, heart and lungs...

Shoulders...

Take a deep breath in... and let go. One more deep breath in... and breathe out.

Relax more and more... Relax more and more.

Become aware of your right hand... all the fingers on your right hand...

Right elbow...

Right bicep...

Become aware of the entire right hand...

Deep breath in... and breathe out...

Relax completely...

Become aware of your left hand... all the fingers on your left hand...

Left elbow...

Left bicep...

Become aware of the entire left hand...

Deep breath in... and breathe out...

Let your attention be on your entire back... Effortlessly feel the places that touch the mattress...

Deep breath in... breathe out...

Neck region...

Head...

Become aware of your forehead... your eyebrows and eyes... your nose... your cheeks... your lips... your chin.

Relax more and more... Relax more and more...

Become aware of the back of the head... Feel where the head is touching the pillow.

Become aware of the entire head...

Become aware of the entire body...

Become aware of the entire body... (say it slower and softer)

Become aware of the entire body... (say this even slower and even softer)

Totally relax...

This entire process can be between 20-30 minutes long. Wait at least 7-10 minutes after the final instruction before waking up.

If you decide to wake up after this, turn to your right side and slowly sit up with your eyes closed. Become aware of the environment around you. Keep a smile on your face as you slowly, gradually, when you feel like it, open your eyes.

Don't be in a hurry to get up. Keep sitting with your eyes open for about a minute before you get up and get on with your day.

If you are doing the Yoga-Nidra right before sleeping, feel the deep, deep relaxation as you drift off to sleep. You will feel much more relaxed and refreshed when you wake up in the morning.

Practise Yoga-Nidra before sleeping every night. Have pleasant dreams and a refreshing, rejuvenating rest. The date with that fair enchantress will be even more fun.

F.A.Q ABOUT MEDITATION

Dinesh and I have been teaching meditation for more than two decades. We have taught hundreds of thousands of people the delicate art of doing *nothing*. We receive a bunch of questions in almost every class. Here they are, along with the answers.

1. What is meditation?

When someone asked this question to Gurudev, He simply looked at that person without uttering a word. A little more than a minute elapsed, and Gurudev didn't avert His gaze. A deep silence filled the entire hall.

Finally, Gurudev said to him in a soft, gentle voice, 'Got it?'

Meditation is Waiting for Nothing. Waiting for something is frustration.

2. How is meditation different from thinking?

Meditation is deep rest combined with awareness. Thinking means you are actively involved with your thoughts. In meditation, thoughts may come and go, but you are detached from them. You observe them as if they were clouds in the sky. When you are thinking, you could classify thoughts as good, bad or neutral. In meditation, there is no such classification. A thought is simply a thought.

3. How is meditation different from concentration?

Meditation is, in fact, the opposite of concentration. Concentration is whipped attention. In meditation, we let go and allow the mind to be as it pleases. However, we observe the mind, and whatever thoughts may be there, without involvement.

Meditation dramatically enhances your concentration and your ability to stay focused on the task at hand. Think of meditation as drawing the arrow and concentration as shooting it. The more you pull back the arrow (meditation), the better you will concentrate (the further it will go).

4. How is meditation different from sleep?

Both are rest. Meditation is rest with awareness. Sleep is rest without awareness. The quality of rest that you get from meditation differs from that of sleep. You have to choose to meditate. If you don't sleep, sooner or later, nature will force it upon you. Both are important and neither can be substituted for the other. Having said that, a meditator will have a much bigger time frame to repay sleep debt (see chapter on sleep) than a non-meditator. A meditator becomes adept at sleep, packing in more efficient REM and N3. A meditator could get by with less sleep too, though I wouldn't recommend that.

5. How is meditation different from relaxation?

Meditation will bring on a very deep state of relaxation, much better than any glass of alcohol or recreational drug could. Alcohol and related vices push the mind into ignorance. As you become oblivious to the environment, you tend to become more and more relaxed and comfortable. Meditation uplifts the mind into sparkling awareness which will make you feel wonderful. It's a different type of relaxation... You can only know and experience it when you meditate: www.happynessexpressbook.com/videos/booze.

6. Where should I meditate?

The place of meditation does matter, especially for a beginner. A cool, clean, quiet, comfortable place is best. When you practise meditation every day in one place, it gets charged. You will see that it becomes increasingly easier to meditate when you practise there. That is exactly the case with the recliner in my room at the ashram. I only need to settle myself in it and close my eyes. And then, off I go! Consistency will add depth to your practice.

7. What's the best time of the day to meditate?

The periods of transition, sunrise and sunset, are ideal. We are transitioning from the wakeful state to the meditative state and these times of the day make meditation easier and deeper. Noon is another great time to meditate. If these timings don't suit you, you can meditate at *any* time of the day or night.

Be mindful that meditation can bring in a lot of energy in some people. They feel fresh and alert right after meditation. If that happens to you, it may not be a good idea to practise it just before sleeping.

Meditation brings down the metabolic rate of the body and for good digestion you require a high metabolic rate. Hence, the only time you shouldn't meditate is immediately after a meal. Wait until you feel light in the tummy before you start—as I mentioned earlier, typically 10-15 minutes after a snack, about an hour or two after a full meal.

8. Should I meditate with eyes open or eyes closed?

It's much easier to meditate with eyes closed. With this, an entire avenue of sensory information is shut out. The brain allocates a massive amount of computing power to process visual information. Closing your eyes relaxes you almost instantly.

Besides, have you noticed that your eyes close automatically whenever you are doing something intensely pleasurable? Enjoying a piece of dark chocolate? A kiss? A rose?

There are techniques that teach you to meditate with eyes open. These are reserved for advanced practitioners and I wouldn't recommend you learn any of these techniques from a book or a video. You will need a trained and experienced teacher to guide you into this type of meditation.

9. Should I listen to music while meditating?

If you are a beginner, you may use a relaxing, soft, ambient music. A solo flute or piano works best. The music provides a hook for the mind and as it listens to it, other thoughts subside faster. However, as you progress, even this music can be distracting. If you ask me, I would discourage you from playing any music at all, even if you are a beginner. It's not a good habit. Enjoy music in your wakeful state.

10. Do I need to blank out my mind to meditate?

You cannot make your mind blank. It will go blank.

Thoughts are not an impediment to meditation at all. Your involvement with the thoughts will result in you thinking instead of meditating. Don't bother getting rid of thoughts. That's as ridiculous as wanting to get rid of a cloud in the sky. To get rid of a cloud in the sky, all you do is wait. It will go away by itself. Ditto for a thought.

11. Can I meditate on a chair or is it compulsory to sit cross-legged?

What's important is that you are comfortable. Sit on the floor in lotus pose, or sit cross-legged, or sit in a chair: Padmasan, Sukhasan or Chairasan! Ensure that your spine is erect, head looking straight up front, body relaxed and palms facing the ceiling on your lap.

12. How do I know I meditated?

Here is a little test. Bring a finger to your nostrils. Breathe in and out a few times and see which nostril is dominant. It could be the right or left. Keep checking this throughout the day. You will find that at different times, different nostrils are dominant. Very few times, both the nostrils are balanced.

Immediately after meditation, bring a finger to your nostrils. You will see that very often, both nostrils are balanced. This means you have had a lovely session. In case they are not, please don't fret. Just keep meditating every day.

Of course, if you have a blocked nose or are unwell, this test wouldn't work.

Instead of worrying about whether you are indeed meditating or not, focus more on how you feel after your practice.

This is one of the most important reasons you should learn meditation from a trained instructor. They can ease things out for you, answer your questions and lay your doubts to rest.

13. I have all sorts of thoughts. Sometimes positive, at other times negative. How can I control my thoughts?

You cannot really control your thoughts. If you meditate regularly, pleasant thoughts and feelings become your nature. This is the easiest way I know of 'controlling' my thoughts.

14. Do I need to make lifestyle changes to meditate?

When you meditate, you will feel calm, poised, confident, happy and relaxed. You will tend to make healthier, greener lifestyle choices. These are ultimately good for you and our beautiful planet.

For me, all the lifestyle changes happened on their own. For example, I didn't give up non-veg food; it gave up on me. It had lost the charm it had over me and I no longer wanted it. A child may absolutely love his teddy bear. As the child grows older, the teddy bear loses its appeal and its importance fades away. Your lifestyle changes will mostly happen like that, especially when you meditate regularly.

15. Can I learn meditation from a book, or do I need a teacher?

Well, you are learning from this book... still, any book is light years away in its ability to teach meditation compared to a good teacher. This book gives an introduction to meditation. It even has a few links to guided meditations online and apps. These are all basics, the veritable tip of the iceberg.

To explore this fascinating state of consciousness further and actually learn to meditate, find a teacher. Come and do a course with Dinesh and me or with some other Art of Living teacher. Do a bit of research about the teacher and make sure you feel comfortable learning with them.

16. When I look at pictures or statues of the Buddha in meditation, he is always portrayed as sitting with his head facing forward. My head lolls forward when I meditate. Am I doing something wrong?

No, no, no. You are fine. When we asked this to Gurudev, He mischievously replied, you pose when a photo is being taken!

While meditating, your head may fall forward. If your neck starts hurting and you return to body awareness, slowly bring your head back to its initial front-facing position and slip into meditation saying, 'I want Nothing, I will do Nothing, I am Nothing' to yourself...

17. I have learned various types of meditation. Which one should I do?

Please don't go spiritual shopping. I have been practising just one set of techniques for the last 25 years. I intend to do that for the rest of my life. Becoming established with one is far better than jumping from here to there. If you are seeking water in a field, dig one well of fifty feet. Not ten wells of five feet each. To cross a river, you need only one boat, not five. Stay with one technique.

I have mentioned it earlier, I will say it again: I cannot comment on techniques other than those I have learned. I have learned Sudarshan Kriya, Sahaj Samadhi Meditation and other core techniques of the Art of Living. I can wholeheartedly recommend these because I know they work. This doesn't mean other techniques don't work. They may. I don't know.

Choose a technique. Practise it for a long time. Stay with it. Then the results will show.

18. I have been meditating off and on. I don't experience anything much. How do I enhance my practice?

Stop the off and on. Maharishi Patanjali to the rescue. He says, for your meditation to really work and for you to be established in that wonderful space, you need to do these once you have learned to meditate:

स तु दीर्घकाल नैरन्तर्य
सत्कारासेवितो दृढभूमिः ॥

satu deergha kāla nairantarya
satkāra sevito driḍabhoomi

☐ You need to practise it daily, without a break. Miss a day and it almost resets.

☐ Practise for an appreciably long time (at least a few thousand hours). Though the benefits of meditation become apparent in just a few days, for these to become your nature takes a long time. Be patient and drop expectations. Trust the technique and yourself and keep going.

☐ Honour, respect and revere your practice. This last step is as important as the other two. Meditation is not simply something you do. Feel it to be sacred and special. Know that you are lucky to have the ability to meditate. Feel immense gratitude. This brings about an undeniable transformation.

19. Which direction should I face while meditating?

Well, there is one shloka that says it's best to face east or north when you meditate. Another shloka says, whichever direction a yogi faces while meditating is east!

When someone asked Dinesh about his preferred side, he replied, Inside!

20. Do I need to chant Om?

Om is the primordial sound. It is part of all major religions of the world, in some form or the other. It's 'Amen' in Christianity, 'Amin' in Islam, 'Ek Omkar' in Sikhism and so on. It's not necessary to chant Om, but for me it feels nicer to begin my practice by chanting Om three times. Chanting Om is deeply peaceful, and it signals my mind that I am going to meditate now.

You can watch my TEDx talk on Om at www. happynessexpressbook.com/videos/allaboutom.

21. Do I need a Guru?

Do you need an answer?

The moment you have asked this question, you proclaim your need for a Guru. In fact, by doing so, you have already made the person who would solve your query into your Guru. Guru means a teacher or a mentor. You can have a Guru for music, dancing, or anything else you wish to learn.

A Satguru is the One who initiates you into spirituality. He is a non-intrusive Presence who watches out for you in the here-and-now and the hereafter.

When we asked Gurudev, Hereafter? He replied, *Mar ke to dekho!!* You die and see what happens! (The English translation of the Hindi doesn't convey the essence, but you get the point.)

22. What is the importance of breath while meditating?

Breath is important. Period. If there was no breath, you wouldn't be reading this book, nor would you be meditating. We usually start and end meditation with some pranayama, some breathing. This gentle attention on the breath makes the transition into meditation easier. The breath is the connection between the body and the mind. Sometimes the breath can become very subtle during meditation.

23. How do I deal with restlessness? Feeling fidgety in the body, some itch or discomfort, or too many thoughts in the mind.

- ☐ Check your diet. Stop white sugar, white flour, non-veg food. Definitely steer clear of tobacco, alcohol and recreational drugs. This will help immensely.
- ☐ Check the place you are meditating in. If there is a lot of hustle and bustle, it will cause restlessness. If you are a beginner, it's best to find a cool, clean, quiet, comfortable spot to meditate in.
- ☐ Be aware of the company you keep. The people you hang out with have a direct impact on the mind.

If there is some itching or any other discomfort in the body, don't react right away. Just observe it and be with it. Accepting the itch or pain usually makes it go away. If absolutely required, slowly move into a more comfortable posture.

Sometimes, even when all these are sorted, you may still feel restless. Chalk this up as just one of those days and leave it be. Keep meditating, and the restlessness will settle in time.

The bach flower remedies can help a lot if this problem is recurrent. Take white chestnut if there are too many random worrying thoughts. If these are worrying thoughts about people you care for, red chestnut might be better.

Impatiens (it's not a typo, it's the name of a flower) is recommended if there is too much irritability or fidgetiness.

Crab apple is known to counter itching.

These are very general indicative remedies. I would suggest a full consultation with a qualified Bach Flower Practitioner who would be able to create a personalised remedy for you. They would even educate you about the Bach Flower Remedy System and involve you in creating your remedy. It so happens that I am a qualified practitioner and if you want a consultation, please write to khurshedbfrp@gmail.com to request an appointment.

See appendix 5 for a short write up about these amazing remedies.

24. What if I fall asleep while meditating? Is that okay?

There is quite a thin line between meditation and sleep. If you doze off once in a while, it's fine. If it keeps happening often, you will need to check your diet and sleep. A sleep-deprived person will nod off very quickly during meditation. Eating too much sugar, or difficult to digest food, can make you drowsy. To have deeper sessions, stick to light vegetarian food.

Exhaustion could be another factor—due to an intense workout, jet lag, traffic jams, or physical work such as household chores. In that case, you will naturally drift off to sleep and that's fine. Your body and mind need that.

If none of these is the case and yet you are falling asleep, there could be two reasons. Your mind doesn't want to meditate and tries to escape by going to sleep. If this is the case, the solution is a mere intention to stay awake.

The other reason is your meditation session may be too long. Keep it to 20 minutes to begin with, and over time build it up to about 30-40 minutes. Better to do half an hour twice a day than an hour at one go. Don't be ambitious about meditating more. Don't turn meditation into another competition.

Olive, one of the Bach Flower Remedies, could help in dealing with tiredness. More about these remedies is outlined in Appendix 5.

25. What percentage of time does the mind wander during meditation? What is 'normal'?

This depends a lot on how your life is at the time you are meditating. If you are relaxed, have eaten light, are feeling happy and in your favourite meditation chair, there typically won't be too many thoughts and your session can be very deep.

If you have just been to a noisy place, eaten junk and feeling stressed, then even a few minutes of calm that you experience during meditation would be wonderful. In my experience, there is really no 'normal'. There are days when everything is fine and I hardly meditate, and other days when there is so much stress and I have really deep sessions.

Don't worry if your mind wanders. Let it. Just don't get involved with the thoughts.

26. How to remain motivated to meditate?

Take a short-term vow. For one week or ten days, I will meditate, come what may. When you pull this off, take another vow—this time for a month. Within a few weeks meditation becomes a habit and you will not even think of starting your day without that special time to yourself.

It's helpful to attach meditation to some habit you already have. For example, if you check your email every morning before doing anything else, make sure you meditate just before you do that. A rhythm emerges, first meditation, then email. Or meditate right after you brush your teeth. Or just before your morning walk. Latching on meditation to an already existing habit will turn it into a routine and you won't need motivation any more.

27. Should I work out, then meditate? Or meditate first, then work out?

It's best to go from gross to subtle. Physical workout, Yoga asanas, Pranayama, Meditation and then Prayer is a fantastic sequence to follow. Be aware that if your workout is too intense and you become physically exhausted, you may fall asleep and not meditate.

For me, meditation after workout removes much of the tiredness I feel and enhances the high that I got from the exercise.

28. Is painting/knitting/cycling/dancing/playing a musical instrument/singing or any such activity a form of meditation?

Meditation is utterly effortless. If you are absolutely adept at a particular activity, there may be times when you just get into a zone. If you are a pianist, it could happen that you merge with the music. You are no longer there; the music is being played all by itself. That, too, is meditation. This is a gift bestowed on you by nature. For this to happen, it requires tremendous effort and years of dedicated practice.

Meditation is much much easier than this.

29. Can meditation help me lose weight?

It definitely lightens the mind. It relieves stress, which is one of the main reasons for weight gain. So yes, meditation can help you lose weight. However, if you eat a slice of chocolate cake every time you meditate, you will not be losing any weight any time soon.

A good exercise routine, a sensible diet and enough sleep combined with regular meditation would be a killer combination to become really fit. Art of Living's Yogic Fitness course is based on these principles. If you haven't yet done this course, do yourself a favour and enroll as soon as you can.

30. Will I look younger and age slower by meditating?

A resounding yes to that. Your body ages much slower than the body of a person who doesn't meditate. Don't take this as an excuse to binge on sugar and skip exercise. Meditation brings a smile to your lips that reaches your eyes, a glow on your face and warmth in your heart. It makes you young and ... irresistibly attractive!

31. What to do when an amazing thought pops up while I am meditating?

A thought is just a thought. You get involved in thoughts, and in a snap, you are very far away from meditation. However wonderful the thought, let it be. Relax and meditate. The 'good' thoughts usually disturb you much more than the 'bad' ones. Just know that you will remember them when you come out of meditation. It would be nice to note them down as soon as you can ... thoughts, especially the good ones, don't have a very long shelf life.

If you truly want to remember a great insight that occurred to you during meditation, a gentle intention that you will remember it when you finish is enough to bring it back to you later.

Don't try hard to remember it after meditation. It will only cause you frustration. Rest assured that sooner or later it will come back.

32. Can meditation be dangerous?

For the vast majority of the population, research and my personal experience say: absolutely not. For most people on the planet, meditation is totally safe and life enhancing. There could be a very few people who have very strong bipolar disorders, ADHD or schizophrenia. Certain types of meditation could intensify their symptoms. If you have any doubts, ask a trained teacher to teach you, and consult a doctor, preferably a doctor who himself meditates.

33. Will I get Enlightened if I meditate?

Yes. Eventually.

34. If it's natural to meditate, why do I need a teacher or a guide?

To drive from one place to another, we use Google maps or ask for directions. Don't you think that to deal with something as complex and subtle as the mind, it would be a great to have someone who knows all the routes? I reiterate, find a good teacher to initiate you into meditation. That's where all the magic really is.

35. You say meditation is not concentration. Isn't taking attention to different parts of the body concentration?

Think of an apple. There. You have it. There is no need for an

analysis of what the apple looks like. Is it ripe or not? Is it green or red or yellow? Where is it from, etc. I say apple, and you get it. There is no effort involved. No visualising or anything. This is the kind of relaxed awareness that you are taking to different parts of your body while doing Yoga-Nidra. It is effortless attention. Taking your attention to different parts of your body is simply, effortlessly being aware of them.

36. Is it better to meditate in a group or all by myself?

Both are great. The collective energy of the group can take you much deeper than you may go by yourself. Meditating alone is that special time I create for myself, an expression of the love that I feel for myself.

When I can love me, I don't require others to praise me. It's when people can't love themselves that they become obnoxious in their need for recognition and appreciation.

Your regularity in your practice can be a direct indication of how much you truly love and value yourself.

37. What is a mantra? Do I need a mantra to meditate?

A mantra is a sound that induces a deep and profound state of meditation in you. In my experience, you cannot pick a mantra to meditate. The mantra has to be given to you by your teacher or Guru. It is the Grace and Power that your Guru embeds into the mantra that makes it work. Learn the Art of Living's Sahaj Samadhi Meditation technique for more on this.

38. At what age should one begin to meditate?

Eight years and above. In Indian tradition Lord Narayana, the Highest Guru, is married to Goddess Lakshmi who presides over Wealth. Even rudimentary knowledge of wealth creation will tell you that great wealth comes by investing small amounts of money over a long period of time. The same goes for meditation. Start as soon as you can. Consistently meditating 30 minutes to an hour a day, every day, for many years will give much better results than trying to cram in 8 hours each day, for a few months, when you are 70.

39. Does meditation work if you are an atheist?

Of course! You don't need to believe in the existence of God to meditate. Indian spirituality has it all. There is actually an entire treatise of Vedic philosophy called *Vaisheshika* which is devoid of any mention of God and could be a superb read for an atheist. Just as you can be awake, sleeping or dreaming as an atheist, you can learn and practise meditation as an atheist. Being in meditation is as natural as being in any of the other three states.

In my experience, though, once you do learn and practise meditation, it will become very tricky for you to deny the existence of a Higher Power.

40. Should I meditate when I am ill and don't even have the energy to sit up?

Yes. Please meditate even when you are not feeling all right. If you don't have the energy to sit up, it's perfectly fine to lie down and meditate. You may fall asleep and that's okay too.

The first step of Ayurveda is Yoga. Giving medicines is the second step. Ayurveda rightly believes that healing happens only when you meditate. The medicines are administered to balance the body, so that it becomes easier to meditate. It's the meditation that brings about rapid healing, not the medicines. Meditation provides a huge boost to your immune system and you will be pleasantly surprised at how difficult it is to fall sick and how quickly you heal if you are a meditator.

41. Can one do too much of meditation?

Don't stretch it beyond an hour a day, unless you are under expert supervision or you are an adept yourself.

42. I exercise and follow a healthy lifestyle. I am successful and happy. Do I still need to meditate?

Short Answer? Yes!

A stressed mind will make you impulsive, reckless and thoughtless in a challenging situation. When life goes well, it will make you take things for granted.

A trained meditative mind is calm, poised, confident and alert. It's an asset in any situation. When life gets tough, a meditator will be able to make rational and intelligent choices, ones that he will not regret later. When life is wonderful, a meditative mind can enjoy it even more. Meditation magnifies the intensity of whatever you feel through the senses.

You are already happy? Fantastic! Meditation will make you happier. I hope you are not allergic to that!

For people who exercise, meditation will enhance your time in the gym or on the field. The same exercises and routines will produce faster, better and longer-lasting results.

Every year, we get a free trip around the Sun. Meditation allows you to totally enjoy that journey. It enriches your experience of almost everything on Earth.

For those who don't meditate, life can often be pedestrian and mundane. For those who do, life is almost always a miracle!

Chapter 4

FOOD

The ancient rishis called a human being Purusha. Literally translated, this means one who lives in or presides over a city. City?! I rule a city?

Did you know that our bodies are a whopping 90% bacteria and just 10% human? One can think of the body as a city and the bacteria as the residents of that city. You and I rule cities!! The ancient rishis did it again!

Microbiome

The trillions of microscopic organisms that reside in and on our bodies make up what is called the microbiome. Just as the quality of a city depends upon its denizens, recent research has almost conclusively proved that our own health is a function of the different kinds of bacteria that are a part of our bodies... especially those that live in the gut.

These guys don't just digest the food we eat, they hold sway over our appetite, our metabolism and our immune system. They influence our moods and can determine how our brain feels—sharp and laser-like, or fuzzy and woolly. They impact the health of our hearts and how our bones develop. They are a source of critical vitamins and minerals. They know how

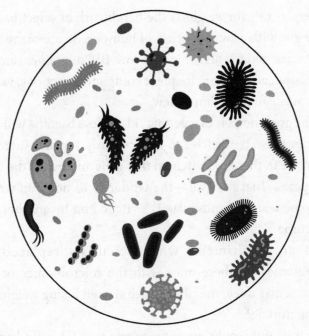

Microbiome

to create natural antibiotics for us. Their job description is endless.

Create an environment where the 'good' bacteria can thrive, send the right type of nourishment their way, and they, in turn, ensure various aspects of our bodies function smoothly, resulting in great health for us. Create an environment that is beneficial for the 'bad' bacteria, feed them what they want and our city becomes a nightmare. Our health is compromised and life becomes an ordeal.

What I found amazing is that these bacteria influence how our genes express themselves. I have often heard people say: I have a tendency to gain weight, it's genetic. I just look at food and a centimetre manifests itself on my waist. This genetic 'tendency' to gain weight is the handiwork of select bacteria in the gut with a twisted sense of humour. So are many other tendencies: skin issues, high or low BP, migraines, anxiety, depression, congestion, frequent colds and infections, various aches and pains, to name a few.

The good news is that getting rid of these bacteria will often result in these tendencies to miraculously vanish! There will be no one in there to switch on that gene and hence the effect disappears. That's not all—the tendency to not gain weight, and to be lean and muscular, is switched on by another type of bacteria.

In an experiment, when scientists replaced the microbiomes of obese mice with the microbiomes of lean and muscular mice, the obese mice started losing weight and gaining muscle!

If we could only evict those yes-to-a-fat-belly bacteria and replace them with yes-to-good-looking-abs species, those workouts and walks would show lightning fast results. That would only be the beginning. We could similarly substitute the high or low BP bacteria with healthy BP bacteria, the migraine bacteria with no-pain-in-the-head bacteria... You get the drift?

And how would we do this?

It largely depends on what we eat. You *really* are what you eat. When we eat, we are feeding all those trillions of bacteria that make up our microbiome.

A good diet needs to create a benign environment for the friendly critters living inside us and to feed them well. The bad fellows would be tightly constrained, and the good fellows would rule. Result? We smile more, suffer less, don't fall ill as often, and generally have a better quality of life.

The Perfect Diet?

It is quite bewildering when you think about how much we eat. Each day, on an average, around 2 kg of food goes through that opening in our body we call the mouth. This works out to around 60 kg a month, which is a little shy of a tonne a year. That's the weight of a giraffe! Keep eating like this for 50 years and you would have consumed the weight of 10 adult African elephants!

There is an assortment of diets and fads that have been created by all sorts of people for all sorts of purposes. There is too much information out there, a lot of it contradictory and quite a bit goes against my principles of being a vegetarian.

Dinesh and I devoted a few years to seeking the perfect diet. We read stacks of books and tried all kinds of food. We finally realised that there is no such thing as a perfect diet. We are all different, our microbiomes are different and what may work for one person wouldn't for another. In fact, what may work for an individual in a particular place, during a particular season, may not work for the same person if they move to another place or during a different time of the year.

Of course, you can consult a qualified dietician, but finding one that suits you, your gut and your principles can be quite daunting and expensive.

The only way to figure out the perfect diet for you is to educate yourself about food, listen to age-old grandmothers' advice and combine that with your own intuition.

Eventually I am pretty sure I will write a full-fledged book on this subject. Until then, here are a few crucial things you should know about food.

Food can be divided into three major groups:

1. Macro nutrients: Carbohydrates, fats and proteins;
2. Micro nutrients: Vitamins and minerals;
3. Water.

Energy

Carbohydrates aka carbs are the quickest, most efficient and preferred source of energy for the body. Carbs or sugars are molecules composed of carbon, hydrogen and oxygen. There are two types of carbs: simple and complex. Simple carbs are those that have just one or two molecules of sugar, complex carbs have longer chains—three or more molecules of sugar. The simple ones are bad for you, while the complex ones are really good for you.

White carbs, especially white sugar and white flour, are the food super villains.

Let me explain…

When you eat carbs, they supply you with energy.

Energy = Sugar.

One of the requirements for the brain to function optimally is a certain concentration of sugar in the blood stream (a minimum of 70-110 mg/decilitre). If this increases, then the brain signals the bouncers, called insulin, to end the party. These bouncers politely escort the excess sugar to various parts of the body where energy might be needed. First, they check with the muscles and ask if they have any energy requirement. If you are an average, typical human being, then your muscles will say we need a tiny bit in the fingers to keep them supple for pressing buttons on the remote control. The sugar is next escorted to the liver which usually has enough to keep it going and will refuse any extra. Finally, the party reaches the fat cells and they greedily agree to absorb all the sugar.

Simple carbs are easily assimilated into the blood stream and cause what we can call a sugar spike.

You relish a rich sugary sweet and suddenly there is way too much sugar in your blood. The brain commands the insulin to end this crazy bash and the insulin goes out with all guns blazing to get the sugar out of the blood, mostly into the fat cells. Unfortunately, the insulin does its job too well. It clears out all the sugar and now there is a fall in the blood sugar which jeopardises the normal functioning of the brain. The brain then desperately calls for sugar. Some simple sugar please, don't have time to process it. So you gorge on sugary sweets which again spikes the blood sugar and the brain reverses its order and calls out the insulin yet again. This vicious cycle continues, confusing your brain, playing havoc with the systems in your bodies. This is the reason why it is almost impossible to stop at just one small bite of a dessert.

White flour too has the same effect. And has one more trick up its sleeve. It coats the inner lining of the intestine with a fine layer, preventing the absorption of nutrients from the food you consume. If you have too much white flour in your system, very soon, even if you are eating the healthiest food in the world, your body will become incapable of assimilating it.

All this seems to be giving carbs a bad rep and there are many 'experts' who recommend a low or no carb diet. Remember that Carbs = Energy and such a diet will mean very little energy and make you feel defeated, frustrated, angry and exhausted.

It is quite interesting to note that the exact same system that feeds fat cells in our bodies can make the body muscular and lean as well. The insulin takes the sugar to the muscles first: if you have exercised, the muscles will be tired and want that energy boost they get from the carbs. Most of your carbs will be absorbed right there. The same carbs that can make you fat can make you muscular if you have exercised and eaten the food at the right time.

You must eat carbs. All carbs are not created equal. Just make sure you eat the right type of carb.

Good carbs are made up of (three or more) molecules of sugar, starch and fibre. In case you are wondering what starch is, it is the compacted form of plant sugar. The longer sugar molecules in plant sugar can be prone to meandering lengths and get a little out of hand. If they were not compressed, a potato would be the size of a dog, or perhaps an elephant. Just like we compress bigger files into zipped files when we want to send stuff over the internet, nature zips up sugar to keep things manageable. This zipped file of sugar is called starch.

The fibre is not digestible; it gives bulk to food increasing the feeling of satiety. It helps in moving the food along the digestive tract.

Whole grains are cereals that contain the endosperm, germ and bran compared to refined grains which are stripped of the germ and bran and retain only the endosperm.

Whole grains contain the seed of life itself and boast of tremendous vitality and energy. Did you know that these unrefined, unprocessed grains don't spoil for over a thousand years?! Brown rice, whole wheat, whole grain barley, quinoa, whole oats and other such cereals are amazing complex carbs and must be included in every diet.

All refined, processed, deep fried or milled fare are simple carbs. These release sugar very quickly into the blood causing sugar spikes and lay the foundation for terrible health.

Placating Your Sweet Tooth

Do not use any sort of artificial sweetener. Those are dangerous and will swiftly create life-threatening consequences.

Watch out for things like high fructose corn syrup (HFCS), corn syrup and other unpronounceable stuff on the ingredients list of whatever you buy to sweeten your food. These are all gobbledygook of sugar.

Organic coconut or palm sugar is a sweetener better than normal sugar but definitely not as good as no sugar. When a recipe calls for sugar, these sugars can be used in almost the same quantity as regular sugar and many people find that very convenient.

Fruit pulp and juices are great sweeteners. Banana pulp, apple sauce and berry juices give distinctive flavours to your desserts.

Dates and raisins pulped or simply tossed into your milkshake instead of sugar are quite nice.

I love the taste of maple syrup in my food. Just make sure that it has not been adulterated with other noxious additives. Simple, plain organic maple syrup is best. There is some research that says that the darker varieties of maple syrup may be better than the lighter golden type.

Stevia is considered to be one of the best sweeteners ever. It loses a few points because it leaves a little bit of an after taste. Stevia can be between 100-200 times sweeter than regular sugar, so you require a tiny bit of it to sweeten quite a big batch of dessert. Don't use the powdered variety, use the tincture or dried stevia leaf.

Jaggery is typically Indian. We have not seen it anywhere else in the world. It is a fabulous sweetener, and many Indian sweets can easily be made with jaggery instead of white sugar. Ensure that you use the organic, non-processed variety. The darker the jaggery, the better it is. As children we would get a huge piece of it as a reward for finishing all the food on our plates... I still have a piece after almost every meal.

Honey has been used since times immemorial to sweeten food. Honey doesn't spoil. Jars of it have been found in Egyptian tombs and is still edible. It has been mentioned many times in the Vedic scriptures. Make sure the honey is raw; not boiled and pasteurised. There are quite a few health benefits of having two to three tablespoons of raw honey every day. Most commercial brands available are not raw. Beware of these. They are sugar masquerading as honey. Use different types of honey; don't stick to just one variety.

There are many who believe that honey is perhaps the best and healthiest way to sweeten food.

Protection and Survival

Other than Sumo wrestlers, no one I know of wants to be fat. Yet fat is an essential member of the trinity of macro nutrients. Our bodies are bags within bags within bags within bags. The entire body is contained in the first bag which we call the skin, followed by the fascia, then deep fascia and muscle (and bone) coats and finally organ cavities in which the organs reside. In between each of these bags is fat. All organs are enveloped in fat. Fat ensures smooth and lubricated movements of the body. It protects delicate organs from the shock waves which routinely happen when we move. It keeps everything where it's supposed to be—for example, ensuring that your kidneys don't end up somewhere near your knees every time you jog.

When an infection poses a threat, the body isolates it by cleverly coating it with a layer of fat. The body's defence system then gets to work to eliminate it. Fat plays an important role in surviving infectious attacks.

Fat protects.

Our brain is nearly 60% fat. A form of fat called lipids, very different from fat cells, but fat none the less. We learn and remember better when our neural pathways are myelinated. Myelination is medicalese for 'coating of fat.'

The fat cells in our bodies are storehouses of energy reserved for emergencies. Fat is a smart evolutionary move. Our bodies evolved over hundreds of thousands of years. Most of the time we have spent on this planet has seen severe shortage of food. Our bodies had to get energy wherever and whenever they could and learn to store it for tough times.

Hence, the fat cell: Energy for Emergencies.

The Battle of the Bulge

My father, thank God, has saved and invested money for my sister and me all through his life. I have been signing various complicated documents every now and then. He has forever been telling me, I would get this money when I am older.

Recently, when I turned 49, I asked him how much older was I supposed to get before I got that money. He said, 'Don't worry. You will get it when I die.' I said, 'That's no fun... I want to see your face when I spend it!' The next day, I got yet another document to sign.

Our bodies' attitude towards storing emergency reserves of energy in the form of fat is the same as my dad's approach with money. If it comes in, it's not going anywhere. That's it!

Our bodies' evolution has not yet caught up with the age of plenty that we are living in.

You starve the body and you are reinforcing its evolutionary insecurity about lack of food. It will stubbornly hold on to fat. If it is forced into burning those reserves, it will stock pile them at the next opportunity. The battle of the bulge would continue with no hope of victory. You know why most of those shed-your-fat diets don't work for too long, and why as soon as you are off the diet, the fat boomerangs back with a vengeance.

For the body to let go of fat, it needs to be convinced that there is enough food for it to survive and that it will receive it at regular intervals. The survival instinct of our body makes it super possessive about fat.

Fat loss has to happen gradually. The body will automatically let go of its fat reserves once it is convinced that food is readily available. But how do we convince it?

There was a time I used to suffer from terrible acidity. I'd get a burning sensation in my food pipe throughout the day, accompanied by those disgusting undigested food burps. I tried all sorts of medicines and cures for this. Ayurveda, allopathy, homeopathy, massage, reflexology... Nothing worked for more than a week.

I discussed my problem with a doctor friend of mine, who simply advised me to eat on time. 'If you have breakfast at 7 a.m., you need to have it every day between 6.55 a.m. and 7.05 a.m. The same goes for your lunch and dinner. Wrap up your dinner before 8 p.m.'

I rationalised to him for 15 minutes about why I couldn't follow all this. My courses start at 7 p.m., I said. I couldn't walk out of them in the middle of the pranayamas to eat dinner. Plus, I travel a lot, and have plenty of late nights...

He patiently listened to my soliloquy. When I finished, he leaned back in his chair and said, Ok, then suffer.

I cleaned up my food habits and meal times from the very next day. Within a month, my acidity drastically reduced, and in three months all symptoms had vanished. It felt fantastic.

Another amazing thing happened to me because of eating on time. Over the next few months, I shed about 5 kilos of weight, which was mostly fat. While I failed to see a connection back then, I now know what had happened. I ate good food, fastidiously sticking to my meal times for a few months. This must have convinced my body that there was plenty of food and it was regularly available. The evolutionary insecurity had been wiped out. My body, at first grudgingly, and then quite enthusiastically, let go of the ugly fat around my middle. I was actually winning the battle of the bulge as a happy by-product of fighting my acidity.

Though I have presented a strong case for fat, it doesn't mean you need oodles of it. A little bit in between each of the 'bags' is more than enough. Extra fat will burden the various systems of your body and invite rapidly declining health.

Bad fat or trans-fat clogs arteries and can lead to heart attacks and stroke. It makes you look ugly and saps confidence. The only way to burn fat is to eat fat. The type that lubricates and protects, and in small, controlled quantities. Picture protecting the flame of a burning diya by adding tiny bits of fat everywhere.

Eat on time. Eat controlled quantities of good quality fat. Throw some exercise and meditation into the mix and, in time, you will begin to look good and feel great. For sure, you will smile more!

Building Blocks

Think Lego blocks. That's protein.

The basic building blocks of life are protein. Protein is what everything is made of in our bodies. Structures in our bodies are being regenerated all the time. For the regeneration to happen, we would need certain pieces to replaces those that are failing. These pieces are created by the body using protein.

Proteins themselves are made up of individual amino acids. NH_2 makes up the amine or amino part and COOH is the carboxylic acid group. Various proteins are just chains of these two groups in different permutations and combinations. The protein required to regenerate tendons is different from that needed to rebuild muscle, which would be different from the protein required to renew the bone and so on.

There are 22 amino acids that the body requires as its Lego blocks. Think of these as Lego blocks in various sizes that the body would use to renew or replace parts of itself. Of these 22, 9 are considered to be essential. Essential simply means the body cannot synthesise these and they need to come from the food we eat. There is a tenth one that is required during childhood in the phase of rapid growth. Though the body can make it, it cannot make enough of it during that time, and so it needs to be supplemented by eating.

The body doesn't store protein, so it is imperative to make sure you get enough of it through food. Likewise, because the body doesn't store protein, if you eat too much, it will just be excreted. But not before it has been broken down into usable form (converted to carbs or lipids or oxidised), which is a tremendous amount of work for the body. It would be like buying the 7541-piece $1000 Lego set with which you can make the huge Millennium Falcon space ship from Star Wars (utterly drool-worthy btw, wouldn't mind getting it as a birthday present) and using about 100 pieces to make a tiny house and throwing the rest away!

Too much protein would mean a huge waste of resources and energy just to create poo. Too little would mean bone and muscle degeneration.

How much is enough?

Experts haven't come to an agreement about this. Approximately 25% of your meal should be good proteins. You may increase this by about 5% if you are actively exercising.

I would go with plant protein instead of animal protein any day. Eating vegetarian food is good for your body, fantastic for the planet and a winning strategy in the long run. We have talked at length about this in our previous book *Ready, Study, Go!* and on our blog www.bawandinesh.in.

Watch my video 'Make the Moon Smile' (www.happinessexpressbook.com/videos/makethemoonsmile) for more information about why choosing a plant-based diet is just the right thing to do.

Vitamins and Minerals

Vitamins and minerals are required in trace quantities to keep certain very specific functions of the body going. When they are present in the right amounts, you don't feel much, everything is humming along smoothly. Their deficiencies, however, can create all sorts of complications. With vitamins and minerals, it can get extremely technical or remain very simple. Let's keep it simple.

1. For each meal have many colours of food on your plate.
2. All the six tastes—sweet, sour, salty, bitter, pungent and astringent—should make an appearance at least once in a day.
3. Make sure you get about an hour of sunlight every day. Sunlight will stimulate Vitamin D production in your body. However, contrary to popular belief, this doesn't happen as efficiently in the early mornings or late evenings. The sun needs to be at an angle of at least 50° above the horizon (90° is directly above) for reaching its greatest potential of stimulating Vitamin D production. A good way to test this is to check the length of your shadow. If your shadow is shorter than you, the sun is in the perfect position to get your body to produce significant amounts of Vitamin D. Of course, you need to make sure that you have exposed enough of your skin while you are in the sun to create that Vitamin D.
4. Eat a little bit of dairy—some A2 milk or products made from A2 milk like yogurt, ghee or butter.

Following these four steps will ensure you have all the vitamins and minerals you require.

Many people believe that animal flesh or secretions (milk) have Vitamin B12 and it is absent in a completely plant-based diet. While it is true that plants are not a source of B12, neither are animals. B12 is made by anaerobic bacteria (these don't need oxygen for survival) in the soil, and is found in dirt and soil where these bacteria grow. For thousands of years, humans got their supply of B12 by eating plants that still had some bits of soil on them. Animals get it the same way and that's how it finds its way into the milk and the flesh.

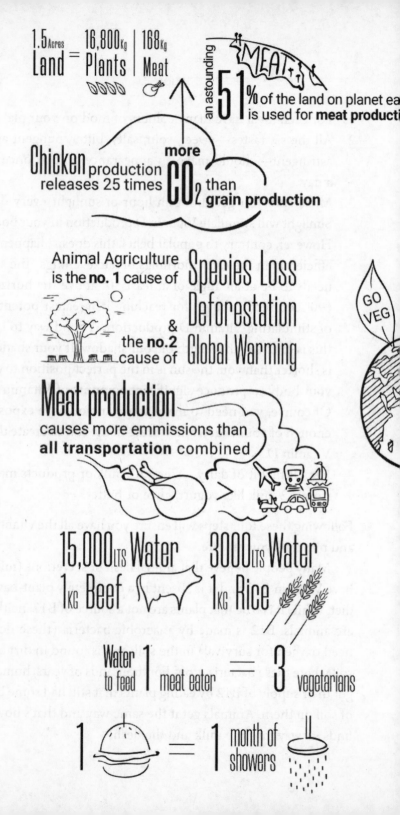

The human body is designed for a vegetarian diet. Our teeth are not sharp and our intestines are longer than our bodies, ideal for **herbivores.** Meat can take up to **72 hours** to pass through our intestines and will rot and ferment inside of us.

World Health Organisation

places **red & processed meat** in the same danger level to our health as **smoking and tobacco**

70% of Food Poisoning

Is caused by **meat consumption, including** exposure to **arsenic**

Chronic Heart Disease

The US economy spends a staggering **$1 Trillion** each year on medical costs due to these diet releated diseases

Stroke
Obesity
Cancer
Diabetes
Osteoporosis

+

Slaughterhouses inject **Hormones** and **antibiotics** into livestock so they grow **faster and bulkier**

this is a serious **health hazard** since they find their way into your bloostream when you eat meat

Nobel prize winner Elizabeth Blackburn discovered that a vegan diet changed more than 500 genes in 3 months

it activated genes that prevented diseases & de-activated genes that caused various **immune system** related illnesses & certain types of **cancer**

These days, we wash our fruits and veggies thoroughly which is a great thing to do—but it removes all the B12 from them. In this case, B12 supplementation may be the way to go for strict vegans.

Some people could have severe deficiencies that may require supplements. Seek a professional's help for this.

Having some pre- and probiotic supplement may be a good idea. A prebiotic creates a good environment for the nice bacteria in your gut. A probiotic will add millions and millions of the good guys to your microbiome.

Please consult an expert for more information about this.

Good Food to Eat

Now that you know the fundamentals of food, you might be wondering which foods are better than others and what macro- or micro-nutrient they provide. Read on ...

Great Carbs

Oats (old fashioned or steel cut), unpolished and unrefined whole grain rice (brown, red or black varieties are way better than white), quinoa, couscous, amaranth (*raajgira* or *raamdaana*), buckwheat (*kootu*), sorghum (*jowar*), barley, spelt are all super grains loaded with complex carbs. Some grains like quinoa and spelt are rich in protein too.

Veggies like sweet potatoes, pumpkin, butternut squash, beet and tomatoes are rich sources of complex carbs. Did you know that tomatoes are 95% water?!

Chocolate was used
AS CURRENCY BY THE AZTECS

Apples, bananas, mangoes, grapes, papayas, blueberries, blackberries, acai berries, strawberries, watermelons, oranges, peaches, pears and pineapples pack in loads of vitamins and minerals along with healthy doses of good carbs.

Powerful Proteins

Nuts and seeds of all types—walnuts, almonds, pecans, pine nuts, sunflower, pumpkin and flax seeds—are superb sources of protein.

Tofu (firmer tofu means more protein), seitan, tempeh, horse gram, beans—chickpeas, kidney beans, pinto beans and black beans, all lentils, chia seeds, edamame, asparagus, broccoli, spinach, artichokes, kale, brussels sprouts, bok choy, zucchini, carrots, green beans, green peas and spirulina pack quite a protein punch.

Fantastic Fats

The healthiest fat you could have is from A2 milk from the Indian *desi* cow. Ghee and butter made from the milk of breeds like the Gir cow, an ancient breed dating back to Lord Krishna's time, are rocking sources of good fat.

95% OF THE AVOCADOS YOU WOULD EAT IN AMERICA CAN BE TRACED TO A SINGLE TREE PLANTED IN 1926 BY A POSTMAN CALLED RUDOLF HASS

Coconuts and coconut oil, avocados and avocado oil, and olives and olive oil are next on my list of great fats to have. The oils should be extra virgin and cold pressed—no refining or heating of any sort. Coconut oil, avocado oil and ghee are good for frying. They have very high smoking points.

My most favourite source of good fat is dark chocolate. 70% or more is fantastic. One or two squares a day is enough. You could add dark cacao nibs to your smoothie or shake.

Good quality organic fresh and aged cheeses are amazing sources of fat and protein. Make sure they are vegetarian and use vegetarian rennet.

Chia seeds, hemp seeds, walnuts and flax seeds are rich in the elusive Omega 3. Other nuts and seeds have very good fat content in them.

Finally, traditionally made Greek yogurt is brimming with great fat.

Super Foods

Super foods are foods that are unusually dense in all sorts of nutrients that our bodies love. Other than all the goodies mentioned above, make sure you get portions of these foods on to your plate.

Turmeric, cumin, mustard seeds, fenugreek, Ceylon cinnamon are terrific spices to bring rich aromas and tastes to your food. Don't forget ginger and garlic. Most Parsi recipes call for a paste made of ginger and garlic—a distinctive taste.

Kale, arugula, baby spinach, lettuce and various salad greens are supreme sources of great health. Don't spoil their health benefits by adding those high-in-bad-fat dressings.

Coriander or cilantro leaves, and moringa leaves are great as garnish and can be cooked with lentils or made into chutneys.

Tulsi leaves eaten just like that or brewed into a tea with a bit of ginger and jaggery can clear most congestions between the throat and the navel.

Shiitake mushrooms in particular, and all the other types of edible mushrooms in general, give great flavour and texture to food. They are rich in vitamins and minerals, fibre and proteins.

Lemons and limes deserve a special mention. Lemon (or lime) juice will alkalise your system brilliantly. A lemon or lime shot first thing in the morning with warm water would be a superb start to your day.

Organic miso added to soups, salads and veggies will give a boost to good gut bacteria—it is considered to be a fantastic probiotic.

Kombucha is another wonderful probiotic Japanese drink fast gaining popularity for its health benefits. A small shot twice a day and the good guys in your gut will be grateful.

I had not heard of kefir till recently, and found it to be similar in taste to Indian lassi. It is full of good fat, probiotics and protein. Most people who are lactose intolerant can drink kefir even though it is made from dairy milk.

CANNED PEACH WAS THE FIRST EVER FRUIT TO BE EATEN ON THE MOON

My favourite Italian herb is basil. It's nutritious, can be eaten raw or cooked, or made into delicious pesto. Basil is perhaps one of the easiest plants to grow. Fresh basil, just plucked from a potted plant, is quite a treat for your tongue.

Nori, the Japanese seaweed, is full of vitamin B12—great news for people who are vegetarian or vegan. It is incredibly tasty when added to a Goan curry. Of course, you could have it as sushi.

The humble Indian gooseberry (*aamla*) has made it to the super foods list. Extremely rich in Vitamin C and many other vitamins and minerals, it is a brilliant anti-oxidant as well.

The little green moong beans are full of protein, fibre, anti-oxidants and phytonutrients.

Green tea is one of the heathiest beverages on planet earth. Full of anti-oxidants and nutrients, studies show that green tea improves brain function, lowers cholesterol and helps with fat loss.

Cucumbers have an impressive list of health benefits—great for the skin, superb detox for the body, alkalising, boosts digestion and makes stronger bones and teeth. Cucumbers are considered to be conducive to meditation.

Sattu flour is the secret Indian super food. Sattu has always been considered a poor man's food—bursting with proteins and rich in iron, this flour can be made into a sweet or savoury drink, or used as a stuffing. It is dirt cheap to buy, and brings on a feeling of satiety because of its high-fibre content. Few outside the Indian subcontinent know about it.

Sacha inchi or the Incan peanut is the new kid on the super foods block. It is a rich source of Omega 3 along with containing other brain- and heart-supporting vitamins and minerals.

When?

Two groups of genetically identical rats were given a high-calorie, full-of-fat diet. Both groups were allowed to eat as much food as they wanted to. The only difference was that while one group ate whenever they wished, the other group was allowed to eat for just eight hours each day. The first group developed the expected health issues: high sugar, cholesterol, lethargy, heart problems, etc. The second group, amazingly, remained fit and healthy. This experiment and many others like it concluded that timing is critical when it comes to eating. *When* you eat may actually matter more than what you are eating!

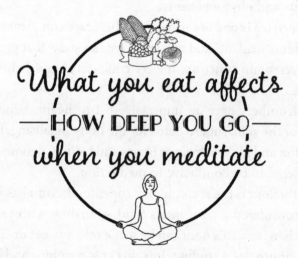

What you eat affects —HOW DEEP YOU GO— *when you meditate*

There is a lot of science that now supports what is called intermittent fasting. The benefits are almost magical and following this 'diet' is quite simple. Restrict your eating time to between 8 to 12 hours daily. If you eat your first meal at 9.00 a.m., your last meal should ideally be by 5.00 p.m. Outside this eating window, you may only drink water.

Start with a 12 hour fast and build that up over a few months to 16 hours a day. If you keep your fast for 12 hours, you will typically not put on any weight. Every hour more up to a maximum of 16 hours a day will double the benefits—your body will start to burn fat and replace it with muscle.

Add a sensible diet and some vigorous physical activity to the mix, and you will become healthier and fitter than you have ever been before.

Some people don't like the word fasting, so they call this system Time Restricted Eating or TRE. Watch out for more about this on our blog and in our next book.

A Liquid Enigma

Combine two atoms of one gas with one atom of another. Make sure both gases are highly inflammable. The result is not a gas. It is a liquid, which can be used to douse fire. It turns gaseous on heating; when frozen it turns solid. Other liquids contract when cooled; this one expands as its temperature drops from 4°C to 0°C, becoming less dense as it grows colder. It manages to float in itself because the liquid is actually denser than the frozen solid it becomes.

This mysterious liquid is the result of a chemical romance between oxygen and hydrogen. Water (H_2O) is one atom of oxygen in love with two atoms of hydrogen. The Sanskrit word for water is *Apah*. *Apah* also means love. Drinking water is loving yourself.

All of us are approximately 70% water. Even our planet is 70% water—quite a coincidence, huh?! Water is the base for most of the chemistry that happens in our bodies. Water is Life.

Thirst is your body crying for water. Actually, by the time

you feel thirsty, parts of your body are already dehydrated and not functioning optimally. Water is critical to great health and the smooth functioning of our bodies.

Your mood is better when you have enough water. You have less aches and pains and your skin glows. Proper hydration can help prevent cancer and stave off migraine headaches. Water is crucial for flushing out wastes and toxins from our systems. Our brain works much better when we have enough water.

CUCUMBERS ARE 96% WATER.
CRANBERRIES BOUNCE
WHEN THEY ARE RIPE.
ALMONDS ARE ACTUALLY
SEEDS, NOT NUTS

If you are thinking about building muscle, you definitely need to have a lot of water because muscle tissue is a whopping 75% water. Any muscle cramp is usually due to insufficient water.

In general, drink a lot of water. Three litres a day for sure. If you work in an air-conditioned environment, you may need to drink a little less. Drink water at room temperature and drink slowly. Sipping water like it is some fine wine is much better than gulping it down. Sipping water regularly instead of gulping a lot of it a few times allows the body to absorb much more of it. The body stays hydrated and urination is up to six times lower. Make sure you are sitting when you are drinking water.

Please don't waste water—there are a billion people on

earth who don't enjoy the privilege
that you and I do. That you and I
can take so much for granted: clean
drinking water readily available.

Every time you drink water,
remember to feel immense gratitude
as it flows down your body quenching
your thirst and nourishing the life in
your system.

How to Tame Your Stomach

The unit pH (potential of hydrogen—
don't ask, I have no idea what it means) tells you how acidic
a substance is on a scale of 0 to 14. 0 being super acidic to 14
being super alkaline. 7 is considered neutral.

Our blood is slightly alkaline with a tightly controlled
pH hovering between 7.35 and 7.45. A pH of 6 in your blood
means you are in coma. Maintaining a pH of 7.35 to 7.45
creates a benign environment for the good bacteria in our gut.
It helps cellular enzyme activity and maintains cell membrane
integrity.

pH is a logarithmic scale. This means that pH 6 is 10x
more acidic than pH 7, pH 5 would be 100x more acidic than
pH 7 and so on.

For digestion, our stomach uses acid. It produces gastric
acid in the range of pH 1.5 to 3.5! The stomach acid is strong. It
is 10,000x to 100,000x more acidic than blood and can dissolve
a stainless steel blade. The stomach can easily digest itself. It
doesn't, because the cells of the inner lining of the stomach
are continuously regenerating themselves. Food that lands in

the stomach is thoroughly churned—think of a blender with
thousands of blades. This churning along with the acids digests
(breaks down) the food into tiny pieces and passes it along to
the duodenum for further processing.

The stomach will play a one-upmanship with whatever
food that comes in. It always wants to be more acidic than the
food that lands in it. Eating acidic food will make it secrete
higher concentrations of acid to aid in digestion and keep its
ego intact. Higher acidic environment in the stomach will
mean higher levels of acid in the digested food as it travels
through the digestive tract.

Eventually, the digested food is absorbed into the blood
stream... but blood needs to be alkaline (pH 7.365) and
this extra acid that is coming in is not helping at all. We have
alkaline buffers in our body and the body will draw on them
to bring the system back to a pH of 7.365. These buffers,
though, can get depleted pretty fast. The body will do anything
to remain alkaline, even sacrificing long-term and/or short-
term health. Various body functions could get compromised.
The body could, for example, begin to draw upon calcium in
the bones or magnesium from the vital organs to maintain its
alkaline levels. Mainly the kidneys work overtime to get rid
of that extra acid.

Many times, if too much acidic food is consumed, the
kidneys may not be able to keep up with the acidic wastes and
the body will then store the extra acid in our tissues. Studies
have shown that over time, this accumulation can have severe
health consequences: kidney stones, muscle degradation,
reduced bone density, even arthritis.

This is why it is so much better to eat more portions of

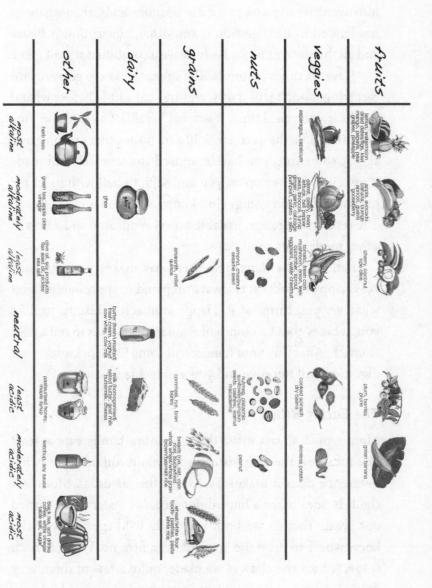

Acid-Alkali Chart

	most alkaline	moderately alkaline	least alkaline	neutral	least acidic	moderately acidic	most acidic
fruits	lemon, watermelon, dried dates/figs, kiwi mango, papaya, pear grapes, pineapple	apple, avocado banana, orange watercress, kiwi gooseberry	cherry, coconut ripe olive		plum, berries prune	green banana	
veggies	asparagus, capsicum	carrot, celery lettuce, bell pepper peas, garlic, turnip parsnip, cabbage pumpkin, potato + skin	tomato, fresh corn mushroom, onion cucumber, celeri eggplant, water chestnut				
nuts			almond, chestnut sesame seed	pumpkin/squash seeds, sunflower seeds, cashew, walnut macadamia		peanut	
grains			amaranth, millet quince	cooked spinach dry beans	cornmeal, rye, bran barley	skinless potato	
dairy		ghee		milk (homogenised) salted butter, goat milk buttermilk, cheese	breads (rye, oat, corn whole wheat/whole grain brown/basmati rice	wheat/white flour foods: pastries, pasta white rice
other	herb teas	green tea, apple cider vinegar	olive oil, soy products flax seed oil, pickles sea salt	butter (fresh/unsalted) fresh cream, yoghurt cow whey, cow milk	pasteurised honey, maple syrup	ketchup, soy sauce	black tea, soft drinks coffee, white vinegar table salt, sugar

alkaline food so the stomach's ego stays intact and it doesn't go into overdrive to prove that it can be more acidic than whatever has landed in it. Digestion is smoother, absorption is better and all the systems of the body heave a combined sigh of relief.

Have set times for meals. The stomach likes to get ready for receiving food. It will start secreting acid a little before what it thinks is your meal time. If you eat breakfast at 8.00 a.m. one day, 10.00 a.m. the next day, 9.30 a.m. on another morning and skip it sometime, you have confused the stomach and made it insecure. It gives up on you and says, to hell with it, let me just keep the acid going; God knows when he is going to eat. The result: acid reflux, irritable bowel syndrome and a host of other unpleasant conditions.

Eating at the same time every day makes your stomach very happy because it is always prepared to thoroughly digest whatever you throw at it. Happy stomach = Happy, healthy you. It takes about a month of regular meal times to train your stomach. After this, your hunger will come like clockwork, your digestion will improve and you will feel fantastic.

The Eating Ritual

Mom would always insist that the entire family eats at least one meal together. My sister and I would roll our eyes: what difference does it make? Turns out that as usual, Mom was right. It does make a huge difference. My sister and I turned out great. Though we both had fairly wild friends, we both knew where to draw the line and say a firm no. We were both respected for the choices we made, quite a few of them very bold. A deep sense of right and wrong was ingrained into us.

Studies now show that children who eat at least one meal

a day with their families are able to make better choices in life. They are more stable and can say no to drugs and other vices that may come their way. Families and meal times can be fantastic support systems.

I recently saw the brilliant animated movie *Coco*. It's all about family and the choices we make, and how sometimes families can be wrong, but in the end how love triumphs, and everything is better than before… Our family has been like that. And one of the places we used to discuss things together was at the dining table.

Dinesh and I now live in a lovely home at our beautiful Art of Living ashram in Bangalore with our extended family—and Mom's rule still holds. We eat as many meals as possible together, celebrating our love for each other, and feeling gratitude that we have been blessed with such a wonderful life.

Meal times are opportunities for rejuvenation. We work and expend energy the entire day. Quality time spent for meals helps us replenish ourselves, so we can perform even better. Meals cannot and should not be hurried. A leisurely, relaxed hour spent at the dining table savouring food cooked with love pays dividends beyond what you might think possible.

Set aside at least half an hour for each major meal. You may choose to eat by yourself and ruminate about the day, or enjoy your food in the company of your loved ones. Whatever you choose, make sure you feel pleasant while eating.

Sit while you eat, down on the ground or on a chair, though the former is better. Don't stand and eat. Sitting nudges your stomach to place so it can better accept the food that comes in. As much as possible, eat with your hands. The tactile sensation of the food in your fingers and the involvement of the other senses signal the stomach to produce the right amount of acid to digest that particular food.

Chew to Poo

Mom used to tell us to chew our food well. She would say 32 times, once for each tooth in the mouth. This was one thing I never did. I would invariably gulp my food down, chewing hardly ten times—until I read about the benefits of chewing as I was researching material for this chapter. It blew my mind to know that more than 70% of the digestion of carbs, our primary source of energy, happens in the mouth. If you don't chew enough, the carbs don't get digested as well as they should, and you fail to get enough energy from your meal, even though you may be eating all the right types of food.

Besides this, saliva is normally slightly alkaline with a pH of just above 7. When you chew well, whatever goes into the

stomach will be more alkaline and the stomach doesn't have to produce as much acid. Just by chewing you are alkalising your system. Chewing can be a deeply satisfying activity once you get the hang of it.

Chewing also helped me deal with pooping issues. I would alternate between constipation and badly formed lumps, rarely experiencing a complete cleanse. If you are like how I used to be, you need to chew. Chew each morsel 50 times. Do this for all your meals this week. Your poo will come out long and smooth, and you will feel that amazing feeling of being totally clean from inside.

For 47 years I didn't listen to Mom. I didn't chew. Now I do. I put a bite in my mouth. I put my hands on my laps and chew. 50 times. Mom passed away more than a year ago, but wherever she is, I can almost hear her say, I told you so!

Wisdom of the Grandmothers

1. Buy your fruits and veggies fresh, organic and preferably local. Eating seasonal varieties aligns your system better with natural rhythms.

2. Grow your own produce as much as possible. Even if you live in a tiny city apartment, you can definitely grow hardy, low-maintenance plants like green chillies, curry leaves, basil, spring onions, coriander, lemon grass and so on. Home-grown veggies bring a new dimension of health and flavour to your food.

3. Cook with convection heat. Steer clear of appliances that use radiation like microwave ovens as they can alter the delicate structure of food and convert it into 'tasty cardboard'. Use microwave ovens to test gravity, not cook food. Stove tops are the best.

4. Don't use aluminum vessels. This metal reacts with food when hot and has been implicated in various brain degenerative diseases and respiratory problems when used regularly. Throw away all aluminum cookware you may have. Do it now.

5. Use cast iron, ceramic or stainless steel cookware. Avoid other materials.

6. Eat whole grain. Eat lots of whole grain. I have seen fads of 'super' foods come and go. Whole grain is uber food!

7. Prefer lightly cooked veggies. The person sitting next to you should hear a crunch as you eat. Overcooking robs them of their goodness. Steam or sauté for fantastic taste and optimal health.

8. Eat ghee. About a tablespoon of ghee should accompany each of your major meals.

9. Eat fermented food—a small portion of any vegetable fermented in brine is adored by the good bacteria in your gut. Kimchi is one of my favourite fermented foods.

SPEED UP THE RIPENING OF A PINEAPPLE BY STANDING IT UPSIDE DOWN

10. Eat freshly cooked meals as much as possible. Avoid reheating. Nothing tastes as delicious as pan to plate fare.
11. A well-balanced meal will have many colours in it and all the tastes. Through the day, eat food so that all tastes make an appearance.
12. Sit and eat food or drink water. Don't stand. Sitting nudges your tummy into place to better receive food.
13. Never skip breakfast. Eat a big breakfast, have a good lunch and then a light dinner. Soups are great for lunch and dinner. Have salads for lunch, not dinner.
14. Don't eat after 8.00 p.m. The body needs at least three hours to process the dinner before bed. Your last meal should preferably be before 7 p.m.
15. Don't drink water with meals. A glass of water, half an hour to an hour before a meal, and an hour after your meal, will greatly aid the digestive process.
16. Drink at least one glass of water first thing in the morning before brushing your teeth. Downing a glass of water last thing before going to bed is a great idea too.
17. Ban cellphones, TV, iPads, books, etc. from the dining table. This is the time for the family to appreciate the bounty on their table, and each other's company. No scolding, complaining or unpleasantness while eating. Meal times should be the most pleasant times of the day and looked forward to by everyone.
18. Food should make you happy. The best silence is the hush that suddenly dawns at a dining table as everyone goes into a state of bliss enjoying every morsel of their food.

Of all my research and experimentation with cooking and diets, the macrobiotic and the Ayurvedic ways stand out. Both are quite similar, as they focus on balance. A balanced, happy microbiome is going to make a balanced, happy you. Check the bibliography for books on these topics.

As you make greener, healthier choices, the vibrant bouncy health you always wanted will be yours. The wooziness in your thinking will vanish and you will be able to take rational, intelligent decisions. The good bacteria in your gut will experience many happily ever-afters. Your face will glow and your eyes will twinkle. Your smile will widen and your laugh will be deeper... and you will wonder what you really saw in that horrible sugar-laden, full-of-white-flour doughnut that you were once addicted to.

Chapter 5

EXERCISE

Jogi, a great friend, used to be a body builder par excellence. He had his bulges in all the right places. He'd shoot me knowing looks and tut-tut about my appearance whenever I complained of aches and pains. Unlike him, I was quite averse to exercise back then. I used to think, why spend time and effort on something as transient as the body? Isn't it wiser to take care of the mind alone? After all, that's what's tagging along with me when I leave my body.

Jogi would huff and puff in the gym; I would meditate. I should point out that Jogi was not disinclined towards spirituality. Quite the contrary. Even though he was huge, unlike most body builders, he had trained himself to be flexible as well. He did brilliant Yoga and was a regular meditator. He was fit, healthy and mostly happy. I was... happy ☺

Jogi was brilliant at body work. I don't meet him often these days and the memory of his massages fill me with nostalgia. One day, after he had managed to get rid of a particularly painful knot in my body, he insisted that I accompany him to the gym. He promised he won't make me work out or anything. 'Just come,' he said.

I knew where my next massage was coming from, so I

didn't argue much and went along. We reached the gym, and Jogi started his workout while I sat and watched. After about 10 minutes, he came up to me with two dumbbells of 2 kg each. He thrust them into my hands and said, 'Hold these.' And he went back to his exercising. To humour him and not look completely out of place, I readily complied. All I had to do was hold them—how hard could that be?!

I realised 2 kg can become very heavy, very quickly. After a few minutes, I went up to him and asked him if I could let go of the dumbbells. He airily replied, 'Just hold them for a little longer.' I did. Three minutes later, I felt as if I was holding 20 kg in each hand. I made some sad groaning noises. Without showing any sympathy, he sternly said, 'C'mon, these are the smallest dumbbells in the gym. Hold them a little longer.'

Another long minute passed, and he was standing beside me, 'Hold them, hold them, hold them. You can do it.' My hands were screaming in pain by now and I lost all track of time. After what seemed like eternity, he quietly said, 'Ok, drop them.'

The dumbbells crashed to the floor and I was quite angry with Jogi. My arms were in pain and I felt exhausted, defeated and stupid. Jogi looked me in the eye and gently said, 'Bau, that's just four kilos you held in your hands for less than 10 minutes. When you let go of them, did you notice how you felt?' Then he put his arm around me and continued, 'You are overweight by 5-6 kg. You are carrying this extra weight all the time. Imagine how you will feel if you manage to get rid of it...'

His method was brutal, but effective. Reluctantly, but resolutely, I started my workouts the next day.

Initially, I would loathe going to the gym. But as I continued with my workouts, I started feeling good. I enjoyed my time there. My resistance to illness improved. I had a lot more energy and didn't get tired as quickly as I used to. I could do so much more with my body. Life just seemed to get easier.

Exercising is now a part of my life.

In time, me being me, I wanted to find out what exactly about exercise made me feel the way I felt. A lot of research, reading and picking the brains of bodybuilder and doctor friends ensued. I learned a few surprising facts about exercise which I believe everyone should know. I hope I can inspire you to start your fitness journey through these words—otherwise there are always 2 kg dumbbells. Hold them for 10 minutes and then let go of them. You, too, will feel exactly how Jogi made me feel all those years ago. Hopefully, like me, you too will begin exercising, and eventually start enjoying it.

Move

Imagine a big, comfortable chair. Picture a few things lying on it. A bottle of booze, whiskey, brandy, vodka, whatever. A pack of cigarettes. A double cheese burger with fries. A large piece of cake, full of icing and loaded with sugar.

In this picture, if you had to pick one thing that was most hazardous to your health in the long run, what would it be?

Some will choose alcohol. It can cause liver degeneration, deprive you of sleep, make you depressed, compromise the immune system, reduce your sex drive, and possibly result in a few types of cancer.

Others insist that it's smoking. Implicated in lung cancer, hacking coughs, premature death, coronary heart disease, stroke, among other things.

Few will choose the burger or the cake... all that white flour and trans-fat are known causes of obesity, poor quality of life and related problems.

All would be wrong.

The most insidious threat to your health in the long run, far worse than all the others is, incredibly: The Chair!

Let me explain.

As our bodies evolved, we mainly did two things. Either we were running after something we wanted to eat, or we were running away from something that wanted to eat us. As hunters and gatherers, we were constantly moving.

In the more recent past, we learned agriculture. As farmers we settled down in one place and civilisation happened. There was still tremendous physical activity. We had to till the land, sow seeds, water and care for the fledgling plants, and harvest them. All this involved movement.

Thousands and thousands of years of evolution imprinted the need to move into our genetics.

It's 2018. We hardly move at all. We wake up. We sit and have breakfast. We sit and drive to work. We sit and work. We sit and have lunch. We sit and drive back home. We sit and have dinner. We sit and watch TV. We even sit to shop online. Finally, we sleep. These days, people sit for an average of 7.7 hours a day.

This is completely opposed to our genetics which scream for movement. Dr James Levine, former director, Mayo Clinic, Arizona State University, an authority on this subject, coined the term 'The Sitting Disease.' All the sitting that we do is wreaking havoc on our bodies. Dr Levine says, 'Sitting is more dangerous than smoking, has killed more people than HIV and is more treacherous than parachuting!'

Sitting too much has been implicated in quite a few diseases: various types of cancer, heart diseases, obesity (of course), compromises in the musculo-skeletal system, depression, anxiety and even type 2 diabetes.

Sitting is the new smoking and has reached epidemic proportions.

Solution: Get up and about. Move!

After every 45 minutes of sitting, get up and walk for around 15 minutes. Your brain works better and you become more productive and creative, as we saw in the Brain 101 chapter. The simple act of standing can improve muscle tone, boost your metabolism, lower your stress levels, improve your mood and reduce minor aches and pains.

A little bit of movement, and your brain rewards you for your efforts—it releases the feel-good hormones, dopamine and endorphins, into your blood. That's the reason people who exercise regularly typically feel wonderful about life. Exercise is the elixir of life.

Movement is good. Movement is life. Move more.

Neurogenesis

The microscopic equivalent of an electrical lightning storm happens in the brain every few seconds. I guess with all that electricity zzzizzing around, a few neurons are bound to get fried every day. That's not such a big deal. Millions of cells in our bodies die and get replaced all the time. The problem is that neurons are incapable of division. Now that's a big deal.

We lose around 3000 neurons a day. We start off with

a billion neurons in our brain. And 3000 is a tiny number compared to a billion. But tiny numbers multiplied by tiny numbers rapidly become huge numbers. As people grow older, we often hear them complain that their brain is not what it used to be. They feel they are not sharp enough, can't remember things and so on. That's mostly the result of all those fried neurons.

For a long time, it was believed that once you lost a neuron, it was gone forever. We had to make do with what was left.

Enter Neurogenesis.

Neurogenesis proved that new neurons are indeed birthed in the brain.

Guess what helps create an impetus for the creation of new neurons?

Yup. It's Exercise.

Exercise is definitely the key to a stronger, fitter, great-looking body. Amazingly, it helps make your brain function better, by keeping it from ageing. That's how deeply encoded movement and exercise are in our genetics.

Exercise regularly. Your body will be healthier and your brain will become younger.

Mind the Body

The grossest aspect of the mind is the body. The subtlest aspect of the body is the mind. The body will never go where the mind doesn't want it to. The first rule of exercising is deciding to do it. If the mind has not agreed, it's not going to happen. Read all of the above once more. Google the various benefits of exercising if you feel you would like to know more before you actually take the plunge. Convince yourself.

Once that's done, the rest is all about technique, consistency and honouring what you are doing.

By the way, this is how you start any new habit. Figuring out and strengthening the 'why' automatically makes you committed, and grants you the resilience to overcome any obstacle that might come.

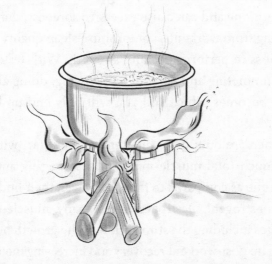

To boil water, you need to have water, something to put the water in like a vessel, and a source of heat. To get the water to boil, you pour it into the vessel, put the vessel on the heat source and wait. Once the water starts boiling, there is no need to continue with the heat. You remove the water from the heat. You have achieved what you wanted.

Exercising is similar to boiling water.

Many people over-train. They do too much. This is like leaving the water on the boil. You don't end up with hot water, you end up with steam—two very different things. Rule of the thumb? Never exercise for more than an hour. Your bones, ligaments and muscles become progressively weaker as you stress them out with exercise, and you may risk injury if you go beyond an hour.

There is a theory which I agree with. When men begin exercising, their testosterone levels increase, which helps build muscle. After about an hour of exercise, the testosterone levels rapidly fall and cortisol levels begin to rise. Cortisol is the stress hormone and can cause excessive soreness, difficulty in recovering from workouts, compromise sleep quality and can lead to loss in performance and strength. With testosterone levels plummeting and cortisol levels rising, doing any more exercise becomes futile. And you will only end up harming yourself.

Women are built quite differently. They start with about half as much total muscle mass and have a tiny amount of testosterone as compared to men. However, their bodies have lots of oestrogen. Oestrogen gives many muscle-building advantages including the stimulation of the growth hormone, speeding up post-workout recovery and increasing metabolism.

Women also produce more growth hormone throughout the day, which is a significant advantage to gaining muscle.

Women shouldn't exercise for more than an hour either. Cortisol will rise after an hour of exercising and will create the same problems as men.

Some people haphazardly go through their workout. They pay no attention to the correctness of their form. They will never achieve the desired results. Worse, there is serious risk of injury. This is akin to leaving a vessel full of water not on the heat source, but next to it. The water might become warm but would never come to a boil.

Yet others are not consistent. They do their exercise in spurts. Every few days, they take a break for a few days. The water is not going to boil if you keep removing it from the heat source and putting it back again and again and again. You need to exercise at least 4-5 days a week and rest for 1-3 days.

Our minds are supremely powerful. A thought can weaken and drain us of energy. Another can make us stronger than steel. Remember this while exercising. If we think tired, we will be tired. This is especially true when we finish a set. Your belief that you are exhausted as you do the last rep will make you feel exactly that. Do that last rep with enthusiasm and vigour, like a warrior tasting his first moment of victory. Finish strong. Then you feel fantastic.

Ever seen a person devoutly performing a pooja? Everything has to be just right. There is great attention to detail. When we consider something sacred, it is natural that we get totally involved and our actions are smooth and graceful with a lot of focus. Lalit is a dear friend and a personal trainer. When he enters the gym, he bows down to the equipment with reverence before he starts his workout. The honour that he gives to his practice pays great dividends. He is supremely mindful about what he does and how he does it because he considers it sacred. Obviously when there is such focus, results come super fast.

Mind the body as you exercise and you will be stunned by what you become capable of doing. Both in the gym and outside it.

Pain

There is no nice way to say this: when you start exercising, there is going to be pain. Parts of your body you didn't even know existed will howl in agony. You will have to make friends with pain. Do not confuse this pain with the pain you feel when you bang into something hard. This pain has a different flavour. It's a healthy sort of a pain. A sweet pain.

Your body doesn't trust you to take care of it. If you injure some part of it in some way, that part grows back stronger and more resilient. It's like the body is protecting itself from your carelessness.

When you exercise, you are literally tearing your muscle fibres apart. It's controlled injury. Your body responds by making these fibres tougher and more robust—that's how your body gets 'built'.

When you hurt yourself, it pains.

Exercise is willingly and methodically hurting yourself. This is going to pain, though this pain is the other kind of pain. As your body grows stronger and stronger, you will start to enjoy the taste of this mellow pain. The pain that magically transforms into power, as you continue to relentlessly push through it.

IT TAKES 12 WEEKS OF AN EXERCISE ROUTINE BEFORE YOU

CAN SEE MEASURABLE CHANGES IN YOUR BODY

Your mantras for Exercising:

Muscle: No pain, no gain. Use it or lose it.

Fat: No pain, no loss. Use it to lose it.

Setback

For more than a year, I had been conscientiously following my exercise routine. I had shed a lot of excess weight and was feeling great about myself. My tummy had flattened; I was winning the battle of the bulge. I had decided to devote 2018 to start putting on some muscle. It was not to be.

Dinesh and I had been to London in late 2017. It was a fabulous trip, but I caught a cold. A cold that refused to leave me as I coughed and coughed for more than a month. After having tried all sorts of alternative medicines, eventually, I had to take antibiotics to get over it. I was very weakened by the entire experience. The constant coughing meant that I had no energy to exercise. I had not worked out in over two months and was feeling quite awful.

When we returned from London, I was in pretty bad shape. The cough, coupled with the long-distance flight and jet-lag, left me drained and washed out. I needed rest. My body begged for it. Instead of respecting my body and taking it easy for a while, I went on a hectic teaching tour over the next couple of weeks. You can imagine how my physical condition would have been when I finally got back home.

One fateful evening, a few days after all this, our bike hit a particularly nasty bump on the road and I felt something bust in my lower back. I had slipped a disc.

A month of severe pain and complete bed rest followed. Walking, climbing stairs, showering, pooing, shaving—just normal day-to-day activities were miserably restricted by the horrible pain. The good news was that I recovered fast. This was largely possible because of the osteopathic and craniosacral therapy given to me by my good friends Dr Ankita Dhelia, Dr Stanley Rosenberg, Thor, Dr Sanket Agrawal, Rashmi Bhatia and Jim Stone. What expedited it even further was the exercise routine I had diligently followed for over two years. This had infused my body with strength and helped it respond remarkably well to these treatments.

After so many weeks of agony, finally being able to walk down the stairs with just a few twinges of pain made me feel incredibly happy!

As I write these words, I can do almost all the normal stuff that I used to, but I still can't exercise without aggravating the pain. I can't move my body the way I used to just a few months ago. I have strictly controlled my diet and put on just a few kilos of weight during this time, yet I am confident I will be able to burn them off soon.

YOU ARE NEVER TOO OLD TO EXERCISE

I learned a crucial lesson from this episode.

There were times in my past when I would be too lazy to hit the gym. 'Not today,' I would tell Lalit, 'I just want to relax.' But now, I have resolved to skip the excuses. I had taken for granted the beautiful ways in which my body could move. I will not do that ever again.

Move while you can. Life is unexpectedly fragile, and what you can do today, you may not be able to do tomorrow. This is not just about exercise. It's about saying I love you, or Thank You, or spending time with people who matter. Don't take life, love or friendship for granted. It's the biggest mistake you will ever make.

Five-Star Property

If someone asks you where you live, you will probably rattle off some address—

Vyas Kuteer, The Art of Living International Ashram,
21st km., Kanakpura Road,
Bangalore 560082

That's where your body lives.

You, actually, live in your body. Make your body a five-star property and living in it will be such a joy! We spend so much time and money on our homes. Interiors, décor, fittings—beautifying and maintaining them. We strive to make them comfortable havens of peace.

Exercising will transform your body into a beautiful, comfortable home for you to live in. It requires commitment, time, effort and money. All one hundred per cent worth it.

This I will tell you—the time you don't spend exercising, you will spend flat on your back being ill. And staring at ceilings is boring. The money you don't spend on yourself will go towards your doctor's bills.

Decide to exercise.

Stick to that decision.

Do it right. Pay attention to correctness of form, have reverence for the space and equipment, and gratitude for being able to exercise in the first place.

Do it right now. Don't wait. Unless you have just eaten. Then do it after two hours.

Health and Fitness

Health and fitness should ideally go together. These days, mostly they don't. Many people compromise their health in the name of fitness. Non-therapeutic drugs, steroids, growth enhancers and injections that promise to make you bigger and more shredded are supremely tempting, especially for the young. They want those gains now. The nicest thing that happens to some who go down this route is that they die. Others suffer from prostrate issues by age 25, are on blood pressure medicines by age 22, can have cardiac arrests, shrunken kidneys, erectile dysfunction, or develop a plethora of physical and mental complications by the time they are 30. No one can really tell how these dangerous chemicals affect the body.

Bodybuilding is perhaps the only sport in the world in which the contender is in his worst physical condition on the day of the event. To make the veins pop while posing, they starve themselves on crazy diets and drink little to no water for two or three days before the competition. I know of some who collapsed the moment they left the stage.

This is utterly ridiculous.

There are no shortcuts to building a great body that you can safely take. A crash diet will do exactly that to you. Steroids and other dangerous supplements may create a great-looking exterior but finish you off from the inside. There isn't much sense in becoming a beautiful corpse, right?

I like to apply the principles of hatha yoga while doing traditional exercise. *Sthiram Sukham Asanam*. Meaning you should be balanced and steady in your poses and feel at peace. Only then it would be a truly yogic pose. That's why doing yoga feels so good. Exercise should as well.

Many bodybuilders push their bodies too much to get that 'ripped look'. I don't agree with this. Instead, I recommend balance, correct technique and doing just a little more than what is comfortable. While doing yoga you stretch just that little bit more, and then relax into the pose. Same way, if you can do 15 reps of a particular exercise, then your form goes for a toss as you grunt another 5—it's no good for you. Maintain the exact same form and maybe squeeze in a couple of more reps. When you finish, you should feel good. Not punished, exhausted or overwhelmed.

Once you have your technique correct, turn your attention inwards. See if you get them to turn off the blaring music that is the bane of most gyms. Bring in an element of meditative mindfulness to your routines by staying with your breath. When you exercise this way, you will truly enjoy the experience and will look forward to your session each day.

Meditation after exercising is amazing. It brings down the cortisol that's on the rise and supplements serotonin, endorphins and oxytocin production. It will enhance the high of the exercise and minimise the associated pain and discomfort.

Art of Living offers a series of courses called Yogic Fitness which apply the principles of yoga to fitness. Exercising the Yogic Fitness way ensures you get all the benefits, feels great and minimises the risk of injury. These courses are designed to bring health back into fitness.

Walking Tall, Sitting Right

There is an art to walking. First and foremost, maintain balance. Keep your weight equally on both feet. Check and see whether you are walking with a tilt to any side or if you are putting more weight on one leg than the other. Are your shoulders equally relaxed, or is one tenser that the other? Are your arms moving freely and equally? Adjust yourself to get balanced if required.

Then square your shoulders—rotate them back and down, far away from the ears. Tuck your tummy in a bit (not as much as when you are about to take a selfie), about half an inch or so is enough. When you walk, feel the movement from your belly.

Lastly, lead with your heart, but walk as if someone is lightly pulling you forward from the belly button.

While standing, square your shoulders, feel as if a hundred balloons have been tied to your head and hold it up accordingly. Keep your chest out and your stomach pulled in about half an inch. Most importantly, smile!

Sit keeping your spine erect and your head in line with the spine. If your chair has a back rest, ensure your lower back is fully supported. Don't leave any gap between this part and the L of your chair. When you sit, your shoulders may tend to subtly droop, closing the chest. Roll the shoulders back and down, and your chest will automatically come out a bit.

Your feet should be resting easily on the ground; otherwise, adjust the level of your seat or use a foot stool. This helps prevent or minimise many of the problems associated with sitting.

You Got to Move It—Move It!

Here is a sample body weight work-out routine that almost anyone can do. It shouldn't take more than an hour or so. If you have never exercised, you may not understand the jargon or how to do the exercise knowing just its name. What does 'mountain climber' actually mean? What in the world is IYTLW? And a Hindu push-up? What's that?

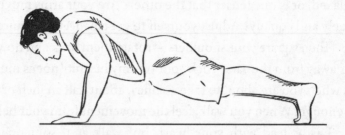

Don't worry about these names. You can find out how to do these exercises through YouTube videos that Dinesh and Lalit have made: www.happinessexpressbook.com/videos/exercises.

There are many books detailing how to exercise and plenty of videos out there. Check out some books we refer to in the Bibliography.

Always start with a bit of warming up. A 10-minute session could include jumping jacks, twists, mountain climbers, HIIT (High Intensity Interval Training). Anything that moves all the parts of your body and gets them prepped for exercise. Even vigorous dancing would work.

Add some yoga at the end of your routine to complete the experience. A few suryanamaskars done at a quick pace will improve your stamina. Slow suryanamaskars, synched with the breath, will bring balance and flexibility. As you unwind and relax, it also creates more space for the muscle fibres to grow.

I have realised that I am more consistent with my exercise routine when I have a workout partner. Find a friend who will work out with you. Both of you can provide support and motivation to each other.

For all the exercises below, do 3-5 sets of 8-15 repetitions. Slowly build up to more reps and more sets. 3 sets of 15 reps is a great goal to aim for. Take your time.

Remember Sthiram Sukham Exercisum!

स्तिर सुखम एक्सर्सैसम ॥

sthira sukham exercisum

I talked to Prashant Jaiswal, Certified Master Trainer by the Australian Institute of Fitness, Strength and Conditioning Coach, about the benefits of exercise specifically for women. Here is what he had to say: 'Many women love cardio and stick to it through their lives. All they do in the gym is treadmill, bike and cross-trainer. Genetically, the female body holds a higher percentage of fat than the male body. Though they may lose weight with cardio, the total fat percentage could remain the same and they could end up being 'skinny fat'. Strength training will help the female body to change its composition, not just lose weight. You get a double win: lose weight and get more toned. For many women this brings a lot of confidence.

Very often, women fear that if they do strength training they will look like some male bodybuilder and lose their shapely feminine aspects. It will never happen because they simply don't have enough testosterone to achieve that.

Strength training for women will make them stronger, have more endurance and eliminate knee and joint pain. They will experience better moods and will definitely feel and look more attractive.'

Legs are very important to develop. Many people neglect legs because they are not seen so much. That's a mistake. Matchstick legs on a broad chest and big shoulders make you look like some drunk Disney artist had a go at you. There is no aesthetic in a body like this.

Women have much more bulk on the upper body than the lower body. Exercising legs will give them that coveted hourglass figure, as a bit of mass, muscle and tone comes to the leg muscles.

Thighs have the biggest muscles in the body and good, strong thighs bring balance, stability and proportion to the body.

Squats, Lunges and Walking Lunges are fantastic for legs. Calf raises and their variations are brilliant for **calves**.

The **lower back** is the most susceptible to injury. I know this from bitter personal experience. Whatever exercise you do, add leg pulls every few sets so you end up doing around 3-5 sets throughout your workout.

Broad **shoulders** give you an air of authority and confidence. Build them up with Pike push-ups. Controlled rotation of your arms holding 1 litre bottles of water in each hand is another great exercise for your shoulders.

Shoulders need to be pulled back naturally for good posture. This doesn't happen because the latissimus dorsi, the back's largest muscle, is weak. Proper shoulder training for women will give their bodies a much better look as well as reduce pain in the neck and the back.

Your **back** gives you resilience and power. The superman pose from yoga is great for the back. The IYTLW set of exercises are perfect for the upper back as well as shoulders.

A big **chest** with all the bulges in the right places can enhance your personality. One arm wall push-up (should be called push-away), both arm wall push-up, push-ups, push-up variations and the Hindu push-up work well. Choose three or four of these and stick to them for a month or so before introducing more into your routine. Push-ups even exercise your biceps and triceps.

Biceps and triceps are the ultimate show off muscles. Flex your biceps and hear a swarm of oohhs and ahhs. For biceps, do the doorway and towel bicep curls. Women shouldn't have the huge biceps and triceps men can develop. However, toned biceps and triceps are wonderful to have and a woman can create just as many oohhs and aahhs by flexing them.

Diamond push-ups and bench-dips will work your **triceps**.

A fantastic **core** is the ultimate dream of anyone desiring a great body. It's perhaps the most difficult (and painful) set of muscles to develop. The core will bring a humungous amount of stability and strength to the entire body. A great core makes back injury almost impossible. Planks and side planks are best for the core. Throw in some specialised exercises for the transversus abdominis and obliques, and you will soon enjoy small victories in the battle with the bulge.

You don't need to do all these exercises every day. Group related body parts together and work them out once or twice a week. Do leg pulls every day, core exercises at least twice a week—more, if you are feeling brave. Make sure you have at least one or two rest days each week. Legs are the most demanding, so I like to exercise them on the day before my rest day.

Burpees are a brilliant all-round exercise and you could do around 8-10 each day. Slowly build up to 3 sets of 10 burpees. Do these at the end of your workout just before you begin your yoga for stretching and cooling down.

Prashant helped us create this exercise routine for both men and women.

Monday: Warm-up, chest and triceps, 3 reps of lower back in-between the other exercises, core, burpees, stretch and cool down, meditate.

Tuesday: Warm-up, back and biceps, 3 reps of lower back in-between the other exercises, burpees, stretch and cool down, meditate.

Wednesday: Warm-up, legs (thighs and calves) and shoulders, core, 3 reps of lower back in-between the other exercises, burpees, stretch and cool down, meditate.

Thursday: Rest day.

Friday: Warm-up, chest, back, biceps and triceps, 3 reps of lower back in-between the other exercises, burpees, stretch and cool down, meditate (you may do only 2 sets of everything on this day to begin with).

Saturday: Warm-up, legs (thighs and calves) and shoulders, 3 reps of lower back in-between the other exercises, burpees, stretch and cool down, meditate.

Sunday: Rest day.

As mentioned earlier, if you don't understand the workout jargon, watch the YouTube videos that Dinesh and Lalit have made to figure out how to do these exercises: www.happinessexpressbook.com/videos/exercises.

Better yet, come and do the Yogic Fitness series of courses with us. If that's not possible, engage a good personal trainer. Just as you would seek the help of an architect to design your dream home for you, a great personal trainer will help you create a superb five-star property for you to be in.

A little caution here: stay away from trainers who want you to consume non-veg food, pump you up with supplements, prescribe diets that go against the principles that we have talked about in our chapter on food, or shame you and make you feel small. Do your own research and feel free to ask uncomfortable questions. A good trainer will assist you to create the body you want, on your terms. You need to be comfortable with the person training you.

If gyms and trainers simply don't fit into your philosophy, be active. Drop the sedentary lifestyle. Walk, play, spend time gardening, clean up your house, dance—pick any activity that keeps you on your feet, keeps you moving, and twists your body into various postures.

Cycling and swimming provide brilliant, no-impact, full-body workouts.

At the very least, go for a brisk walk and do some stretches every day.

Here's to a healthy, fit body and a happy, confident You!

Chapter 6

LEARNING

Hopefully, you have started making some lifestyle changes by now. You have sorted out your sleep. You have learned and are practising meditation. Your diet is wholesome and delicious. You are engaged in adequate physical activity every day.

The next stop is the brain.

The Learning Advantage

John Salinas in his nineties decided to challenge himself and learn about computers. He said this renewed a zest for life.

Doretta Daniels bagged her associate degree in social sciences from the College of the Canyons in Santa Clarita, California, in 2015. She worked for six years to get that degree. She was 99 years old and she did it simply to better herself.

Doretta and John may have known something that many have missed: life-long learning can help improve and maintain mental well-being. Research suggests that a year of education can add more than half a year to a person's life span.

An abundance of books, online resources, personal and professional development programmes, podcasts, etc. are super accessible. This makes learning almost anything you want to much easier than it was earlier.

Learning something is akin to giving your brain a fantastic workout. The brain thrives on getting out of its routine and chewing on new and complex things. Continuous learning has been shown to increase intelligence, keep the mind sharp and buffer the brain against ageing. It delays and could potentially prevent the onset of dementia and other brain degenerative diseases.

Learning increases brain size and develops better neural connectivity within the brain. This results in a host of life advantages:

- ☐ You become better at planning, prioritising and decision-making.
- ☐ Your ability to focus and pay attention to what's going on is enhanced.
- ☐ You are more aware of your environment, picking up cues and acting on them.
- ☐ You don't fall for marketing hype.
- ☐ Your memory becomes sharper and you gain mental flexibility.

- ❐ You are more creative and productive in whatever you do.
- ❐ You make peace with delayed gratification and gain the ability and motivation to work on long-term goals.
- ❐ You gain confidence as you learn more and more. Your social circle widens and you enjoy better relationships. You get to be on top of all that yummy new technology.

I am always in awe of my friends Prama and Ranji Bhandari. They are 80 and 90 as I write this, and the way they embrace and enjoy life is a wonder to behold. Prama bhabhi would tell us that in the 1950s, a telephone call to another city would take more than a week to get through, while a call to another country would mean a wait for a month or more. And if you booked an emergency lightning trunk call, you would get a terrible connection, with lots of static and a mere three to five minutes to talk. She related all this to us while unpacking her brand-new iPhone! She knows all about WhatsApp and iTunes and regularly Facetimes with her daughter in the US.

Much before I was born, Ranji bhai owned a Morris 14/6; he was one of those privileged few to drive a car on Indian roads way back in 1938. He reminisces fondly about all those old, old cars as he navigates his beautiful new Skoda Superb.

Prama and Ranji Bhandari are the youngest old people I know... right there in the hall of fame with Doretta and John.

There is no doubt about this. Learning keeps you young and makes you live longer. It improves the quality of your life and of those around you. For me, it is as important as meditation, sleep, diet and exercise in my formula for Happiness.

The Learning Slump

We saw earlier that the brain (as well as the body) works on the use-it-or-lose-it system. Many adults barely learn anything new after their formal education is over. Possibly because the 'learning' part of most people's lives is usually associated with a lot of pain. All of us have our pet peeves. Math, History, Economics, Statistics, French… The subjects we loved to hate can bring up agonising memories and can make a lot of us shy away from the process of learning.

I still remember that feeling of exhilaration I had after writing the last exam of my life in IIT. As I walked out of the hall after my exam on Statistical Inference, there was such a deep sense of relief. No more exams. Ever. I could finally get on with life…

It was not always like that. I remember, as a child, I loved studying. I would look forward to getting brand new textbooks at the start of every school year and read them long before school started. I enjoyed learning. In fact, I don't know any

PLAYING WITH **BLOCKS** INCREASES THE NUMBER OF NEURONS IN CHILDREN'S **BRAINS**

child who is averse to it. Somehow, as we grow older, the drive to learn diminishes. For some people, it vanishes altogether and few even develop anxiety issues around it.

Have you noticed how most young children are like sponges? They soak up knowledge from everywhere. They can learn things at breakneck speed. The younger they are, the faster they learn. They brim with curiosity and wonder. Age seems to rob us of our enchantment with learning. As we grow older, even though we do the same things day in and day out, we don't seem to get any better at doing them. We work hard at them, because we care for them… but we tend to stagnate. We fail to become better spouses, better parents, better teammates or better friends.

Compared to the phenomenal growth in our childhood, we hardly improve as adults, be it professionally or personally.

Learning a language is widely accepted as a great benchmark to figure out how much one is open to learning new things. Research reveals some fairly scary figures.

A child knows around 50 words at 18 months of age. 1000 words at age three and 4000-6000 words by the time she is seven. As a teen, her vocabulary hovers between 20,000 and 40,000 words, though most teens use around 1000 words in their interactions. At 25, you know nearly 42000 words—just 2000 more than you knew at 13 or 14.

Your vocabulary rapidly declines till you learn hardly any new words as you grow older. Most adults learn only one new word every two days. This means that by the age of 60, they would have added only 6000 more words to their vocabulary from the time they were 25.

Check the learning rate:

Age 0-20, normally, most people learn up to 42,000 words. Age 20-60, we add just 6000 more words to our repertoire. This is an incredible decline considering that there is so much more to learn. Most languages have around 250,000 words in their lexicon!

A new word
IS ADDED TO THE DICTIONARY
EVERY 2 HOURS

It's not just about learning more of a language. It's about learning anything. Most people simply stop wanting to learn new things as they grow older. Unfortunately, these days there are quite a lot of children, too, who have become learning-averse. What's going on?

Learning Zone and Performance Zone

Edwardo Briceño, co-founder and CEO of Mindset Works, gave a brilliant little TED talk titled 'How to get better at things you care about'. He talks about the learning zone and the performance zone.

The learning zone is for improvement. Here, we increase our knowledge of the things we know little or nothing about and hone our existing skills. This is the place where we expect to make mistakes so that we can learn from them.

The performance zone is where we action all our knowledge and strive to do our best. We really want to shine here. There is tremendous pressure in the performance zone with barely any room for making mistakes.

Both these zones have to be a part of our lives. The performance zone maximises our immediate achievement, while the learning zone maximises our growth and future performance.

When I learn a new piece of music on the piano in the privacy of my home, I don't worry about making mistakes. In fact, I know that I will make many mistakes and that would be the only way to learn this new music.

I would keep the score (musical notation) in front of me. I would play very slowly and repeat difficult phrases over and over again. I would experiment with different fingering. I wouldn't care too much about expression, being loud or soft. My goal would be to get the music into my fingers and my head. As I become better and better, I would strive to be more precise with the music, bringing in the speed, the pedalling and, finally, the expression.

I would still be absolutely okay with making mistakes. If I found something really challenging, I would seek guidance from a teacher. Once I am confident with the music, I would play it to a few friends. It would still be okay for me to make a few mistakes here and there, because I would still consider myself in the learning zone. Only when I am absolutely confident about my virtuosity with the music would I go public. This brings us to the performance zone.

If I am performing a piece of music for an audience, I would be mortified if I made a mistake, even if I was the only one who noticed it. Sometimes you practice an entire year for the five minutes that you get in front of an audience. One wrong note, one place you falter or make even a semblance of a mistake, and all that effort feels futile.

the original name FOR BUTTERFLY WAS flutterby

Performance zone can be nerve-wracking to be in.

You may think that the performance zone is all stress and pressure. That may be true, but it can be very motivational, even inspirational. It is much required. It is where the real work happens. Most importantly, it gives insights on where to focus next. It tells us how we could be even better at what we do… taking us back to the learning zone.

Dinesh and I have been teaching Art of Living courses for more than 25 years. Conducting an Art of Living programme is a richly rewarding experience. It requires great presence that one needs to develop through one's own practice of meditation. It requires authenticity and honesty to facilitate meditation, teach knowledge from Vedic sources that has been contemporarised to be relevant today, and conduct group activities that would make people realise some deeper truths about themselves and the world we live in.

Even after all these years, and after teaching thousands and thousands of people from all over the world, after every course, Dinesh and I still discuss what we could have done better. After each foray into the performance zone—delivering a course—we return to the learning zone to think again and again of how best we could enhance the experience for our students.

This back and forth between the two zones is critical for success in life. And you will go into an ever-increasing spiral of superior capabilities. You will develop skills that will enable you to do things way better than you could have imagined.

What would we be doing in the learning zone?

❑ We need to believe that we can improve. Many people feel they are already perfect at what they do. Others feel there is nothing more that could be done, even if they wanted to. Gurudev once said something amazing which I implement all the time: You are perfect the way you are. Move from one level of perfection to another! A seed is perfect as a seed. As it sprouts, it is still perfect. It grows into a small plant and it is perfect. As a fully grown tree bearing fruits and flowers, it is perfect yet again. We need to feel at all times that we have done the best we could and then see how we can do it better.

❏ Be aware that it takes time and effort to improve. The last 20% will take up an inordinate amount of time compared to the first 80%. We need to really care about what we want to improve; otherwise it will feel like we are wasting time and we will end up feeling useless about ourselves.

❏ There needs to be a methodology in place for improvement. Practice makes one perfect, but wrong practice makes one perfectly wrong. It is wise to seek help from a mentor, a teacher, or a coach.

❏ Learning thrives in a friendly, low-risk zone. Mistakes are expected here, and making them shouldn't have significant consequences. Rookie pilots would learn to fly in a simulator, not on a commercial aircraft. A chef would try out a new creation for himself and people he trusts around him, not put it on the menu to experiment on customers.

❏ After every event, Dinesh and I make it a point to answer these four questions:
  ❏ What else can we do?
  ❏ What can we do better?
  ❏ What should we continue doing?
  ❏ What should we stop doing?

Adults spend far too much time in the performance zone. If the stakes are always high, and there is no freedom to make even small mistakes, learning will continue to elude you. Even if you slog it out, you would see hardly any improvement.

IF YOU ARE GOING TO TEACH SOMEONE SOMETHING YOU ARE LEARNING, YOU REMEMBER IT BETTER

I attribute the growth of the Art of Living and all our teachers and volunteers to Gurudev's philosophy on this: You are allowed to make mistakes. Even big mistakes. Just make new mistakes! Keep learning.

If flawless execution is the norm, then the team will feel too scared to try out new things. This means that the company will not be able to innovate and improve, and stagnation will set in.

Even if you have to continuously function in high-stakes zones, it's a great idea to create islands of low stakes. Being able to talk things through with a friend or a mentor, having informal feedback meetings, etc. are fantastic ways to do just this. My friend, Dr Rangana Choudhary, has 'feedforward' (instead of feedback) meetings with her team. The term itself changes everything!

Schools, colleges and universities are places of education. Of learning. Or, are they? Instead of being safe learning zones, these once-venerable institutions have become high-stake performance zones. It's no wonder that most people learn very little when there is such minimal scope for making mistakes.

Result? Countries full of 'educated' people too frightened to make mistakes and thus doomed to mindless middle-class mediocrity. Maybe this is probably the reason why more and more of us are becoming so averse to learning.

If we give ourselves more time in the learning zones, our performance will be in ever-increasing spirals of success. We will be able to embrace learning all over again and become like sponges that can easily absorb knowledge from everywhere. The enchantment of learning will sparkle within us once more and the world will become better for it.

All the best!

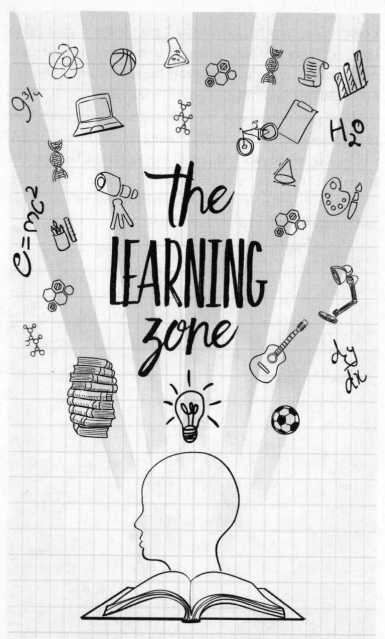

For those who have decided to return more often to The Learning Zone,
the next few chapters will make your adventures here productive and enjoyable

Chapter 7

THE FEYNMAN TECHNIQUE

The derivative of a function $f(x)$, denoted by $f'(x)$ is:

$$f'(x) = \lim_{h \to 0} \frac{f(a+h) - f(a)}{h}$$

Wonderful!

Did you instantly switch off as your eyes hit these dreaded symbols, reminding you of horrible times in calculus class? Or, maybe you never studied calculus and were left wondering what a derivative is, what those symbols meant, and what all this is doing in a book called *Happiness Express*.

For a person who has studied mathematics, the definition above is familiar and something they can take in their stride... with maybe just a small wince or two. For the rest of the world, this looks like the beginning of some nightmare.

Enter Richard Feynman.

Richard Feynman was a Nobel Prize-winning physicist and a brilliant scientist. His memoir, *Surely You're Joking, Mr. Feynman!*, was one of those books I have read again and again. He was known as the 'Great Explainer' and was famous for his ability to explain complex ideas to others in simple, intuitive ways. He (or Einstein or somebody) is known to have

THE THING THAT DOESN'T FIT
IS THE THING THAT'S MOST INTERESTING

said that if you cannot explain something in plain language stripped off jargon, you have not really learnt or understood it.

The Feynman Technique for studying is all about dejargonising content and being able to explain to a lay person what it all means. If you can do that, it means you yourself have understood it and are not likely to forget it in a hurry. Besides, if you teach it to others, you cement it into your memory.

On a side note, this is the way I always used to study. I wrote my M.Sc thesis such that my mother, a BA in French, could understand it. Mr Feynman has done a lot more for physics than I ever will; he was before my time; so we will continue calling this The Feynman Technique, not Bawa's Study Methodology.

Stay with me while I apply The Feynman Technique to the concept of a derivative. I am not trying to do some hardcore math here, expect a few omissions, assumptions and some sweeping generalisations. Not at all acceptable in a math textbook. But this is not a math textbook, so we are going to be impetuous. My goal is to make you understand what a derivative is, and if you read the next few pages with an open mind, I am quite convinced that you probably will.

Possibly you may even see the elegance and beauty in that formula. Or, possibly that's hoping for too much!

Functions

Let's start off with the definition of a function.

What's a function? What does it mean when you say $y = f(x)$

In English this simply means, tell me what's happening to as I mess around with x.

If is x 42, what is y? If x is 0.655, what is y? If x is -34, what is y? If x is 0, what is y? If x is 350001, what is y? ... You get the drift.

There are a few rules about how a function should behave for it to be called a function, but let's not get into that. If you are curious, I have made a YouTube video to explain that. Check it out at www.happinessexpressbook.com/videos/functions.

Slope

See this line below?

Let's make a triangle out of it:

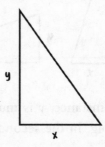

Traditionally, we call the vertical side and the horizontal side x.

Slope for some reason is denoted by m, and defined as

$$m = \frac{y}{x}$$

What does this mean? And what do you mean by slope? Let's apply The Feynman Technique to this. If you had to explain slope in English, without using those symbols, what would you say?

I would ask you to roll a marble from the top of that line. The faster the marble rolls down, the greater the slope; the slower it trundles along, the smaller the slope.

Or,

Say I am walking from here to there. When I get 'there', how high did I go with respect to my starting position (here)? I went very high, big slope; not so high, smaller slope.

Now, let's check in with the mathematical definition of slope:

$$m = \frac{y}{x}$$

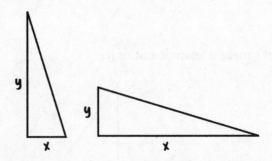

In the first instance, y is much bigger than x and so m is going to be big. In the second instance, x is much bigger than y, so m will be small. This is exactly what our English definition says.

Instead of saying, I am walking from here to there; when I get 'there', how high did I go with respect to my starting position (here)? if I went very high, it's a big slope, etc., we simply say:

$$m = \frac{y}{x}$$

Concise, precise and elegant! Do you see how you can appreciate this little formula only when you have truly understood what a slope means?

Going further, this means that slope changes depending on the changes in the height (y) and width (x). We could as well look at slope to be the ratio of the change in to the change in x.

How do we figure out the change in y and x?

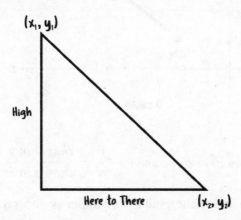

Think of the walking again. Here to there is and how high is y. These turn out to be just the length of the two sides of that right-angled triangle above. If the end points of our original line had coordinates (x_1, y_1) and (x_2, y_2), then change in y, meaning the length of y, would be $y_2 - y_1$. Similarly, change in x would be $x_2 - x_1$.

If this is confusing you, take real numbers and check it out. For example, a segment with end points $(2,1)$ and $(5,3)$ when plotted on a graph paper, will have $y = 3 - 1 = 2$ *units* and $x = 5 - 2 = 3$ *units*. These lengths are easily seen as illustrated below:

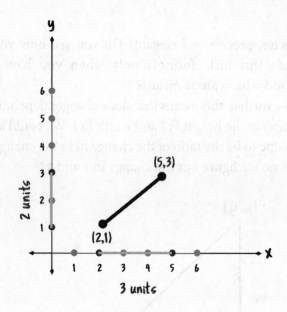

Finally, we have slope as $m = \dfrac{y}{x} = \dfrac{change\ in\ y}{change\ in\ x} = \dfrac{y_2 - y_1}{x_2 - x_1}$

This is an important result to remember as we foray onwards.

Bending That Line

Slope of a line is all very well. Bend the line, it becomes a curve. How about the slope of a curve?

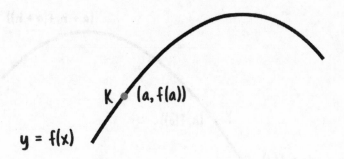

It is quite obvious that the slope of this curve will keep changing at every point on it. We don't even talk about the slope of a curve, we simply talk about the slope of a curve at some specific point on that curve.

To find out the equation that represents this curve, we ask the question, what's happening to the y coordinate as we change the x coordinate? Remember functions from earlier?

To represent the equation for this (or any) generic curve, we can say: $y = f(x)$. Keep telling me what's happening to y as x changes.

Let's take a random point K on the curve. If the x coordinate of that point is a, then the y coordinate will be $f(a)$. The point K will have coordinates $(a, f(a))$. We want to find the slope of the curve at the point K.

We don't know how to do this, but we do know how to find the slope of a line. Let's draw a line, so that the first point is K $(a, f(a))$, and the second point is a little farther down the x-axis, some h units further and still on the curve we are working with. The coordinate of this point is $a + h$, and the coordinate will be $f(a + h)$. This second point will have coordinates $(a + h, f(a + h))$.

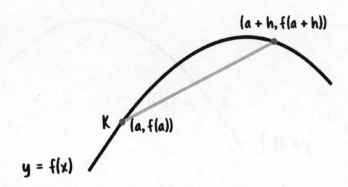

The slope of this line is change in divided by change in x, meaning:

$$\frac{f(a + h) - f(a)}{a + h - a}$$

Remember $\dfrac{y^2 - y^1}{x^2 - x^1}$

This becomes:

$$\frac{f(a + h) - f(a)}{h}$$

We don't want to know the slope of that line. We are actually still interested in the slope of the curve at that original point K. Let's start sliding the second point closer and closer along the curve towards K... meaning h is becoming smaller and smaller. We make h so small that the second point has slid almost on top of the original one. They are kissing each other.

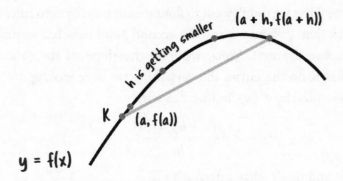

You may ask, why bother with making smaller and smaller? Just make $h = 0$? Isn't that what we are after? Well, $h = 0$ will means division by 0 which screws things up and is the equivalent of a mathematical sin. Curious why? Watch this video which is all about division by 0: www. happinessexpressbook.com/videos/divisionbyzero.

So, what to do now?

Mathematicians are crafty little fellows. They came up with the concept of a 'limit' to handle these prickly situations. The exact mathematical explanation of a limit is a bit too tedious, so here it is in reckless English:

$$\lim_{h \to 0}$$

read limit of h tending to zero, simply meaning h is getting closer and closer to 0. h is super super super super close to 0. It's sitting sooooooooooooooooo close to 0, it's for all practical purposes 0… **But it's not 0.**

They whisper, actually $h = 0$. It's not. But it is. Just don't tell anyone. It's our little secret. And we get out of that unfortunate division by 0 business.

Coming back to that equation we had where we needed h

to be 0 but we didn't want to flout the division by zero rule, we stick that $\lim_{h \to 0}$ into it and the second point now has virtually become the first. Voila, we have the slope of the original point K on the curve, the very thing we were looking for! It is denoted by $f'(x)$ and we can write:

$$f'(x) = \lim_{h \to 0} \frac{f(a + h) - f(a)}{h}$$

And that's what a derivative is.

It's just a glorified slope.

The Derivative in English

You have a curve. You want to find the slope of the curve. This is not possible because the slope of the curve changes at every point. Let's pick some random point on the curve. You need to find the slope of the curve at that point.

Well, remember you know how to find the slope of a line. Draw a line from the original point on the curve to another point on the same curve. Can we find the slope of this line? Great.

Shrink the line. Make it smaller and smaller; the second point has now slid all the way to be almost on top of the first point. It is virtually the first point, but not quite. So we still have two points and that means we still have an infinitesimally small line. Find the slope of that miniscule line and you have figured out the slope of the curve at the original point. All you need to do is pretend that the length of that line is zero—knowing that it is not. It's our little secret. Don't tell anyone and we are done.

The slope of the curve at a point is called the 'derivative' of that curve. Derivative is simply slope—glorified!

Mr Feynman, do you approve?!

The Feynman Technique (with a few tweaks from me)

This technique is primarily used to make sure you have understood and can explain a concept you are grappling with. It's quite important that you use some paper and a pen for this. Preferably avoid using a computer. Go as low-tech as you can with it.

I was born not knowing and have had only a little time to change that here and there

Study your concept from your source material till you feel you have a good grasp of the subject and are comfortable with it.

Step 1: Title

On a blank sheet of paper, at the very top, write the name of the concept you are wanting to learn. I have used a math example; you can use this technique to get around a concept from any field of study.

Step 2: Initial thoughts

Write out whatever you have understood about the concept in your own words in plain simple English. Pretend you are teaching someone else with little or no knowledge of the subject. How would you say it to them? Sometimes it may help to think that you are going to be talking about this to a child—how would you explain it all? Write it out.

Step 3: Fill in the gaps

Review your notes and compare them to your source material. See if there's something you didn't know or understand. Go back to studying those parts and incorporate them in.

Step 4: Dejargonise

Once more, go over your notes, tidy up if required, and check if your explanations are really without jargon. If there are parts with too many technical terms in there, challenge yourself to write them out in simpler language. Is there stuff that could be explained in even simpler words? Are you assuming some sort of knowledge that already exists about the subject? Redo those parts till you are satisfied that anybody with little to no knowledge about your subject could read your notes and grasp the concept you are talking about.

Step 5: Ask impertinent Whys

My buddy Gowrishankar makes the most amazing videos, but he is desperately math challenged. I asked him one time, 'Gowri, what is -2 times -3?'. Without missing a beat, he replied -6. I said no, it's +6. He asked, why? If +2 times +3 is +6, -2 times -3 should be -6. I didn't have an explanation. Telling him it is a rule didn't work. He kept asking why again and again. I had to do quite a lot of thinking before I could come up with an answer that could satisfy a supremely math-challenged person. Check the video: www.happinessexpressbook.com/ videos/minustimesminus.

As you go over your notes, think like Gowri and keep asking 'why?' to things you may take for granted because of the knowledge base you already have acquired through the study of your subject. For example, you know the Pythagoras Theorem and you know it is universally applicable to all right-angled triangles. Ever wondered how that got verified? How can we be so sure it works for every single right-angled triangle in the universe? See this video to find out: www. happinessexpressbook.com/videos/pythagoras.

Answer your own 'whys' till you are happy that no more remain.

Step 6: Mind Map

Once you have got your notes done, it would be a great idea to mind map your material, especially if the material you are studying is mind-map friendly. This step is optional, but it can give even more insights to you about what you are learning.

We have outlined how to mind map in the next few chapters. We have discussed mind mapping in great detail in our earlier book *Ready, Study, Go!*

Step 7: Forage for Fun Facts

This step is optional too. Check if you can unearth some interesting and little-known facts about what you are studying. Stuff that people can throw at each other during a dinner conversation and sound intelligent.

Step 8: Go public

Grab a friend and explain the whole thing to him or her. Show them your mind map from step 6 and definitely weave in a few of those facts from step 7.

They understood it?—Good.

They loved the way you explained it?—Fantastic.

You managed to spark curiosity in them for the subject?—Absolute brilliance!

This style of learning will constantly challenge and engage you. Taking the time to dig deeper into a subject can be richly rewarding. It will transform the process of studying considered by most to be dull drudgery, and avoided as much as possible, into something that is interesting and fun.

There is an amazing, incomparable high you get when you have finally cracked a concept that's been eluding you. Here's to many of those highs!

THE IMAGINATION OF NATURE IS FAR FAR BETTER THAN THE IMAGINATION OF MAN

Chapter 8
MIND MAPPING AND
RADIAL THINKING

We have elaborated on the technique of mind mapping in our earlier book *Ready, Study, Go!: Smart Ways to Learn*. This chapter is a refresher on the topic before we jump into a specialised way of mind mapping which I call Focused Mind Mapping.

Our brain has a big, wonderful, enchanting, chaotic mess of neurons in it. Definitely not a neat, orderly list! Sequential or linear thinking is one of the biggest impediments to learning and recall.

a. Making lists.
b. Then ticking them one at a time, until we are through.
c. Making more lists.
d. Rinse and repeat.

It's borrrrrrringggg!

Linear thinking makes learning drudgery and recall wishful thinking. These patterns (of linear thinking) are a bad habit society and families forced upon us.

Linear thinking doesn't allow us to use our brain the way it was supposed to be.

Enter Mind Mapping. A British psychology author Tony Buzan has laid claim to having originated mind maps, though people have been making such drawings for years.

Mind mapping is just a few circles and lines really. But beneath its simplicity, there is power. It's a profoundly easy way to use the brain how it's meant to be used.

This is not a 'read' chapter. It's a 'do' chapter. Remember that actually drawing the mind maps are going to grow the 'drawing' mind map dendrites in your brain. Merely reading the text and glancing at the pictures will not bring you the proficiency you require to use this technique.

Before moving on with this chapter, make sure you have the following things at hand.

☐ A few pencils and pens in an array of colours: red, blue, black and green pens and a box of Crayola are enough.
☐ An eraser.
☐ Plenty of A4 blank sheets of paper, preferably unruled.
☐ If you are feeling artistic, get more colours, felt pens, etc.

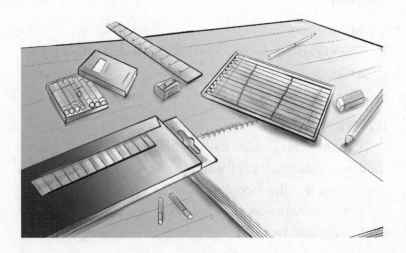

Now, you will have an exercise to do. It will take you less than 20 minutes to complete it. Please don't skip ahead and ensure you follow the order it is presented in. By the end of this exercise, you would have learnt the basics and purpose of mind mapping.

The Vacation

A good friend of yours inherited a beautiful cottage in the woods. He has invited you along with a few others to go with him for a few days and check out the property. Though the place is comfortable, he has warned that it is rustic. You will be spending five days there over a long weekend.

Make a list of the stuff you would pack for this trip. Don't write it out on an electronic device; use pen and paper. Think of all the things you would require and jot them down. Bear

in mind that you will have to make do with only these during your five-day trip. Nothing else.

Don't read ahead please until your list is ready.

Here is the list I made for my vacation.

Vacation Packing

Clothes-
5 vests   5 pairs of socks
3 pants
7 shirts & tshirts
3 undies
Medicines - Ayurvedic, homeopathy, Bach flower, inhaler
Supplements
iPad, iPhone, Chargers, extension box

Books & Magazines

Snacks - Chocolates, Khakharas, Biscuits.

Toiletries - soap, shampoo, Conditioner,
                    nail cutter, toothbrush, toothpaste
Chappals

Meditation iPod & Kriya Tape

water Bottle

As I thought more about the trip, I got a few other ideas. I penned these into the original list. For example, I had totally forgotten about taking along a personal identification card and swimming trunks.

You, too, should give yourself some time to list things you may have missed. You could get ideas from either of my lists or google vacation packing. Add everything you think you may want to take along. Feel free to delete any item—just scratch those out. Don't worry about being neat. Focus on getting everything onto that piece of paper.

Here is my revised list.

Vacation Packing

Clothes - Make sure to get proper directions to the place, ask if sleeping bag needed
5 vests eye mask 5 pairs of socks, laundry bag
3 pants neck pillow 4 shorts, 3 handkerchiefs
7 shirts & tshirts hat, swimming trunks
3 undies   towel, sweater

Medicines - heal cream, shakti drops Rescue Remedy
Ayurvedic, homeopathy, Bach flower, inhaler
Div Vati
Supplements, Crocin, Nux Vomica, Carbo Veg, Arnica
Sunscreen & lotion Bandaid, swiss knife
iPad, iPhone, Chargers, extension box, frisbee, playing cards
power bank
Books & Ready, Steady, Go! Yog Vasishtha,
Bhagwad Geeta Knowledge sheets from Sri Sri,
Snacks - Chocolates, Khakharas, methi Biscuits.
Cheeses dark, green & blacks
Toiletries - soap, shampoo, Conditioner,
Shaving foam, razor, nail cutter, toothbrush, toothpaste
Chappals blades hairbrush
hiking shoes
Meditation iPod & Kriya Tape

water Bottle, foldable bag to carry stuff
Personal id - Passport, credit cards, money, driving liscence
tickets,
house warming gift for my friend - Grandma's photo

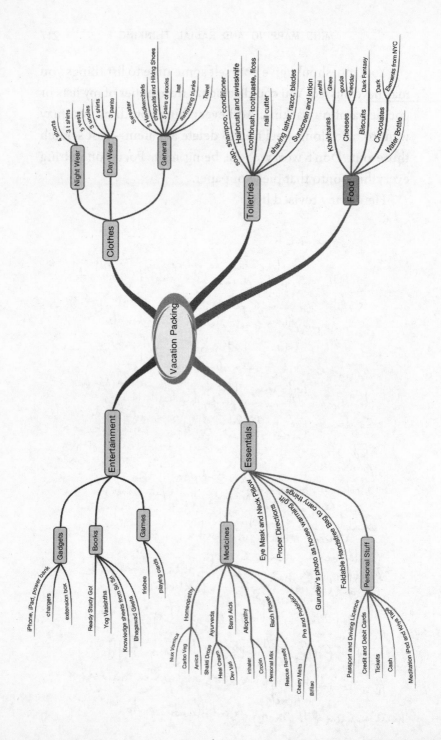

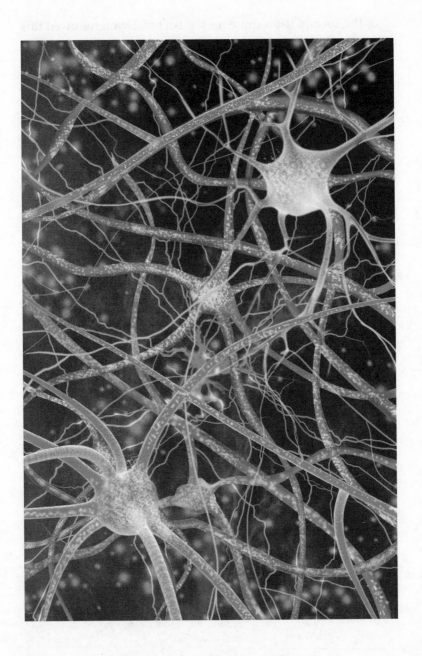

The second list is quite messy, isn't it? If you followed this exercise, I bet your list is equally messy!

Did you notice how tough it was to add new ideas to your first draft?

Here is a mind map of my vacation packing (see p. 218). Compare it with both my lists.

Look at this artist's impression of the wonderful mess of neurons and neural pathways in your brain (see p. 219).

What resembles the way your brain is wired?

What is easier to look at?

Do you see how simple it would be to add an idea to this mind map?

A line and a circle, and voila! We are done.

It gives a bird's eye view and a worm's eye view at the same time. I can see the whole as well as get into the details if I wish to, at any node.

I don't have to 'finish' the food node before moving onto the electronics node and so on. As I get ideas, I can capture them as I jump from node to node, simply penning them down.

The structure of our brain and the way the neurons are organised make ideas pop randomly, not neatly and sequentially. The ability to jump from one node to another as ideas come makes the process of recording thoughts far more organic and natural than any list would allow.

Welcome to the world of Radial Thinking!

When you think radially, ideas flow naturally and the process of learning and recall is enhanced. Using the brain is so much easier.

The 1-2-3 (and 4) of Mind Mapping

1. Start with a central idea for your mind map. You may want to take some time thinking about what it should be. For example, if you had to mind map Romeo and Juliet, what would your central idea be? 'Tragedy' or 'Love Story' or something else? As you can imagine, the resulting mind maps for the two words would be quite different. The central idea gives a perspective to your mind mapping project.

2. Draw 4-5 lines (branches) radiating out from the central idea. Jot down whatever ideas come to you that are related to the central idea. Don't worry about how important or relevant these ideas are.

3. As you get more ideas for the various nodes you created, add them in, creating more nodes and branches as required. Keep doing step 3 until you are satisfied that you have got whatever ideas you have in your head about that project onto the paper.

4. If an unrelated but brilliant idea comes, don't discard it; just start another mind map and put it down. Then come back to what you were working on.

The 6 Cs of Mind Mapping

C1: Central idea: This will be pivotal to the perspective your mind map will take. It can be decided in advance; or it may be resolved in retrospect, if you are unclear about what the topic is going to be. For example, when you are using a mind map to take notes.

C2: Conciseness: Write briefly on the nodes and branches— use just enough words to capture the essence of the ideas.

C3: Craziness: Our brain loves new and crazy. Make things as funny as you possibly can. You will remember it better.

C4: Curves: Use curves instead of straight lines. Our brain loves curves. Curves make things far more visually attractive. This makes things more interesting and the relevant dendrites required for learning grow faster.

C5: Colours: This one is a no brainer. Colours appeal to us. Unless you are a professional photographer. In which case, you use a $5000 camera to take out-of-focus, black and white photos and call them art. Use some colour in your mind maps. Vary text sizes and alignments. You could use particular colours for coding stuff: red could be used for important and urgent, orange may denote work in progress, green for things that are already done, and so on.

C6: Cartoons: Draw a few doodles here and there to symbolise information on your mind map. Instead of writing first aid, for example, drawing a small red cross would be enough to convey the idea. Pictures and cartoons trigger emotion and that strengthens memory.

'I can't draw' is a myth. Everyone can draw. Maybe they draw badly to begin with, but that's all right. Start somewhere. Keep at it and the correct dendrites will grow over time and you will learn to draw.

Typically, you will not be able to create the final version of any mind map in the first draft. Start with a rough version. Get all the nodes and the branches with some details radiating off those nodes onto the paper. For the next draft, draw it again, ensuring everything is more or less in place. You may want to shift a main node under some other node, or create a new main node, etc. Finally, use colours and cartoons to make your mind map as neat and pretty as possible. When you have done this work, it's highly improbable that you will ever forget what you have mind mapped. Even if you do, you only have to look at your mind map and you will remember everything in a few minutes!

Of course, you need not do all this for every mind map you make. For example, when it's a mind map about what you are going to do today, a simple rough one would suffice. Otherwise you may end up only drawing mind maps and never getting to the actual work.

Pros and Cons

There is a very interesting side effect of using mind maps extensively. Mind maps bring obvious clarity and help you organise yourself. They create reliable road maps for the way ahead. Over time, as you gain the ability to think radially and logically, your ideation skills will grow exponentially. This clarity is contagious. In a little while of using mind maps, as your dendrites start growing and forge all the right connections, you will suddenly, almost magically, find answers to other things that you have not mind mapped at all. Problems that you may have relegated to the back burner for a long time may abruptly get resolved.

The biggest disadvantage of mind maps is that they can only show you the way. They bring clarity to your plans and create actionable items for you to execute. They lack the ability to make the actual 'doing' happen. A beautifully created mind map about weight loss will only tell you how to shed those kilos, it will not make you actually lose weight. A mind map shows the way, the action is up to you.

Mind maps and their use are limited only by your imagination. Unfortunately, they are also limited by the amount you practice and use them as well. You will need to diligently mind map for a few months to start seeing real results. Fortunately, mind maps are such fun to create and work with that these months just zip by.

Take five minutes each morning and mind map your day. You will be amazed at how much you get done. Check in with the map at night, so you get an idea about what you need to do the next day.

You need to prepare for an interview or a speech? Mind map it. You will find yourself being able to create fantastic presentations in a fraction of the time you would normally have spent.

Are you stuck for ideas on how to handle that new project? Mind maps will help conjure up ideas out of the blue for you.

You and your team are going to brainstorm on something? Use mind maps to effortlessly take notes. After the meeting, create a final version and send it off to everyone in the team. Recap the next meeting will be quick, and each person will be crystal clear about what they are required to do.

Mind mapping makes you so efficient that you will finally have the time to do all those things you have always wanted to do: being with friends and family, going on that vacation, learning to play the piano...

Have fun with mind maps!

Chapter 9

FOCUSED MIND MAPPING

This technique is an extension of regular mind mapping and tweaking the way mind maps are created. It will require a bit of expertise with the fundamentals of mind mapping. If you are new to mind mapping, please read the previous chapter and draw a few mind maps before proceeding with this one.

You need to study something? Jumping right in then, these are the steps to create a focused mind map.

Phase I: The Foundation Mind Map

First, we decide how much of a particular subject we wish to study to meet our competency goals. Typically, this phase should not take more than a few hours to complete. You could plan to do this phase over two or three days if the subject matter is vast, new or complex.

The time you spend on phase I and creating your foundation mind map will increase your focus and efficiency when you get to the second phase of more detailed studying.

1. Scope

Decide how much you want to learn about a particular subject. Are you appearing for an exam? Interviewing for a job? Or, do you just want to sound intelligent during an after-dinner conversation? The scope of how much you intend to study will depend largely on this.

Heard about the 80-20 rule?

Vifredo Pareto was a famous Italian philosopher and economist. He grew green peas. He saw that 80% of the peas that he got from his garden came from only 20% of the peapods. He called these the vital few. He then went on to show that 80% of the land in Italy belonged to 20% of the population. If you check out world incomes, 82.7% of the global wealth belongs to 20% of the population. This 80-20 rule applies to various areas.

80% of work is done by 20% of the people. 80% of sales comes from 20% of the customers, and so on. This rule can have a huge impact on all aspects of our lives. When you realise that you need to study only 20% of a subject to achieve 80% proficiency in it, learning suddenly seems so much simpler—if you don't care too much about the remaining 20%.

If you want to learn a new language, here is some more good news. Most languages have around 250,000 words. However, to understand 50% of the language, you need to know the meanings of just about 1000 words. Mastering 2000 to 2500 words means you have acquired 80% proficiency in that language. This means you need to know a mere 1% of the words of a language to have an astounding 80% proficiency in it!

These 1000-2000 words can easily be learned in about six months. Of course, there are diminishing returns after this, and to have greater proficiency levels in a language could take years. The question is whether you really require that high a level of expertise.

Before you embark on your learning adventure, you will have to decide how deep you want to go down that figurative rabbit hole, and how much of your schedule you can devote to it. Be realistic about your goal and the amount of time you need to pursue it.

If you want a working knowledge of Ayurveda, enough to give a speech at a Rotary Club event, one to two hours daily for two or three days will suffice for your study. However, if you would like to treat common ailments using Ayurvedic medicines, you would need a lot more time, possibly an hour or two a day for a few months, along with expert guidance.

2. Graze

Once you have decided how much you want to learn about a particular subject, gather the material you think you would require to accomplish this. It could be a few books, some online resources, your own notes or someone else's. Skim over all the material you have collected doing a cursory read. You are getting a rough idea about what you are getting into. Once you have done this, go back to step one to redefine your scope if required, and graze again.

3. The Initial Mind Map

Draw out a mind map including whatever you know and remember from your grazing, referring to your material minimally. This step will set the stage for further learning.

4. Fill in the Blanks

Go back to your study material and do a more detailed survey of it. You are still skimming, but this time paying more attention to elements such as chapter titles, paragraph headings, diagrams, summaries and whatever else catches your attention. Keep adding these as branches or nodes to your Initial Mind Map. Don't worry about being neat and organising things. You only have to capture your scope into your Initial Mind Map. Get it all down on that paper.

5. The Foundation Mind Map

Tidy up the mind map from step 4. Organise all your information into relevant nodes. You will have created your Foundation Mind Map. It defines the scope of what you need to work on. You would mostly stay within the confines of this mind map for the remainder of your studying.

Phase II: The Focused Mind Map

This is the part where you will do detailed studying of your subject. Phase I will have provided you with what and how much you need to work on.

1. Detailing

Work on the nodes of the Foundation Mind Map. Study from your source material, this time doing a more thorough reading. Make notes. Gather your facts until you have detailed each node and its branches with as much information you feel you require.

Sometimes a node could be complex enough to become a mind map by itself. Other times, a node would be easier to work with as a separate mind map because that information could be the basis of many other nodes or mind maps. Work through your study material and create all the mind maps required.

Your Foundation Mind Map will have transformed into a Focused Mind Map(s). It should ideally give you a bird's eye view and a worm's eye view of your subject at once. If you have followed all the steps above, you will have created a fantastic pictorial representation of your subject. It will guarantee a logical collection of your thoughts and a thorough understanding of the topic. In times to come, you will be able to recall your work with minimal effort. It will allow you see in a few glances almost everything you need to know about your area of study.

2. Beautify

Now that you have more or less finished studying your subject, tidy up all your mind maps and beautify them keeping the 6 Cs in mind: Central idea, Conciseness, Curves, Colours, Cartoons and Craziness.

You may think this step should be optional. After all, isn't this just cosmetic? Instead of 'beautifying', think 'cementing'. Bringing the 6 Cs into your mind map will reinforce all that you have studied and embed them into your memory. Perhaps you may even get some amazing insights into your subject that never crossed your mind before.

3. Go Public

Use your knowledge and mind maps to write a blog post (or a series of posts) about what you learned.

4. Diving Deeper?

Optionally, if you feel you want to explore your subject further, go back to phase I, redefine your scope and repeat the steps above.

If what you have learned is important to you, reviewing it is critical. When you have finished Phase II to your satisfaction, revisit your mind maps and notes once a week for a month.

Apply the Feynman Technique to the knowledge you have acquired. Write out what you have learned, eliminating all jargon, so that even a novice can understand it. Better still, teach what you learned to a friend who has little or no idea about your subject. If you keep teaching what you have learned to others, you will be pleasantly surprised at how much you can remember.

It's easy to fall prey to the illusion of competency—make sure that you redraw your mind maps from memory after a week, a month and a year. See how much you can recollect. Review everything: your original mind maps and notes, with a focus on what you may have forgotten.

After this, revisiting and refreshing your work once a year would be enough to cement this knowledge into your long-term memory.

AN EXAMPLE

Here is how I wrote the chapter on Memory using focused mind mapping. Please come back and re-read this section once you finish the chapter on Memory. It might make more sense.

Phase I: Creating the Foundation Mind Map

1. Scope: My target was around 5000 words on Memory, with a few techniques on how to improve it.

2. Grazing: I browsed through many books and online resources on the subject. Next, I spoke to Rajesh Krishnamurthy (Myla), a memory expert and a dear friend. He taught me the Memory Palace technique, the Spaced Repetition System (SRS) and ANKI. I practised these myself and taught the basics to a few friends. I experimented with other memory techniques such as The Link method, Mnemonics, The Journey or Story Method and The Major System which I picked up from the internet.

Rajesh gave me a stack of books to refer to. I researched about them and other books and finally picked three books: *Fluent Forever: How to Learn Any Language Fast and Never Forget It* by Gabriel Wyner, *Brain Rules* by Dr John Medina and *The Memory Book* by Harry Loryane and Jerry Lucas. I also referred to *How to Memorise Anything* by Aditi and Sudhir Singhal.

3. My Initial Mind Map (tidied up): This combines steps 3 and 4 together.

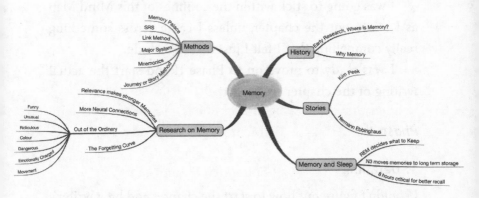

4. The Foundation Mind Map: I began writing a first draft of the chapter, simultaneously doing more experimenting with the memory techniques I had learned. I confined my reading to the nodes and topics on my Initial Mind Map and made a few decisions. The part on Memory and Sleep had to go. I had talked enough about sleep earlier in the book. I loved the Memory Palace technique and SRS. The other techniques were great, but there are many books out there detailing them. I could point my readers to good books on the subject.

I needed to create some interesting hooks and stories for my content. My Foundation Mind Map looked like this:

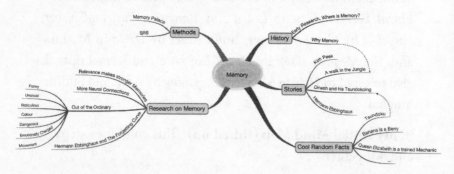

I was going to stick within the confines of this Mind Map as I wrote out the chapter, unless I came across something really compelling that I felt I just had to include.

I was ready to move on to Phase II and start the actual writing of the chapter in earnest.

Phase II

1. Detailing

I couldn't figure out how to start the chapter and hit a writer's block for a few days. What to say first so I could draw my readers into the fascinating world of the Memory? I finally decided on the 'walk in the jungle' story that establishes the role of Memory in our survival as a species—this is how you are here, and alive, and reading this book! From there on it was fairly smooth sailing.

I put in the facts after that. Those facts needed to be there because I wanted people to realise that they forgot a lot by the time they got to the end of the chapter. I was confined to bed for almost a month because of a back injury while I was doing this part of the book. I had insane fun finding those facts on the internet and then spouting them out at all the people who came to visit me.

Kim Peek is a Memory Hero. His story just had to be there. I watched many YouTube videos on him to create those few paragraphs.

The search for where memory is in the brain was quite intriguing. I presented a quick snippet.

A bit about how memory works went in next. I could have done a book on this as many people have; I resisted the urge to write more, simply writing enough so I could establish that better memory = more neural connections. And more neural connections happen when what is happening is relevant to you. I added a paragraph about the preference of the brain to remember things that are out of the ordinary. Dinesh and his tsundokoing story went in here.

The Memory Palace technique was next on the agenda and took a long time to write. It's so easy to teach, but to put it down in words and make it readable was quite a challenge. I hope you enjoy this section. It's a lot of fun when you can make it work for you.

Then, I went on to talk about Forgetting: Hermann Ebbinghaus and the Forgetting curve. And how to get past the natural tendency of the brain to forget things using the SRS technique which I described very briefly, considering there is vast online data available about how to use it. I talked about the amazing software ANKI that almost flawlessly implements SRS and gave a nod to its generous developer Damien Elmen.

2. Beautifying (Editing?)

As I revised the chapter, I felt it needed one little goad to make it complete and that's the section on the Test. It tied in beautifully with what I had talked about in the Brain chapter and our earlier book *Ready, Study, Go!*. It made perfect sense to introduce it here. Nothing better to drive home the point that dendrites grow for exactly what you do—something I feel we need to be constantly reminding ourselves about.

My final mind map looked like the image on p. 235.

I didn't feel any need to beautify or add any more detail to this mind map. It served its purpose. I could write out and finalise my chapter. I must admit that I got caught up in writing that chapter, and many finishing touches on this mind map were done after I had finished writing it.

It is apt that we use mind maps, which are a fantastic tool for memorising, to remember things about the Memory!

3. Diving Deeper and Going Public

I didn't feel the need to delve further into this subject for now. I had written 5278 words on Memory, exactly what I set out to do. I was satisfied with my effort. For going public, I asked a few people to read the chapter, and they loved it. More of the going public phase would happen when you read this book.

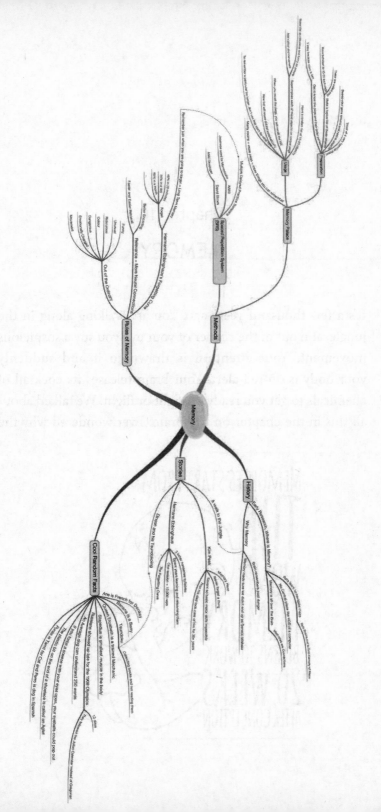

Chapter 10

MEMORY

It's a few thousand years ago. You are walking along in the jungle, and out of the corner of your eye you spy a suspicious movement. Your attention is drawn to it and suddenly your body is on red alert. Your brain releases its cocktail of chemicals to get you ready for fight or flight. We talked about all this in the chapter on the Brain. Ever wondered why the

MEMORIES START FROM THE WOMB MEMORY BEGINS TO WORK 20 WEEKS AFTER CONCEPTION

brain releases those chemicals? Why would that movement in the bushes make it happen?

The brain remembers similar incidents and their consequences. The last time a movement like this had happened, there was a hungry predator intent on making lunch out of you. You had managed to escape. Your brain remembers this and reacts accordingly.

Memory just saved your life, and made sure you didn't become some sort of a genetic mistake—and our species went on to rule planet Earth.

Some Cool, Random Facts

'Ane' is the French word for donkey, 'Punae' is cat in Tamil, and 'Perro' is Spanish for dog.

The stapedius is the smallest muscle in the human body.

Tsundoku is the act of acquiring books without reading them.

If you had a Premature Extraventricular Systole, it means your heart just skipped a beat.

Queen Elizabeth II is a trained mechanic.

The Russians showed up 12 days late for the 1908 Olympics in London because they were following the Julian calendar instead of the Gregorian one.

An average dog can understand up to 250 words.

If you had an Autosomal dominant Compelling Helio Opthalmic Outburst (ACHOO), you sneezed on seeing light.

A banana is a berry.

If you force a sneeze with eyes open, your eyeballs could fall out.

The plastic bit on the tip of a shoelace is called an aglet.

By the time you finish reading this book, chances are that you will have forgotten almost all of these facts. What would be the point of learning something new if we are simply going to forget it?! My biggest frustration in the process of learning stemmed from my memory not behaving itself. Many times, I would remember useless bits of information and forget critical things. For any sort of learning to happen efficiently, we need to understand how memory works. Figuring out how and why we remember stuff will help us remember stuff better.

Meet Kim Peek

The undisputed King of Remembering was a man called Kim Peek and nothing written about memory would be complete without a mention of him. The blockbuster film *Rain Man* was based on a fictitious person like him. He was a savant and had one of the most incredible, prodigious memories recorded in recent times. He remembered everything. Forever. He would read eight books a day. And remember every single word of every single line. He would read two pages at a time, one with each eye. He would go to the public library in his hometown of Salt Lake City and sit and read and read and read. He knew every single postal code in the US, every single street name. He knew historical and geographical facts that would put Google to shame. He knew the lyrics to thousands of songs. He was a repository of all the scores of every single baseball player of the last few decades. If you told him your birthday, he could tell you in an instant what day of the week you were born. I can go on… but you get the drift.

Kim was born deformed. His cerebellum was damaged. The corpus callosum in his brain was missing and there was

ALEXANDER THE GREAT
HAD A PHENOMENAL MEMORY.
HE COULD REMEMBER
THE NAMES OF EVERY
SINGLE ONE OF HIS SOLDIERS
30,000 OF THEM!

almost no connection between the left and right hemispheres of his brain. The neurosurgeon, who saw his reports as a baby, took a cursory look at them and advised his parents to give him off to an institution and forget about him, remarking that he was late for his game of golf.

Fran, his father, didn't listen to the doctor and brought him home. Fran took care of Kim for more than 30 years. Though Kim had a phenomenal memory, brushing his teeth, taking a bath and other simple motor skills were beyond him. Fran helped Kim with all these daily tasks of life.

When Fran was asked in an interview about what it was like to take care of Kim, he replied it's like working 30 hours a day, 10 days a week! It's a testament to a father's indefatigable love for his son that the world got to witness the power that a human memory can have. Kim died in 2009. During the last years of his life, he acquired many abilities that he shouldn't have had, being a savant. Scientists from many universities in the US are still figuring out what was going on inside Kim's head—as well as in ours.

Memories Are Connections

Scientists began the search for where memories are stored in brain cells in the early 1940s by doing some fairly brutal experiments on rats. The rats learned how to navigate a maze. Then the scientists cut off parts of the rats' brains to see if the rats forgot the maze, hoping that they could therefore pinpoint where the rats were storing information. No matter how much of the brain was cut away, the rats still managed to find their way through the maze. This approach was abandoned by 1950.

It was then that the search for memory went to the junctions between the cells rather than the cells themselves. We saw in Brain 101 that learning something is simply making sure that a certain bunch of neurons and their dendrites fire their synapses in a particular sequence forming a neural circuit. This circuit represents that bit of information.

Remembering that bit of information is getting all those neurons to fire again in the same way.

The maze was all over the brain of the rat. There is no central place in the brain like the hard drive of a computer where memories are stored. Data related to every experience is spread across the brain.

The Vitamix is a powerful blender with the motor of a small bike. Its blades move so fast that through sheer friction, it can heat up water to boiling point in a few minutes. Imagine putting several chunks of an assortment of fruit in a blender like this. Leave the lid open and switch it on at full speed. Pause for a bit and picture the mess…

Incredibly, our brain does much the same thing when it encounters new information. It slices, dices and splatters bits of information all around itself.

Most of what we experience involves many or all of our senses.

Just reading this line will involve your visual, tactile, olfactory and possibly your aural ability. Your eyes are processing the letters, your hands are feeling the book or

reading device you are reading this line on. Your nose smells that new book/old book smell, and your ears are detecting noises around you. If you are munching on something, then the taste and smell of that snack are added to the mix. The processing of all these senses happens all over the brain. Even for each particular sense, processing of specific bits is done in different parts. The vertical lines of a picture are in one place, the horizontal in another. Colour occupies yet another. And so on… The brain takes whatever we encounter and chucks it all over the place, to make sense of it for us.

Little wonder then that the rishis of yore said everything is an illusion. It actually is! You are definitely not experiencing the world as it is… but as your brain is interpreting it for you.

That's just experiencing. Let's come to remembering that experience. The brain has to now recreate all those connections for you. Amazingly though, the more connections there are, the easier it is for the brain to piece them together later. This is supremely counter-intuitive, but it is actually simpler for the brain to 'remember' something when there are more senses and multiple connections involved. It can pick up any thread, build on it and recreate. More threads mean easier recall.

The point when we meet with new information is remarkably important to remembering it. The more connections it generates, the more you are invested in it, the more emotional charge there is, the more likely you are to remember it.

Relevance

Do you remember what tsundoku is? It is a Japanese word and is the act of collecting books without reading them. If you are like most people, by now, you would have forgotten that. There wouldn't have been enough connections inherent in that word for you to remember it. For some people, though, that's the one thing they may remember from that list of random facts at the start of this chapter.

When I came across that word for the first time, I immediately connected it with Dinesh. He has been wanting to learn Spanish for as long as I can remember, and has collected tonnes of books on that subject. He has never managed to get through more than the first few pages in any of them. He just keeps getting more and more of those books home. I think he thinks that if there are enough books on Spanish around the house, the language will somehow seep into his system.

I have been wanting to give those books away and reduce the clutter, which has led to a few arguments between us. It is not restricted to Spanish either. He will get a random weird title on some obscure subject and keep it on his desk. Then that book will go to the bookshelf. Finally it will be relegated to the stack of books lying all around the house which I call clutter.

Just when I am about to get rid of it, he will ask for it and it will return back to his desk. He has an amazing knack of noticing when a book is not in the house any more, even if he has not touched it for five years. Give the book away and he promptly asks for it. He is an absolute tsundokist, if that's a word.

The word tsundoku rang a loud bell in my head when I first read it, because Dinesh who I love so much and is close to me, does exactly that. It formed numerous connections in my head and I could effortlessly recall it, precisely because there are so many connections which made it relevant for me. Perhaps you know someone like that in your life, and, when you read the definition for the first time, you smiled (or frowned) at the thought of them. If they play a significant role in your life and their tsundokoing has impacted you, then you will love to have a word that describes that infuriating habit. A parade of memories in your head related to the word ensured you remembered it.

If you are not a Tamilian, or no significant person in your life is a Tamilian, or you have no interest in cats and no interest in the Tamil language whatsoever, then your brain dismisses 'punae' means cat in Tamil as utterly irrelevant and promptly forgets it.

This, then, is one of the keys in the process of remembering. If you want to remember something, the brain needs to be convinced that the information is relevant. Relevance is just many, many connections. The more elaborately we encode things into our brain at the point of learning, the more relevant it feels to the brain, and the better we remember it.

Memory Palace

The brain is primed to remember things that are not what it considers to be normal. When new things happen, the brain goes on hyper-alert mode, recording the experience. Unusual, funny, ridiculous and dangerous are all turn-ons for the brain. It favours colour over black and white, movement over static, and out of the ordinary over mundane. Add emotional charge and you have a memory that will remain with you for a long time.

Let's bring all these elements together for a little bit of fun. The Memory Palace Technique for remembering things is astonishingly simple to learn and is a great party trick. If you really develop it, it can become quite useful to remember things.

Here is a list of 15 random items:

1. Pizza
2. Race cars
3. Book
4. Needle
5. Spectacles
6. Waterfall
7. Roller skates
8. Mosquitoes
9. Photo frame
10. Eiffel tower
11. Black hole
12. Unicorn
13. Keys
14. Yoga mat
15. Servants

Take five minutes and read this list as many times as you want. Close this book and write out as many as you can remember.

How did you do? Did you get the order correct? If I asked you what was after Mosquitoes or before Yoga mat, would you remember? Chances are you won't.

The Memory Palace technique will enable you to remember this list almost effortlessly.

For now, our palace is just one room. For the sake of this book, it's going to be my room at the ashram. You need to have one room in your head that you are really familiar with.

Sweep your gaze around the room and notice the objects

that make it up... Check out the photo of my room. Going round the room I can see: an earthen water pot, a desk, a standing lamp, the pooja table, an air conditioner, book shelves, a side cabinet, a bed, a recliner, a small cabinet, a rocking recliner, clothes hooks, a toilet door, an attic and cupboards.

It's important that you take in these 'pegs' as we will call them in the order they are in your chosen room. You will need to remember these pegs in their correct sequence. This is very easy considering that you are familiar with the room in the first place.

Before you go further, ensure you have my room firmly in your head, and clearly remember the order of pegs in there.

To repeat, as you sweep your gaze around my room, it is:

1. Earthen pot
2. Desk
3. Lamp
4. Pooja table
5. Air-conditioner
6. Book shelves
7. Side cabinet
8. Bed
9. Recliner
10. Small cabinet
11. Rocking recliner
12. Clothes hooks
13. Toilet door
14. Attic
15. Cupboard

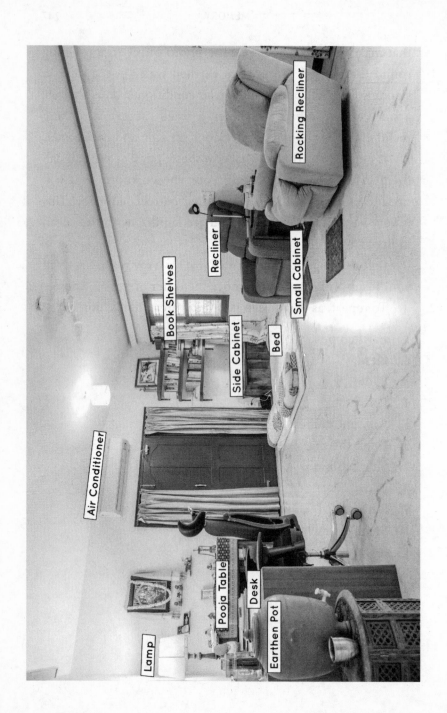

You may want to write this list out once or twice. You need to get the order effortlessly correct before we proceed. Of course, you could do this with any other room of your choice. Make sure you have at least 15 pegs and you know exactly which order they are in.

Being in Nature boosts memory. A person walking in the park had 20% better recall than another who walked in a street

Let's get back to the original list. For your brain to remember it, we need to superimpose each item on each of our pegs, make it as ridiculous or funny as possible, and animate it. Let's do this now. Read what I have written below and take your time to visualise everything. If you can add more details, and make it even funnier or stranger, that's even better. You don't need to spend more than 5 minutes on the entire exercise.

1. **The earthen pot and pizza**. Think of a yummy, luscious, steaming hot pizza with earthen pots as topping. As you bite into the pizza, the pots explode with different types of cheeses and sauces.
2. **Desk and race cars**. Imagine a full-on race track on the desk and little race cars zooming around and the smell of

burnt rubber. These race cars can even have a collision with the hair brush on the desk!

3. **Lamp and books.** The lamp is standing in the corner, reading a book. Every time it understands something, it lights up! If it's funny, it blinks. If it's sad, the light goes dim.

4. **Pooja table and needle.** Lord Shiva is meditating on the table and Parvati is thinking it's getting late for dinner, shall I poke him with this needle to wake him up?! Think of Parvati sitting beside Shiva, getting a little wet because of the Ganga flowing from His locks, with a needle in her hand and sumptuous food spread out in front of her... thinking if it's okay to give the Lord of the Universe a poke with that needle.

5. **Air-conditioner and spectacles.** The air-conditioner has made the temperature so cold that the spectacles have frozen solid, turned a little blue with some icicles on them.

6. **Book shelves and waterfall.** Imagine a huge waterfall cascading down the shelves and a man in a barrel just about to go over the edge.

7. **Cabinet and roller skates.** The cabinet has grown legs and has donned roller skates. It is careening all over the room, its contents spewing in all directions as it laughs and skates.

8. **Bed and mosquitoes.** The entire bed has got irritated by the 'singing' of the mosquitoes and is jumping all over the room trying to kill them. Imagine the bed with sheets swishing, throwing pillows with deadly aim and squashing the mosquitoes.

9. **Recliner and photo frame.** The recliner is posing, showing off its cushions and bulges for a photograph which is then framed and hung on the wall.

10. **Small cabinet and Eiffel Tower.** As soon as you open the drawer in the cabinet, an Eiffel Tower pops out and grows and grows, breaking the ceiling of the room, reaching into the skies until it touches the clouds.

11. **Rocking recliner and black hole.** A black dot appears on the rocking recliner and slowly starts growing and becoming bigger... Its gravitational force is so great that even light can't escape. Everything in the room is being pulled towards that black hole that is there in the rocking recliner.

12. **Clothes hooks and unicorn.** Imagine the clothes hooks as the horn of unicorns. Those unicorns have been very naughty, eating only chocolate and pizza, and as punishment, they have to come to our reality and are allowing people to hang their clothes on their magnificent horns.

13. **Toilet door and keys.** The toilet door is locked, you desperately need to use the loo and you keep turning different keys in the lock but the door doesn't open. The pressure is building and you want to kick the person who thought of locking the toilet door with a key, and then keeping so many keys in a bunch.

14. **Attic and yoga mat.** Open the attic and there are all these people doing all sorts of weird yoga poses on these shiny, super colourful yoga mats. The yoga mats turn green and have stars when people do a pose correctly, and turn bright red and make booing noises if people do a pose wrong.

15. **Cupboard and domestic help.** You open the cupboard and there is a domestic help inside, altering the clothes so that they become tight when you wear them again. She is

horrified that you caught her doing it. This one is for you, Anjana! For everyone else, please ask Anjana about the mystery of cupboards and domestic helps!

And that's it.

Go around the room in your mind and see how it has become easy to remember that list.

You think 'bed' and that ridiculous image of the bed swatting mosquitoes simply pops up. You think 'rocking recliner' and you will see that black hole sucking everything in the room to itself, and so on.

Just to make sure, here is a test. Write out all the things in the list in the correct order. To help you, I have written out the pegs from my room. Write the corresponding object in the list in front of them. You will see that you will have recalled every single one of them.

1. Earthen pot
2. Desk
3. Lamp
4. Pooja table
5. Air-conditioner
6. Book shelves
7. Side cabinet
8. Bed
9. Recliner
10. Small cabinet
11. Rocking recliner
12. Clothes hooks
13. Toilet door
14. Attic
15. Cupboard

And if I ask you, what comes after 'unicorn'? Unicorn is clothes pegs; after clothes pegs is the toilet door; and toilet door is keys. And what's before the 'spectacles'? Frozen spectacles is air-conditioner and before the air-conditioner is the pooja table and on the pooja table we have Parvati wanting to poke Lord Shiva with a …? Needle! See how easy it is?!

In less than 10 minutes, you have got a list of 15 random objects in your head!

What's truly amazing about this technique is that if you get another list of 15 things and make new correlations just like I showed you earlier, these correlations that you have in your head now will just magically disappear to be replaced by the new list. You can do this again and again for as many lists as you may need to learn.

Of course, if you want to remember a specific list for a longer time, don't use that particular room for any other list.

Finally, you can have as many rooms like this in your head; you can potentially remember hundreds of things, maybe even thousands. These rooms need not even exist in real life. They can all be a figment of your imagination. They just need to be as detailed as possible and your pegs should be in logical order. That's when it becomes a Memory Palace.

For the record, I can manage to remember a list of around 50 things now, using three rooms.

There are many other techniques to remember objects, long strings of numbers, countries and their capitals, the periodic table, etc. See the list of resources on memory in the Bibliography.

I would like to touch upon one more aspect of memory, along with another technique which I consider one of the most useful ever. So far, we have mostly talked about remembering. How about forgetting?

Hermann Ebbinghaus

Hermann Ebbinghaus was a German psychologist. Through his life from the late 1800s to the early 1900s, his single biggest contribution to the world was all about forgetting. Much of what we know about forgetting is from the absolutely astounding, yet crazy work that he did.

Ebbinghaus created around 2300 nonsensical words, each a three letter consonant-vowel-consonant combination, where the consonant wasn't repeated. These 'words' had to make no

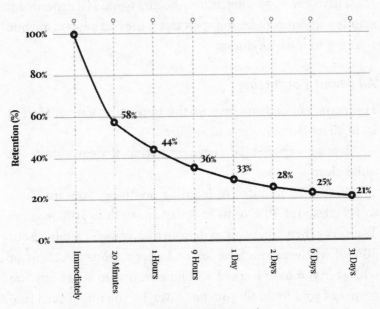

THE EBBINGHAUS FORGETTING CURVE

Lapsed Time Since Learning

sense at all. DOT, for example, was not allowed because it was already a word with a meaning. Neither were MAD or SAD. Or PAP or LUL because the consonant was repeated. He felt words with meaning or repetitive consonants would be easier to remember and skew his experiment.

He then spent years memorising these three-letter nonsense 'words'. To the sound of a metronome and with the same vocal inflection, he would repeat random words he pulled out from a box to see how many he could remember. One such session would involve up to 15,000 repetitions.

He figured out how quickly or slowly he forgot by comparing how long it took him to learn and then, after a period of time, re-learn the list. His savage persistence and tenacity gave us the Forgetting Curve. It's an absolute triumph of the human will to push through years and years of what must have been gruelling, utterly boring work. His experiment stands without parallel and spelt out some bad news to anyone wanting to learn anything.

All About Forgetting

Hermann Ebbinghaus gave us the Forgetting Curve. Here it is, in all its glory, for you to admire.

It is an exponential curve and what it demonstrates is quite clear.

Within 20 minutes of learning anything, you are likely to forget about 40% of it. In a day, more than 70% is gone. The curve then tapers off to denote that you will retain about 20% of whatever you have learned after a month. A ghost of whatever you have learned will lurk around in some obscure corner of your brain till you die... Maybe you might even take some of it with you, who knows?

The strategy most of us used as students to fight this tendency of the brain was to learn, and re-learn, and re-learn yet again, and make sure we managed to get through those exams. This is called overlearning and, in the short term, it might help just a bit: it will get you through that test—we are living proof that it works. But, in the long term, it is absolutely useless. Do you remember a single fact from a test you crammed for? Do you even remember any questions from that test?

Overlearning is definitely out when it comes to lodging stuff you learn firmly in your head so it can be of use to you later in life. Working harder, as we have seen, doesn't work.

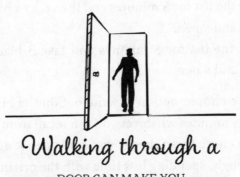

Walking through a DOOR CAN MAKE YOU **FORGET THINGS.** *Weird huh?! Now we* KNOW WHY WE DO *badly on exams. We* WALK THROUGH THOSE DOORS INTO THE EXAM HALL!

There is a sneaky way out. The great news is that it involves working as little as possible. I always knew there was a strong reason for the inherent laziness I have in my genetic make-up!

The Test

You have a list of random facts like the ones at the start of the chapter. Or a set of words in a language you don't know. You are allowed to read that list and study it for about 10 minutes. Then you go home.

Come back after a week and you have 3 options before you attempt to recall it.

1. Study the list for 10 minutes again.
2. Study the list for 5 minutes and then take a blank sheet of paper and a pen.
3. Study the list for 5 minutes and take 3 blank sheets of paper and a pen.

If you have chosen option 2, write out on the blank sheet of paper for 5 minutes whatever you can recall from the original list. If you chose three sheets, you could pen it down thrice.

Amazingly, spending less time with the original sheet and instead writing what you remember gives you the ability for much greater recall when you finally put pen to paper and attempt to write out the list. And if you did that three times, the recall improves even more.

Just study the list and you will remember about 30% of it.

Study and write out once what you remember and the figure jumps to about 40%.

Write it three times after studying and your recall could be more than 50%.

How is this happening?

Remember 'dendrites grow for exactly what you do'?

When you simply study the list, reading it over and over again for 10 minutes, you only become better at reading it over and over again! *Not* remembering it.

When you study the list for 5 minutes, and then write out what you remember, you are creating connections in your brain to REMEMBER!!! Do it thrice and you strengthen these connections even more. You remember more because you practised remembering, not reading.

Challenging the Brain

Have you ever had a word, name or an answer to a question on the tip of your tongue and you simply couldn't remember it?

Your brain goes into a tizzy when this happens. Fragments of things you want to remember dance around tantalisingly as your brain fights to recall them. If it succeeds, there is a sense of triumph. A feeling of achievement of a job well done and there is a chemical party in your brain as it celebrates this feat, and makes a note to itself to remember this fact. More connections are made. More relevance is added. That information becomes even more crystallised in your memory.

If you simply remember what you were trying to, all this doesn't happen... So, to ensure you don't forget something, you need to try to remember it just at the point when you are about to forget it. When you challenge the brain like this, it will create memories that will last a lifetime.

Multiple delayed practice sessions like this will mean that you will keep more and more of that information with you for longer and longer periods of time.

Your new forgetting curve will look like this:

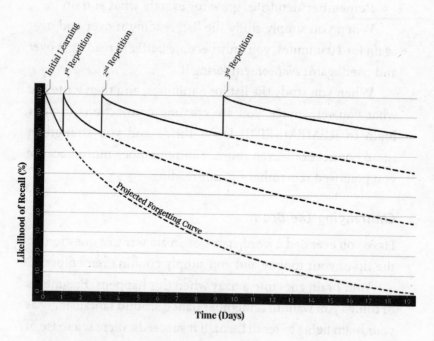

This is Hermann Ebbinghaus's gift to us. Through years of painful experimentation on himself, he had figured out how soon we would forget and concluded that if we practised recall just at the point of forgetting, we would remember more of it for longer periods of time.

ANKI and the Spaced Repetition System (SRS)

SRS is about putting all this into action. You can create a DIY kit to accomplish this, but there is an amazing piece of software that will do exactly that. It will save you the bother of making physical flashcards, drawing pictures, etc.

ANKI is the software. It is free to use, has more than 400 add-ons by third party developers, and is my go to application when I want to work on something and keep it in my head. You can use ANKI to learn new languages, coding, or anything else.

You begin by creating flash cards. You can add images and sound too.

During your review sessions, the software pops them out at you and you check if you can remember or not. If you do remember, the software will test you again in a later review session, calculating for you the time in which you are most likely to forget that piece of information. If you don't remember, it will show it to you again on your next session.

The entire calculation of when you are most likely to forget a fact is done by the software. The fact that this piece of software is absolutely free to use, with no strings attached at all, is a tribute to the generosity of the developer Damien Elmes.

If you are serious about wanting to learn and remember things, download ANKI, thank God for Damien, and get to work. Just google ANKI Spaced Repetition System, and it will throw up pages where you can download the app from. It's quite easy to use ANKI. However, if you require help, there are multiple online resources that will show you how.

IT IS ACTUALLY POSSIBLE TO IMPLANT A FALSE MEMORY "UNDER LABORATORY CONDITIONS" 70% OF PEOPLE IN A STUDY COULD "REMEMBER" A CRIME THEY DIDN'T COMMIT

Remember that to understand around 80% of any language, you would need to know only 700-1000 words. With ANKI, SRS and about 30 minutes a day, you could learn these within a period of 6 months to a year. Your new year's resolution could be: This year I will learn a new language!

For more on language learning, ANKI and SRS, refer to *Fluent Forever* by Gabriel Wyner. It is a fabulously written book.

One last thing about remembering. For me, when I teach something to others, I remember it better and for longer as my brain makes all sorts of connections every time I teach. I understand things differently and with more clarity. Once you have learned something well, teach it to others. They thank you for it, you feel great about yourself and, most importantly, that bit of knowledge gets pretty much wired into your system. You are going to remember it for a long time.

By the way, Anki is the Japanese word for memorisation. Happy Ankiing to you!

Chapter 11

PROCRASTINATION

There was this subject called Number Theory. It should have been an engaging wonder-filled romp, but because of the horrible teacher who was assigned to us, it became a monotonous, dull grind. His lectures would be long and tedious. His assignments even more so. Naturally, I kept putting off doing the assignments. They accounted for only 20% of the credit for the course and I was pretty sure I would get enough marks to scrape by. The teacher was a sadist, though, and a few days before the exam casually announced to the class that students who had not submitted all assignments would be barred from writing the paper.

It was most inconvenient to say the least. I would have to slog through his pathetic questions when I would rather be working on other things. Even with the hammer of doom hanging over my head, I still kept postponing…

Does this sound familiar?

Procrastination is defined as 'the action of delaying or postponing something'.

It sounds quite innocent.

'Will do it later.'

'We have plenty of time.'

TOMORROW WILL BE TODAY TOMORROW

'There is no hurry.'

But do you notice when most people say these things? It's when they **don't** want to do what they are postponing in the first place.

Your brain is hardwired to do two things:

1. It does it's best to save you from pain.
2. It does whatever it can to move you towards pleasure.

You are feeling bored, irritated, frustrated or angry with something you *have* to do, and you simply *don't* want to do. You know that at some point you will have to do it, yet you keep postponing it. This is your brain at work. It will conjure up all the reasons it can to make you avoid it. These reasons will sound plausible and absolutely logical. Most often, you are too weak to fight them, and you will end up not doing what you needed to do.

I enjoy playing the piano. There is no instrument quite like the piano. I love its sound. I love that I can make beautiful music with it. The only thing I don't like is practising scales or doing the exercises. Going up and down the keyboard… again and again... on and on... I know that practising dramatically improves my playing. But it is tiresome and laborious. And so I don't do it as often as I should. Until I come across a piece that I really want to play and my technique is simply not good enough to tackle it. Then I become regular with the scales for some time. Just enough so I can play that particular piece of music. Confession: a few times I give up on the piece. It's too much work. I get a great recording and listen to it instead of doing those scales.

Come across something you don't like doing and your brain goes, Oh no! Not this please. Pretty pleeeeeease. It's soooooooo borrrrrriiiinnngggggg. I don't think we need to do this. Can't we do something else instead?

Why scales? There are so many lovely things we know how to play. Forget about the scales. See, people in the house also get up and go away when you start the scales. Let's not do the scales. We will manage somehow... and so on. And the scales don't happen enough times. So instead of becoming an absolutely brilliant pianist, I have settled for mediocrity. The piano is a very relaxing hobby for me, and I have made peace with this.

Number Theory was another ball game. Not submitting those assignments would mean flunking the subject, and the possible termination of my master's degree. I had already flunked too many times and I was still postponing my work.

Can you believe it? I was actually getting ready to forego my degree!

THE BEST WAY TO GET SOMETHING DONE IS TO BEGIN

When Number Theory happened to me, I was already an Art of Living teacher. I was teaching people how to meditate and was soaked in the wonder of my budding spirituality. Number Theory and meditation didn't quite gel... at least as far as my addled brain was concerned. It came up with an amazing story.

What difference does it make if I get a master's degree or not?! Who really cares. I know I am going to be dedicating my life to teaching the Art of Living series of courses. What use is math then? Why torture myself like this? I have already decided what I am going to do with my life and math doesn't have much place in it.

And, then, the clincher! I can always tell people that I *went* to IIT. I don't have to tell them if I made it out of there. If anyone asks me what qualification do you have, I will simply reply that I went to IIT to do my M.Sc in math. No one is going to ask, did you actually get the degree?

I was totally convinced in my head that the degree made no sense anymore. That I was just wasting time there in IIT when I could be out in the world teaching people meditation. Before doing the final opt out though, thankfully, I felt I should tell Gurudev Sri Sri Ravishankar about my plan. I was 100% sure He would say, yes, yes. Go ahead and teach courses.

Off I went to the Bangalore ashram to meet Him. At that time, there were not the crowds that surround Him now, and we could easily meet Him and chat with Him about the goings-on in our lives.

I sat down in front of Him and started my spiel. I said, Gurudev, I want to give up my degree. And, to my surprise, He started laughing and giggling. I wondered what the joke was. He kept looking at me and laughing.

After a minute or so, He very gently said to me, how can you give up something you don't have? Go back and finish what you started. After that you can become a full-time Art of Living teacher and travel the world and teach people meditation. Get that degree. I want you to move from success to success. Not from failure to failure.

With those words ringing in my ears, I went back to IIT with a completely different mindset. When I knew there was no exit option, and that I had to get that degree, things inside me changed. I have to admit, though, I still procrastinated those assignments till the last minute, but I finished them and passed the subject. And eventually got the degree. I can now tell you that I went to IIT and got out of it! I made it a success and have since then moved from success to success.

Procrastination is not simply delaying stuff for doing later. It is you convincing yourself that you hate doing it, so you will do it later. If you hate doing it, typically, unless you have your arm twisted, you mostly don't end up doing it. This can prove to be very expensive.

IF YOU WANT TO MAKE AN EASY JOB VERY HARD JUST KEEP PUTTING OFF DOING IT

One assignment not done quickly becomes two, then five, and suddenly you have a backlog on one subject. Which could add up to the point you start to feel you are not made for this, and you want to leave it and move on. Only you don't move on. You move backwards. One failure will breed another, and you will find yourself in a hopeless spiral of botched-up attempts, ever twisting downwards. Careers and lives have been wrecked by this bane called procrastination.

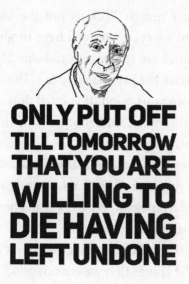

ONLY PUT OFF TILL TOMORROW THAT YOU ARE WILLING TO DIE HAVING LEFT UNDONE

Failure and Mistakes

There is one more reason we procrastinate. The 'What if I fail?' or 'What if I make a mistake?' are immobilising thoughts. There is a deep-seated fear in almost every one of making a fool of themselves. This makes them prefer to not even attempt something they feel they won't be able to do, or that they perceive they are not good enough at doing.

A year from now, you may wish you had started today

Failure simply means, 'This is not the way to do it.' If you truly want to succeed, you will have to give yourself the permission to fail. I am not saying you *should* fail. Don't get me wrong. Just have the *permission* to fail. This will banish the fear of failing from your mind. If you fall down, pick yourself up and do it another way. And another way, and another, and another until you get it right.

You are welcome to make as many mistakes as are required to get to where you have to get to. Just don't make the same mistake over and over again. Progress is all about making new mistakes and learning from them.

We keep putting off doing things we don't like for as long as we can, but the things that we are not good at, or think we would not be good at, we almost never end up doing.

Procrastination is indeed the Dark Lord of all vices, and I feel if you can conquer this one, mostly everything else falls into place.

S.T.A.R. Technique

Dealing with any Dark Lord is tricky business. Dinesh and I developed what we call the S.T.A.R. technique to vanquish this particular Voldemort from your life.

Make a list of at least three things you know you should be doing, but you are not. Don't read further until you have done this.

Start Now

This is the first, most crucial and critical step. It's very interesting how we resolve to start doing something from Monday. Or on the weekend. Or on the first of next month.

Any day or time other than now. You want to lose weight. You know you need to exercise and watch what you eat. You don't do it now. Not today at least. You will begin on the weekend. On weekdays too much is going on… and the brain goes into its loop of creating a fantastic story of why it will be so much better to start exercise on the weekend.

Of course, if it is the weekend, the story changes. Weekends are for rest and relaxation and to get over the stress of the week. Definitely not a time to exercise or be picky about what to eat… and so on. And so you postpone exercising and restricting your diet. And keep get bigger and bigger.

Don't wait for the first of the month. The 26th is a good day too. Don't wait for the weekend or a Monday. There is nothing wrong with a Wednesday. Don't wait for 10:30. 9:17

works just as well. Don't wait for tomorrow. Today is great. Don't wait for later. Right Now Rocks!

Chose any one of those three things you wrote. Make a beginning right now.

Is it too big and overwhelming? You don't know where to start? Which brings us to...

Take small steps

If you want to lose weight and become fitter, maybe it is not a good idea to start with 108 Suryanamaskars twice today. You may not get out of bed for a week after that. But you can do four. Do that. You can walk instead of using a bike or a car when going to buy groceries from the neighbourhood market. Do that. You can climb the stairs instead of using the lift. Do that. You live on the 25th floor? Ok, don't climb all the way. But you can climb to the third floor? Second? Do that. And you can definitely say no to all that sugar and white flour. Please do that.

Don't focus on the end result. If you are 20 kg overweight and want a body like Arnold Schwarzenegger's, you will give up the moment you look at yourself in the mirror.

Take baby steps. Focus on the process of getting there.

You have been postponing that long, tedious presentation you need to make? I am not saying you sit down and finish it off right now. All I am saying is you make the first three slides right now. You can do that, right? Do it!

How much time should you give to this? Well, it should be a minimum of 20 minutes to a maximum of an hour. Start with 20 minutes. Tell yourself that you will do nothing else other than this work for 20 minutes. Get up now, set an alarm for 20 minutes and take those baby steps towards any one or two of those three things you have been procrastinating.

You are inspired to start as you read this. Then your phone beeps a WhatsApp notification. As we saw in an earlier chapter (Brain 101), the brain is not designed for multi-tasking. If you attend to that notification, you will find it very difficult to go back to what you had decided to do. Make sure you are distraction-free for those 20 minutes that you will dedicate to this work.

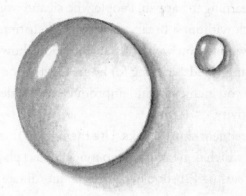

A drop of water is nothing. But then, a waterfall is just billions of drops of water... Start with a drop and build on it, and pretty soon you will be amazed at the deluge inundating you.

Work for at least 20 minutes. Then you are ready for the next step, which is really easy.

Add a break

Whatever it is you are working on, take breaks. The part of your brain that does focused work is notorious for its limited attention span. For most human beings, the mind starts wandering after about 20 minutes. Definitely after an hour. After working on anything for an hour or so, move away from it. Do something else. Preferably something that you don't have to focus too much on. Take a bath, play with your dog, or go for a walk.

Remember the focused and diffused modes of the brain we discussed earlier? It's paramount that both modes are used for efficient learning to happen. People who sit and work for hours at a stretch without a break are wasting their time. It's never about how long you work. It's always about how much you have accomplished. Slogging for hours together on something will make you inefficient and unproductive, besides killing off your creativity.

Add frequent short breaks. Use them to do things you like to do and which don't require too much focus (playing Candy Crush or surfing Facebook requires an inordinate amount of focus by the way), and you will be astounded by the amount of work that gets done. A few rounds of pranayama or a session of meditation are superb ideas for breaks.

And the R? That's my favourite!

Reward yourself

Congratulations! You just did a little part of something you had been procrastinating. This is a humungous step. The Dark Lord has met his match in you and you deserve a reward. Go on and get that reward. It could be anything—a short shopping trip for retail therapy, a nibble of some delicious dark chocolate, a quick phone call to a good friend. Just see to it that the reward does not counter the goal. Don't eat a box of gulab jamuns after walking for 20 minutes if your goal is to lose weight.

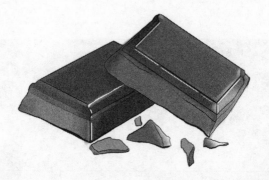

The reward is very important. We procrastinate because our brains are convinced that the activity in question is boring, tedious and painful. If, at the end of the activity, we get a treat, and this happens consistently a few times, the wiring in the brain changes. It will start associating that activity with pleasure. Remember, the brain steers you away from pain and pushes you towards pleasure. In just a little bit of time, you will find yourself looking forward to that activity and the need for the reward will fade away. You don't reward yourself for things you like doing, do you?

More importantly, as you keep doing that particular activity, you will get better and better at it. That monumental paralysing fear of making a fool of yourself or of failing will vanish. It will be replaced by a quiet confidence in your abilities and a glow of satisfaction in your heart.

Start Now
Take Small Steps
Add a Break
Reward Yourself

The Dark Lord is dead. The drop of water has become a waterfall!

Chapter 12

HAPPINESS SUTRAS

Make a quick list of all the things you want. Go on. I will wait.

Okay, at least make a list of 10 things you would really love to have in your life.

Done?

Go over the list and ask yourself why you want any of these things. What will happen if you get them?

The short answer? You will be happy! It doesn't matter what's on your list. If you give it a few moments of thought, you will realise that all you want can be boiled down to a single word: Happiness. It's all we desire. Isn't that amazing?!

Whatever you want, you want it because you feel having it would make you happy. It could be money, fame, power, good health, excellent grades, a promotion, a superb vacation, time with the family, great relationships, opportunities to help others, etc. Each of these is on your wish list solely because you want to be happy.

Whoever you aspire to become, you wish that because you feel when you become that, you will be happy. You may want to be a CEO, or the prime minister. You may want to become a doctor, a mountaineer, dancer or pilot, less angry, more caring and patient—the list is endless. It's all so you can be happy.

IF AND WHEN WERE PLANTED.
NOTHING GREW

All we ever wanted is to be happy. All we will ever want is happiness.

In this book, we have highlighted a few of our secrets behind our smiles. Good sleep. Meditation. Healthy, tasty food. Some physical exercise. A lasting curiosity about things, and a willingness to keep learning. These form a solid foundation to a healthy, happy you. Here are a few bonus aphorisms to make sure that your smile stays and grows even broader.

A Seed Will Inevitably Become a Tree

The first great Truth is this: 'Everything changes.' Change is inevitable. Yet most people want to cling to the way things used to be, refusing to accept that things have already changed. This becomes a great source of misery.

A seed is perfect. You plant it, and it sprouts into two tiny leaves and that seedling is perfect. That grows into a thin little plant, and that too is perfect. In time, it becomes a young tree. Again perfect. The tree matures into a grand symphony of leaves, flowers and fruits, giving shade and shelter—and that is perfect too. Just as a seed which is perfection changes into a majestic tree which is another perfection, we too move in life from one perfection to another.

You are perfect as you are. Change will move you to another level of perfection. The seed is simply becoming a tree.

Dr Rangana Choudhary introduced me to this Change Graph. It's a fantastic way to look at how you can or should deal with the change that is anyways going to happen.

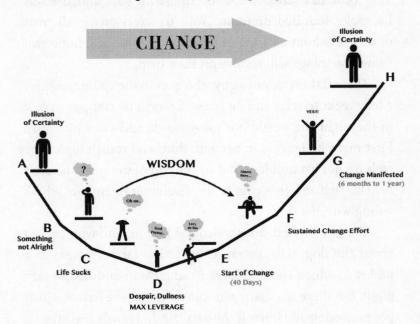

The Change Graph

A: Illusion of certainty: The feeling that nothing will change and that things will remain the same forever.

B: Something is not all right: You know something is amiss, but you refuse to acknowledge it. You hope it will sort itself out. That back pain when you wake up in the morning? You tell yourself everyone has it. Nothing to worry about. Or the strange, sad looks you are getting in your office? You ignore them feeling maybe your colleagues are having a bad day. Or the way your fiancé is looking at someone else? You think it's just your imagination.

C: Life sucks: You have now accepted the problem that you were once in denial about. The back pain is not going away. Your boss has scheduled a meeting with you, and the way he spoke sounded ominous. Your fiancé is giving all sorts of excuses about all sorts of things... But you still hope that somehow things will resolve on their own.

There is this story of a guy who goes to the countryside for a few weeks to relax and de-stress. Everything is super, except in the night the neighbour's dog howls and cries piteously. First night he ignores it. Second, third and fourth nights, he feels it's not his problem. But by the end of the week, he can't help himself and goes over to the neighbour to find out what's wrong with the dog.

The farmer next door welcomes him in, and when asked about the dog, tells a strange story. The farmer points to a basket in which the dog loves to snuggle in and sleep every night. But there is a sharp nail somewhere in the basket which pokes the dog and hurts it. And so, the dog howls and cries...

The man is bemused and asks the farmer, if the nail hurts, why doesn't the dog get up from the basket and go sleep in some other place?

The farmer shakes his head saying, it doesn't hurt him enough.

How many times do we go through life complaining, even crying about our circumstances, but doing almost nothing about it? It's not hurting enough. Which brings us to...

D: Despair: That thing that you dreaded? It's happened. Your MRI showed a disc out of place. Your boss more or less tells you that you may have to resign. The relationship is not working. You are plunged into pain and despair. Everything seems dark and gloomy. Nothing feels right. At least about that aspect of your life.

This is a very uncomfortable place to be in. However, this is a super powerful place to be in as well. This is where you will have maximum leverage. This the spot from where change really becomes inevitable as you bravely accept that your life cannot go on like this anymore. The pain is now unbearable and will force you into action.

If you happen to hit a D, remember this quote from Gurudev: 'Pain is inevitable, suffering is optional.' However bad your pain is, you still can maintain a healthy attitude. This will help you move through this tough phase with relative ease. Yoga, meditation and spiritual knowledge will help you tremendously at this point.

E: Start of change: You begin taking your first baby steps. You look at alternative therapies to fix your back. You join a yoga and meditation class to heal your mind. Sit your fiancé down and have a firm and decisive chat with them and resolve your issues. Look for another job or plan that business venture you always wanted to begin. Learn a new skill set, even if it means going back to school. You clean up your lifestyle. Things are still tough, but life is not dreary and dismal any more. Though outwardly things may seem to be the same, inwardly you have started to feel different.

F: Sustained change effort: You keep up the change effort and stick to your new regime. In a few months, the change that you were aiming at starts becoming evident.

G: Change manifested: Through your intention and attention, the change is now undeniable. Others have started commenting on how nice and fit you are looking. You know you are smiling more. The business worked. You had no idea learning something new would be so much fun. A new person has entered your life, and you wondered what you ever saw in your ex-fiancé! Things are brighter and life is good.

H: The next illusion of certainty: And now you start holding on to this new life… Perhaps because you have still not learned that even this will change—and you will inevitably move from this new perfection to yet another newer perfection.

Wisdom is jumping directly from B or C to E. Though D is a powerful place to be in, it is painful and usually wastes too much of life.

In general, expect to spend around two months at E (Start of change) and six months to three years at F (Sustained change effort) before you see G (Change manifested).

Experiences Rock! Things Don't

'Fooooorrrrwwarrddd!!!'

As our guide shouted the command we had all been waiting for, ten oars dipped in and out of the whirling water as our raft shot into the white churning foam of the Ganga. We whooped and shouted in delight, tinged with just a little bit of fear as our raft was tossed up and down, the wild waters pulling at our oars. Ice cold currents drenched us from head to toe as they slapped us from all directions.

We were in the middle of the rapid when a veritable wall of water suddenly came upon us; we rowed and rowed for what seemed like an hour, but was actually was just a few seconds. The little raft crested a huge wave and was suspended in mid-air, almost flying, for a second or two, before it crashed down into the swirling emerald green waters which suddenly turned calm and limpid. The raft floated on leisurely as the swishing, gushing sounds of the rapid we had been in faded. It was such a rush. Mother Ganga can indeed be quite a thrill!

Another story.

Around 20 years ago, I had been to IIM Ahmedabad to teach an Art of Living course there. Dinesh was beginning to show great promise as a volunteer and a potential teacher of Art of Living. He had become my right-hand man and I had already started to rely on him for many things. I wanted to surprise him with something special, and I decided I could just about afford to fly with him from Ahmedabad to Bombay.

He had never been on a plane before, and I thought it would be a fantastic treat for him. I didn't tell him anything about my plans. I just called him and told him I wanted him to come to Ahmedabad and teach yoga during the course I was giving there. He promptly agreed. He travelled overnight from Bombay by train in an unreserved compartment, more or less standing on one leg. He didn't tell me anything about his journey. He went and taught yoga early in the morning, then came back to our room and collapsed for a few hours. Only when he woke up did he tell me about his ordeal in the train.

We finished the course, and left early the next morning by rickshaw. I told the rickshaw-driver to take us to the airport. His face fell, because he probably thought I would fly to Bombay and expect him to board a train. I let him think that. We reached the airport. He gave me a tight hug, and started haggling with the rickshaw-driver to take him to the train station. I told the rickshaw-driver that wouldn't be necessary as I fished out Dinesh's flight ticket and gave it to him. The look on his face was priceless. He was so thrilled and happy he looked like he would burst with joy!

He was like a curious child, his eyes roving everywhere and taking in all the details. We settled into our seats in the aircraft. I have never seen anyone listen to the in-flight passenger announcements like he did that morning. He paid rapt attention, as if he was Arjuna listening to Lord Krishna speaking the Gita.

The plane gathered speed, going faster and faster until that magical moment when it began to soar—up, up and away...

Dinesh had the window seat of course, and he delighted at the beautiful vista that unfolded beneath us. The plane went higher into the clouds, and he gasped as he saw the top of the clouds for the very first time. He had everything that was there to eat and drink, oohing and aahhing, as if it were cordon bleu cuisine from some exotic seven-star hotel.

It was a very short flight, and it was time to land in less than half an hour. We sailed down into Bombay and then the thump and bump of the landing and the whooshing sound of the aircraft braking and coming to a halt, all amazed him. Dinesh was in his version of Willy Wonka's chocolate factory.

As we were disembarking from the plane, his face took on a slightly worried, quizzical look. I asked him if anything was bothering him. He, oh so innocently, remarked: how come I am not feeling any jet lag?!

I shrieked with laughter as I explained time zones and jet lag to him.

We have shared many flights together over the years and he has had a chance to get utterly jetlagged quite a few times. This story, like our rafting trip, is one of our cherished memories and I always smile when I think about it. I am so lucky to have had many such amazing memories of thrills and spills, of love and friendship, of beauty and adventure. They lift me up when I feel down and out.

Instead of spending money on stuff like clothes, gadgets and jewellery, spend your money to create a bank of fantastic experiences for yourself.

Many people tend to spend money on objects. These can make you happy for a few hours. I am sure if you got an iPhone, it would delight you for some time as you explored its many features and marvelled at its elegant design. But, in a short while, you would get a bit paranoid about it. When you spend

100,000 rupees on a phone, you will want to be extra careful with it. Are the children in the same room as my phone?! No no no no no no no…

Clothes will make you feel great, the first few times you wear them. Then they totally lose their ability to cheer you up… and jewellery will get relegated into a safe somewhere, to be worn only on special occasions. It's more or less the same story with almost any other thing you may buy.

Things are very limited in their ability to please us.

Experiences, on the other hand, thrill and delight you as they unfold, and become cherished memories for you to go back to, time and again. They bring a smile to your face, and uplift you. They become stories to be told again and again, bringing such joy to you and to the people around you.

It is said that if you have three positive things happen to you, for each negative thing, the stress and trauma of that negative event is nullified. Create an array of wonderful experiences for yourself as you go through life. Then, when things look glum, just pull up an experience or three, think about them, relive those memories and you will see that life doesn't feel quite as gloomy any more.

Spend money on experiences!!

People Matter

'Have a nice day.'

How many times have you heard this phrase from a flight attendant whose smile doesn't quite reach her eyes, as you exit an airplane?! 95% of the times this is such an artificial

gesture. What she really wants to say is, get off the plane quick, we need to prepare it for the next bunch who are waiting.

Many people's worlds are filled with meaningless phrases: How are you? What's up? What're you doing? What did you have for lunch? Senseless chatter that tires everyone.

'Have a nice day.'

These very same words from my grandmother as I went off to school each day brightened up my day. It's not the words that matter as much as who says them and how they are said. It's the energy and the love behind the words that make a difference.

We are social beings. Unfortunately, in the name of being social and polite, most people share shallow, one-dimensional relationships with those around them. These relationships only tire everyone out and sap energy.

When we surround ourselves with people who matter, whom we care for and who care for us, everyone's life is enriched.

Create deep, meaningful relationships around you. One of the major factors that contribute to living longer, meaningful and happier lives is having rich social connections. More friends = longer time on the planet! And I don't mean friends on Facebook or Instagram. Friends are real people who you know all about, and who know all about you... and still love you!

People matter. Relationships are important. Spend time on the ones that matter.

Give!

Ever enjoyed a really good movie? Savoured superb food at a fantastic restaurant? Did you notice how you immediately started telling others about it? You were not getting paid or recognised for this. You just did it. Social media is full of such reviews and recommendations by people like you and me. You have a great experience and you instinctively want to share it with the world. Encouraging people to enjoy what you just did.

We love to share. Inherently, we have altruism built into our DNA.

A long time ago, Gurudev had talked about the four types of sharing. It had struck a very deep chord within me. Allow me to share it with you.

1. **Share Materially**: Only the rich can give. How much you can give is an indication of how rich you are. Just ensure that what you give is something you would miss. Otherwise you have not really given. You have just created space in your cupboard.

2. **Share Responsibility**: Delegation requires a big heart. Many people are such control freaks they refuse to give any sort of authority to anyone—even to very capable people. My mother had a boss who would insist on signing even routine documents such as stationery requisitions. He was a poor leader and frustrated many capable staff members. Being able to effectively lead a team involves the delegation of responsibility and trust to others.

3. **Share Credit**: When things go right, only truly secure leaders will be able to praise their team and share the glory of their success with the people who helped them acquire it. Very few people are capable of this type of giving.

4. **Share Yourself**: The realm of volunteering begins when you can say, I am here for you. I am here to see whether you will allow me to contribute to your life to make it

better. Selfless service is when you don't want anything for yourself. Not even recognition. You simply give. This is the highest form of giving.

All four types of sharing will make you feel great about yourself, and are a key to being happy. The last type, however, makes you feel absolutely wonderful.

Over the years, Dinesh and I have led scores of fantastic teams for the many service activities of the Art of Living. Dedicated, committed people have done amazing work to make a difference to their communities. Schools have been started in slums and remote areas where children who couldn't even dream of an education got access to it. Thousands and thousands of trees have been planted, oceans have been cleaned, rivers rejuvenated, suicides prevented... the list is endless.

Being part of a team that gives back to society can be a source of immense joy, fulfilment and gratitude.

Give more. Give what matters. You will smile often.

Rewire Your Brain

It was my first math lecture in G.N. Khalsa College. I was in my graduate programme there and quite excited to be taught by Prof. Marzban Dumasia. I had studied from a textbook he had authored. He was known to have a quick wit and a fiery temper. He walked into the huge lecture theatre, went up to the array of blackboards, and with a piece of chalk, made a small mark, right in the centre.

He then turned around and boomed at us: What do you see?

Many hands went up: a mark, a circle, a point, a tick, or something like that. He smiled, and then thundered, you guys don't see the blackboard? A little mark is all you see? How did all of you miss this huge blackboard?!

Years later, I was reminded of this incident when Gurudev remarked a little mote in your eye can prevent you from seeing and appreciating the vast, infinite expanse of the sky.

Many people live their lives as if they have a mote in their eye. They look for reasons to complain. Take them to the most amazing place, and they will find something wrong with it. They are almost never happy. In fact, they are happy being unhappy. They moan and groan about their fate as they flounder pathetically through life.

It's just a bad habit. And like any other vice needs to be replaced with something pro-life.

Here is a little exercise to do every night before you sleep:

Write down or tell someone five things you are grateful for today. The challenge is that you cannot repeat anything you have said on previous nights.

Like me, you will probably start off nice and easy—

1. I am grateful for having Gurudev in my life.
2. I am grateful for Art of Living.
3. I am grateful that Dinesh happened.
4. I am grateful that I am an Art of Living teacher.
5. I am grateful I get to live in the Bangalore ashram.

The next night—

1. I am grateful for Mom.
2. I am grateful for Dad.
3. I am grateful for my sister.

4. I am grateful that my sister is married.
5. I am grateful for my dog.

Then—

1. I am grateful for all my friends—Gowri, Abhi, Salman, Ankita, Devang and soooo many others.
2. I am grateful for Café Vishala.
3. I am grateful I get to travel and teach meditation to so many amazing people,
4. I am grateful that I have good health.
5. I am grateful that our first book *Ready, Study, Go!* became a bestseller.

I continued like this for a few days and quickly realised that I was running out of things to be grateful for, and I have to write at least five before I sleep. So I spent the day actively looking for things to feel grateful for and started noticing the small things that are such blessings. These days my list looks like this—

1. I am grateful for the shower in my bathroom and the supply of refreshing hot water.
2. I am grateful for electricity.
3. I am grateful for mangoes!
4. I am grateful for air-conditioners.
5. I am grateful the bike didn't work, and I had to walk to satsang. It was lovely weather, and a delightful evening. I would have missed so many beautiful things if I had just zipped off on a bike.

Research shows that if you do 40 nights of writing in your gratitude journal, it completely rewires your brain. You become a much more positive person. You smile more and make others smile more. You look at problems as challenges and opportunities. MRI scans show that parts of your brain visibly grow as you continue to feel and express gratitude.

Rewire your brain to be grateful. It can be done in just 40 days, and years and years of the dead weight of negativity will drop off, leaving you feeling fresh and energetic. You will start living each day to its fullest, accepting life to be the blessing that it is.

The Best Idea of Them All

This book is full of fantastic things you can do so you can be happy. There are lots and lots of great ideas. I have some bad news for you though. Merely reading this book is not going to be enough. Reading it again and again would flatter Dinesh and me a lot, but that wouldn't be enough either.

It would be like joining a gym and never going there to work out. You don't get a great body by joining a gym. You get it by exercising. Even the best gym on earth cannot build your muscles if you don't exercise.

Similarly, a great tip from your friend about the share market won't make you rich. Doing something about that information could. You could choose to heed his advice, buy shares, wait for the right moment, and then sell them. This, hopefully, will create wealth.

Same with all the ideas in this book… Or any book.

Good ideas are no good if they just remain ideas. All the ideas in this book are fabulous. An idea better than all of them, though, would be to actually implement at least a few of them in your life.

It's a good idea to implement a good idea.

The important things in life are actually quite easy to do. They are also easy not to do.

One more thing before we let go of you ... Be careful about reading this part. It's very easy to misinterpret, and I was almost not going to include it, but a book about happiness would be incomplete without it.

The Happiness Express

I am sure we have all heard this: get a great education, get a job, get married, have children, settle down in life, then you will be happy. This is the middle-class mantra, parroted again and again by our parents and by almost everyone around us. Until it begins to feel like some great truth Lord Shiva revealed to Goddess Parvati about Bhairava.

We are made to believe that class 10 is an important year. We are pressurised to work hard and score great marks. Ditto for class 12. That's supposed to be the crucial year. We have all heard the litany: just one more year you have to slog it out. Get into IIT. Or medical school. Or architecture. Then your life is made. Then you will be happy.

You do that. You manage to get into IIT. That's when the real trouble begins. After the first few lectures, you start thinking, I am going to be happy only when I get out of IIT.

Ok. You got your graduation done. Now?

Post-graduation of course. Either in an IIM or some university abroad. Only then will I have any chance at a great life, you think. Ok. That too happens. Then, you get your dream job. It turns out to be a nightmare. But that's alright. Everyone is in the same situation. That's how life is.

Next stop? Get married. Have children. Now your thoughts

are, I will be happy when this product of mine learns to pee in the right place all by himself. I will be happy when he goes to school. I will get my life back. I will be happy when he gets into IIT. I will be happy when he gets a job. Gets married. Has children...

You think, I will be happy when we move to that new house. When I get a promotion. When we manage to buy that fantastic home theatre system. When we get a jacuzzi. An iPhone. When the season changes. When we go for a vacation. When we go to Bali for a vacation...

This goes on and on and on, all through life. Your happiness is always on the horizon. It's tantalisingly close, yet just like the horizon, even though you can see it, you never ever reach it. Yes, there will be glimmers of joy. But like fireworks on Diwali, their effect will be over within a few seconds. You long for something that will bring you joy that wells up in your heart and stays with you. You go through life trying desperately to find it.

You lead a life pursuing happiness, almost never actually being happy. Or being happy for a few fleeting moments, gone like dew drops in the morning sun.

Here is an invitation.

Check out the list you made at the start of this chapter. Do you realise it's full of if-then or if-when statements? I will be happy when I bag a promotion. If my backache heals, then I will be happy. And so on. You hinge your happiness on specific conditions and so push it to the horizon. Do remember that these are all decisions *you* are making. If the decision to be happy is yours to make anyway, why not drop the if-thens and the if-whens and simply say, Come what may, I will be happy!

Doesn't sound practical, I hear you think ☺

It actually is.

Happiness is your very nature. You truly need nothing to be happy. Let me show you how.

Think of a few things that make you unhappy.

If you observe carefully, there is just one way to be unhappy. It's when something happens (or stops happening, which is actually a happening). Ask anyone who looks unhappy the reason for their sorrow and you are likely to get a story. Something had to happen to make that person feel miserable.

On the other hand, have you noticed that there are days when you get up in the morning and feel good about life for no reason whatsoever? You go through the day with a cloud under your feet, and a song in your heart, feeling light and easy. And when people ask you, what's the matter? How come you are so happy? You shrug and say, I don't know.

You realise there is no reason? You are feeling wonderful for no reason at all!

To be unhappy, you need a reason. To be happy, you don't necessarily need any reason. Happiness is your ground state! This is a humungous realisation.

Being happy is synonymous to being yourself.

The middle-class mantra was wrong. You don't do stuff to be happy. You do stuff *because* you are happy.

Happiness is an attitude. Happiness is a habit. Everything in this book will nudge you in this direction. Finally, though, you have to realise that you can be happy just like that. It is supremely simple. There is nothing to do. Just be.

Instead of living life in pursuit of happiness, live your life as an expression of happiness!

How about boarding the Happiness Express?

All the very best!

Jai Gurudeva!

Love,

Bawa & Dinesh

P.S. Someone asked Gurudev, 'How to be happy always?'
He replied, 'Drop the always. Then you will be happy!'

Appendix 1

SRI SRI RAVI SHANKAR

Gurudev Sri Sri Ravi Shankar is a universally revered spiritual and humanitarian leader. His vision of a violence and stress-free society through the reawakening of human values has inspired millions to broaden their spheres of responsibility and work towards the betterment of the world.

He is a multi-faceted social visionary whose initiatives include conflict resolution, disaster and trauma relief, poverty alleviation, women empowerment, prisoner rehabilitation, education for all, and campaigns against female foeticide and child labour. He is engaged in peace negotiations and counselling in conflict zones around the world.

In 1981, He established The Art of Living, an educational and humanitarian Non-Governmental Organisation. In 1997, Gurudev founded the International Association for Human Values (IAHV) to lead sustainable development projects. He is also a co-founder of India Against Corruption (IAC).

He has reached out to many millions of people worldwide through personal interactions, public events, teachings, Art of Living workshops and humanitarian initiatives. He has brought to the masses ancient practices that were traditionally kept exclusive, and has designed many self-development techniques that can be easily integrated into daily life to calm the mind and instill confidence and enthusiasm. One of Gurudev's most unique offerings to the world is the Sudarshan Kriya, a powerful breathing technique that facilitates physical, mental, emotional and social well-being.

Gurudev has received numerous accolades, including the highest civilian awards of Colombia, Mongolia and Paraguay. In 2016, he was conferred the 'Padma Vibhushan', one of the highest civilian awards of India. He has addressed several international forums, including TED 2010 at Monterey, the United Nations Millennium World Peace Summit (2000), the World Economic Forum (2001, 2003) and several parliaments across the globe.

Gurudev travels to nearly 40 countries every year, exemplifying his call to globalise wisdom.

His universal and simple message is that love and wisdom can prevail over hatred and distress.

Appendix 2
THE ART OF LIVING
FOUNDATION COURSES

It's a well-established scientific fact that happy people are more productive, creative, efficient and effective. Who wouldn't want all this and more in their lives? Gift yourself this Happiness Advantage by engaging yourself with Art of Living's various programmes for individuals and communities.

And if you are thinking, but, I am already happy... surely you are not allergic to more happiness? Right?!

The Happiness Programme
Weight gain (or loss) without a diet change, hair fall, stomach ache and stomach disorders, forgetfulness, sleep disorders, headaches, frequent colds, high or low blood pressure and infections are only a few symptoms of stress.

Most people just accept stress and tension as an inevitable part of their lives. They feel that they simply have to 'cope' with the problems associated with stress and get on with life.

The Art of Living Happiness programme includes techniques that allow you to de-stress and live your life without all the associated distress.

Positive psychology is a powerful new branch of mental health founded on the belief that people want to lead meaningful and fulfilling lives, to cultivate what is best within themselves, and to enhance their experiences of love, work and play. The Art of Living courses feature yoga, meditations and interactive processes that allow you to do exactly that.

The profound and powerful Sudarshan Kriya that is taught in the Happiness programme enables you to effortlessly let go of your stresses and tensions and introduces within you a tranquillity you never knew existed.

You can be what you have always wanted to be: healthy, poised, calm, relaxed and confident.

The YES!⁺ Programme

Anyone who is 12 or 13 can't wait to be 18. A 35-40-year-old yearns for his youth. Everyone wants to be 18, except the ones who *are* 18!

The age group 18-30 is a wonderful time in life. You feel you can do absolutely anything. That you can conquer the world! Your body and mind are at their peak. Unfortunately, so is the confusion. There are too many options and challenges. To top it off, you have raging hormones. Things you do or don't in this period can profoundly affect the rest of your life.

You desperately need a calm, poised mind to be able to take sensible decisions. The YES!⁺ course was created by me and Dinesh under the guidance of Gurudev Sri Sri Ravi Shankar to address all these issues and more.

The course sparkles with dialogue, is peppered with fun and

humour, and liberally sprinkled with insightful interactive processes. This allows our participants to explore a dimension of the mind most people don't even know exist. This course is a delectable treat for a young person who is going places.

The Sudarshan Kriya is taught during this course, along with a few other techniques to enhance focus and concentration levels.

You will have the tools and the ability to be able to live the life you *want* to live instead of the life you *have* to live.

Sahaj Samadhi Meditation

Everyone has experienced a meditative state in moments of deep joy, or when completely engrossed in an activity—the mind becomes still, light and at ease for just a few moments. Almost all of us have sporadically experienced such moments of utter calm and peace, but we are unable to repeat them at will.

The Sahaj Samadhi Meditation programme teaches you how. This technique almost instantly alleviates the practitioner from stress-related problems, deeply relaxes the mind and rejuvenates the system.

'Sahaj' is a Sanskrit word that means natural or effortless. 'Samadhi' is a deep, blissful, meditative state. 'Sahaj Samadhi Meditation' is hence a natural, effortless system of meditation.

Regular practice of the technique can transform the quality of one's life by culturing the system to maintain the peace, energy and expanded awareness throughout the day.

The Advanced Meditation Course

The AMC is a 4-10-day residential silence programme. It begins early in the morning with yoga and Sudarshan Kriya, has guided meditation sessions through the day, and ends with blissful chanting and knowledge from Gurudev in the evening. Tasty, healthy food is served to all course participants at meal times.

The course helps you recharge and rejuvenate yourself so that you are better equipped to respond with equanimity and poise to the stresses and challenges that contemporary life throws at you. It is an intensive work-over for the mind and body. People who have undergone this course report feeling refreshed, their faces aglow and with their hearts at peace.

After more than two decades of practising meditation, Dinesh and I still attend one AMC every year, and we recommend that you do too. Take a few days off, unplug yourself from the world and totally relax.

Though AMCs are now conducted in cities and towns all over the world, we feel the best way to get the most out of them is to go do them at one of Art of Living's many ashrams.

Our favourite places to do an AMC? The Art of Living ashrams in Bangalore, Rishikesh, Gujarat, Germany, the US and Canada.

The Divya Samaj ka Nirman Course (DSN)

There are rivers to cross and mountains to climb... but the biggest mountains are mostly the mountains in our own minds.

The DSN is an evening and three full action-packed days of learning about our self-imposed limitations and breaking them. It is an emotional, physical and spiritual roller-coaster ride, an exciting challenge for the courageous and an inspiration for the ones who want to be so.

All of us have good intentions and fantastic ideas, for ourselves, our families and friends, and for society. Regrettably, these good intentions hardly ever translate into action. These wonderful ideas remain as ideas and frequently we are forced to compromise on our dreams and ambitions.

The mind stuff disempowers us and doesn't allow us to lead the life we are born to live. It buries us in the humdrum and the mundane and keeps us from reaching for the stars. It is quite a journey to get rid of these limitations and the DSN programme provides a fantastic start.

The DSN overflows with knowledge sessions, group discussions, games, advanced yoga techniques such as Padmasadhana and many chances to go out into the world and make a difference during the course itself. The DSN experience will leave you enriched and empowered.

Discover your inner superhero and start to live the life you have always dreamt about.

There are many other courses that Art of Living offers, from learning yoga to vegetarian cooking and almost everything in between.

The teachers and volunteers of the Art of Living Foundation strive to create a better world for themselves and their communities through various services like planting trees, rejuvenating rivers, running free schools in villages and slums, empowering women, providing vocational training for village youth, helping disaster victims and more. You can find descriptions and details of all this and more on www.artofliving.org.

Appendix 3
WORKSHOPS OFFERED BY
KHURSHED & DINESH

Study Sutras

'Everyone used to tell me to use my brain. No one told me exactly how to do it.'

You could be a student working your way through university, a professional struggling with new concepts you have to study, or someone who is simply curious and wants to know more.

Our brain is a super advanced piece of organic technology. Unfortunately, we inherited it without a user manual. Study Sutras is a three-hour, fast-paced workshop delving into the intricacies of how to make the brain work with dazzling efficiency.

This workshop, which is based on a few chapters from our book, *Ready, Study, Go!: Smart Ways to Learn,* will create a paradigm shift in the way you learn. It will make the process of studying efficient, enjoyable and more meaningful. It will transform the way you think and possibly even the way you live.

Facts about the brain, study tips, brain hacks and, if time permits, a guided meditation await you in this workshop designed by me and Dinesh.

Do read our book. It is available at online and offline bookstores around the world. With tips and techniques to make studying an intriguing activity, it has sold more than 50,000 copies.

For more about the book, visit www.readystudygobook.com.

To buy it from amazon.in, follow this link: bit.ly/readystudygo

To get it from amazon.com, go here: bit.ly/readystudygointl

Note: In some countries, Study Sutras is called Study Smart.

Mind Maps & More

The system of thinking most of us have drilled into our minds goes against how our brain is naturally tuned to function. We have fostered the unproductive habits of sequential thinking and making endless, often meaningless, lists.

The Mind Maps & More workshop teaches natural and organic ways of thinking and helps you use your brain the way it was meant to be.

Using just a few circles and lines, the powerful technique of mind mapping can open up a world of ideas and solutions to problems that may have stumped you for a long time.

Mind Maps & More is an interactive and introspective

experience peppered with fun and games, aimed to help you reverse incorrect thinking habits and thus open up your brain to a flood of ideas. It will develop and hone your skills in problem-solving, communication, recall and time management.

In just ten exciting hours, spread over three alternate days (or over a weekend), the workshop will enable you to realise and implement effectiveness in your life by bringing about a transformation in the way you think and therefore in the way you act!

Note: This workshop is designed for people aged 18 years and above.

A Delightful Romp through Classical Math

I hate math. This is such a familiar refrain. Studying math, for most people, is usually an exercise in frustration, for some even terror. This is largely because of a lack of interest in the subject, which is compounded by uninspiring teachers and insipid prescribed textbooks that utterly malign the subject.

There is hardly any life without math. Math pervades all we do, yet most people are repelled by it. This is sad, because Mathematics is a subject of magic and exquisite beauty. We had had enough of people berating this lovely subject and decided to do something about it.

We put together a workshop that would primarily eliminate the almost irrational fear that many people have of the subject, as well as effortlessly reveal its intrinsic beauty.

Starting with some frivolous playing around with numbers and multiplication, the workshop quickly moves on to cover some of the basics of real analysis, calculus, number theory and finite mathematics. We focus on fundamental concepts and disclose the elegant logic that hides behind rigorous mathematical proofs. A few fascinating stories from the history of math and mathematicians are woven into the material.

The entire workshop is peppered with healthy doses of humour as well as a few interactive exercises for the participants, so that they can discover the joy of applying logic to solve problems for themselves.

Initially Dinesh and I taught the workshop ourselves, but owing to increased demand, we now have a number of trained and talented teachers besides us. Through this workshop you too will feel the passion and love that we have for math.

We will soon be offering it as an online workshop.

Mathemagic has been designed to be a thoroughly entertaining two-hour learning experience, a delightful foray into the basics of some fairly advanced math.

An Introduction to the Bach Flower Remedies

Dr Edward Bach discovered that certain flowers in nature have the ability to affect our emotions positively. His original Bach Flower System of 38 remedies and their combinations are easy for anyone to understand and use.

The Bach Flower Remedies can work in conjunction with herbs, homeopathy and any other medication. They are safe for

everyone, including children, pregnant women, the elderly, pets and even plants.

You are invited to a workshop on the Bach Flower Remedies conducted by me. I am a registered Bach Flower Practitioner and have had a few years of experience in using them.

The contents of the workshop include:

- ☐ The Origin of the Bach Flower Remedies
- ☐ An overview of the 38 Flower Remedies
- ☐ Creating and using a Personalised Remedy Mix for Yourself
- ☐ Personal Stories about their usage and effects

Each participant will get to take home a 30-ml bottle of the Remedy mix that they will create in the workshop for their own use. You will have clear instructions on dosage and how to integrate the almost magical Bach Flower System into your lives.

The workshop will run for about two and a half hours.

Reality Reloaded

This workshop is based on principles of coaching and gamification along with a few chapters from our books, *Ready, Study, Go!* and *Happiness Express*. It promises to create a shift in the way you think, act and live. It will give you clarity on what you *really* want in life, and help you create a road map to achieve it.

Reality Reloaded comprises three action-packed sessions spread over a week. Each session is three hours long, and will have you laughing, wondering and introspecting. You will delight in the clarity and focus that would finally dawn as you figure out your destiny and take steps to realise it.

For a richer, more fulfilling, enjoyable and rewarding experience of the magic called life, come and gain the skill of reloading your reality. Transform your life into that of your dreams.

This is a fairly intensive workshop and it is recommended that you sign up for it only if you can devote a chunk of time to some serious soul-searching. It involved quite a bit of homework and you need to do it and participate fully in all the sessions to make the most of your time on the course.

Happiness Express: The Workshop

Why do we do anything we do?

Why do we want anything we want?

All our desires and wants can be boiled down to one word: Happiness.

Happiness is what all of us want. Actually, happiness is the *only* thing all of us want!

For most of us, happiness can be quite elusive... We smile, but the smile doesn't come as often as we would like it to, nor does it stay as long as we would want it to.

Two decades ago, after going through a few devastating failures, I had a great big think about life. I took a decision then: I would do things that would make me and others around me happy. I realised that happiness needs to be practised. I developed the Habit of Happiness.

Result? I became more creative, productive and efficient.

Success became easier to achieve. Failure didn't affect me as much as it would before. I developed a resilience towards the 'downs' of life and enjoyed the 'ups'.

This workshop is based on the book you are reading right now, *Happiness Express*. In about an hour and a half, we will share the secrets of our Happiness, stuff that has worked for us and for the tens of thousands of people we have taught over the years.

We invite you to join us on the Happiness Express, your ticket to a smile that will light up your eyes and warm your heart!

Yogic Fitness Act I

An Introduction to Holistic Health and Fitness

Congratulations! You have a body. Not just *any* body—a human body. It can be very easy to take this for granted.

It has taken many millennia for our bodies to evolve into the astounding pieces of super complex organic technology that they are. We experience life through them. For an optimal experience of our time on the planet, we need to ensure that our bodies stay fit and healthy. Disease happens when we forget this.

Time, money and effort invested in building robust good health will not then be wasted being ill, staring at ceilings and feeling miserable.

YF-I is a unique programme that starts you off on that most precious journey: Great Health!

In three sessions of 3-4 hours each, you will be introduced to the art and science of health, strength and fitness.

YF-I brings together three elements required for vibrant good health: Exercise, Diet and Rest.

You will be taught foundation exercises that will get your body moving the way it has been designed to.

Diet can be a game changer when it comes to fitness. Knowledge of what to eat, what not to eat and why is paramount for success. You will learn the basics, enough to whet your appetite. Besides, you will be served a fantastic meal in class each day.

The critical importance of rest will be explained, the why and how of sleep, along with an introduction to meditation. Each session will end with deeply relaxing stillness.

Continue your journey online. All exercises taught and full-body workouts based on the exercises you have learned will be available for you to view online, so you can refresh and fine-tune what you learned in class.

Enroll on the YF-I course to experience the magic of great health for yourself.

Watch out for Acts II and III—coming soon!

Appendix 4

Recipes

There are plenty of online and offline resources for amazing, healthy, delicious vegetarian recipes. The Bibliography includes some of my favourites.

Making Butter and Ghee

Ghee is considered to be a superfood, and rightly so.

It has a very high smoking point of 250°C and will not break down into dangerous free radicals like other oils when heated. It can be safely used for cooking and frying.

Ghee is a rich source of vitamins A and E. It has anti-oxidants with anti-viral qualities if the milk it is made from is sourced from grass-fed Indian desi cows. Ghee can help you lose weight because it has medium chain fatty acids that the body uses to burn 'bad' fat. Ghee is anti-inflammatory in nature and has been used by Ayurvedic doctors for centuries to counter gut issues.

Most commercially available ghee is not made the right way.

Everyone should know how to make it at home, or source it from someone who makes it the traditional way. Here is my recipe to make it the correct way. Butter gets created along the way.

Heat full-cream A2 milk to a boil and allow it to cool. A2 milk is milk from the Indian desi cows, not the hybrid Jersey ones. Skim off the cream or *malai* into a container. Store the container in the freezer. Do this every day until you have 500 ml of the cream. When you are ready to make your butter, bring the container out of the freezer and let it come to room temperature.

The next step is crucial and almost always skipped by commercial companies that make butter or ghee. Add three heaped tablespoons of curd to the cream and mix thoroughly. Cover this and keep the mixture to ferment overnight, for 8-10 hours. Curd infuses your butter or ghee-to-be with vital probiotics and virtually eliminates all the 'bad' cholesterol.

The fermented cream-curd mixture is our base for making butter or ghee.

For making butter, transfer the entire cream-curd mixture into a blender. Add a generous amount of cold water till it completely covers the mixture (around half a litre) and toss in a few ice cubes. We want the mixture to remain cold through the blending process.

Whirr this until the butter separates out, in about 3-5 minutes, depending on the power of your blender. With your hands scoop out the butter from the liquid, squeezing it so that all the milk solids are removed, and put the butter into a container. The liquid remaining is buttermilk.

Heat a little ghee in a pan, add in a slit green chilli and a teaspoon of grated ginger, and let it cook for about a minute. Add a teaspoon each of mustard seeds and cumin. Let them splutter. Add this to the buttermilk and you have a yummy and healthy drink.

Coming back to the butter, you will need to rinse the butter 5-8 times. Do this by adding cold water and squeezing out the milk solids. The water will turn opaque white. Throw away this water, and repeat this process until the water is clear.

What you will have is delicious, healthy, unsalted homemade butter. Taste this once and you will wonder what made you eat that commercially created gunk all your life. Store this in a fridge and it will keep for a few weeks.

To make ghee, there is one additional step.

Put the homemade butter in a big, heavy-bottomed iron or steel pan. Heat until it melts and foams. Bring the heat to medium-low and let it cook for about 10-15 minutes, stirring continuously so it doesn't stick to the bottom. Be careful with this step. Too much heat will give the ghee a burnt flavour—not something everyone will like. Soon, a brown crumbly substance will start to form and collect at the bottom, while the ghee will separate out as a liquid. Turn off the heat and strain the golden yellow liquid into an air-tight glass bottle.

The brown stuff can be made into a nice sweet. Add some jaggery and crushed nuts and you have a tasty snack.

When the ghee starts cooling, it will start to solidify into a dropping paste consistency. If you live in a very cold climate, it might even become a sort of solid paste. The perfect ghee is a very soft paste with a granular consistency and a heavenly fragrance. This ghee is perfectly all right for most people who are lactose intolerant, because all the milk solids have been eliminated in the process of making it.

Ghee will not spoil easily, so it doesn't need refrigeration. Water and sunlight though can degrade it. This is why you need to store it in a dark place in an air-tight glass container.

Sita's Homemade Cereal

I like cereals with cold milk. Unfortunately, the commercially available brands either have copious amounts of sugar or are very expensive. The packet will say the cereals have almonds in them. They don't lie. There will be all of three almonds cut into microscopically thin slivers.

I was in Jakarta at my friends Ram and Sita's home when Sita made me cereal for breakfast one morning. I loved it and asked what brand it was. She said she had made it herself. I asked for the recipe and she happily gave it to me. Here it is. It's quite simple and deliciously tasty.

Mix 1 cup of maple syrup and ½ a cup of avocado oil. Add in a few pinches of salt and a teaspoon of cinnamon powder. Stir this well as you heat it until it boils. Let it cool to room temperature.

Add 8 cups of old fashioned rolled oats, ½ cup pumpkin seeds, ½ cup sunflower seeds and ½ cup pine nuts to the cooled mixture. Mix well with your hands.

Pre-heat the oven to 170°C. Spread the mixture on a flat baking tray and bake for 15 minutes. Remove from the oven, toss, and bake again for another 12 minutes so that everything is evenly baked. Mix in 1 cup of chopped almonds and pistachios and bake for another 3-5 minutes. Remove from the oven and let it cool.

Store in an air-tight container.

You may add your favourite nuts and flavours to this basic recipe. Experiment with vanilla, cacao powder, dried figs, cashews, walnuts, etc. You may decrease or eliminate the maple syrup depending on your taste.

Eat as a snack, or with hot or cold milk.

Almond Milk

Many people are lactose intolerant these days, or cannot get good A2 milk, or choose to be vegan. Almond milk is a superb milk substitute. Commercially made almond milk has a long list of questionable ingredients. That's bizzare and I have no idea why they put all that in, given that all you need is almonds and water. As a bonus, you get to make a delicious herbal almond spread from the leftover almond pulp.

Almond milk with no additives has a very low glycemic index, which means that sugars are released slowly into the blood, so will not convert easily to fat. It contains plenty of the B vitamins, fibre, calcium and vitamins D and E. It's good for your skin, muscle growth, healing and digestion.

Making almond milk at home is a breeze.

Soak a cup of raw almonds in filtered water overnight, about 8-10 hours. Drain off the water. Peel off the skin of the almonds.

Put the almonds into a powerful blender. Add 2-6 cups of clean (not chlorinated) water and blend till smooth, usually for about a minute or two. Add less water to make it creamier.

Use a fine mesh or a cheese cloth to drain the milk out into a vessel. Add a pinch of cinnamon powder and a teaspoon of vanilla for flavour. Store in air-tight glass bottles. Almond milk doesn't need to be refrigerated, but I put mine in the fridge anyway, because I love it cold! Use within 2-3 days. For a touch of sweetness, sneak in a bit of maple syrup or honey.

Almond milk is very versatile and makes a fantastic milk replacement in any recipe that calls for normal milk. Of course, the taste will change a bit, but not much. Drink it just like that, have it with cereal, add some cacao and make a chocolate milkshake out of it. You can heat it and add some cacao for a hot chocolate drink... The possibilities are limited only by your imagination.

What to do with that leftover almond pulp?

Spread it out on a sheet and bake at your oven's lowest temperature until it dries out. Crumble it and use it as a topping instead of bread crumbs. Store in an airtight container in a cool place. You could combine some chopped nuts and raisins into it, and make it into a munchy snack.

You could make a superb almond spread with the pulp. Chop

2-4 cloves of garlic, ¼ cup of sundried tomatoes, and some fresh or dried herbs. Add all this, 5 tablespoons of lemon juice, and a cup of the almond pulp along with a few glugs of olive oil to a mixie and blend until smooth. Add salt and pepper to taste. The spread should be smooth and moist. Slather it on toast or crackers or use as a dip with slivers of carrots or cucumber. Store in a glass container in the fridge.

For more recipes, visit www.bawandinesh.in.

Appendix 5
A BRIEF OVERVIEW OF THE BACH FLOWER REMEDIES

As we go through life, different types of moods and emotions lodge themselves in our minds. Some of them are fleeting, like soap bubbles, others more enduring. Quite a few do not stay long enough to bother us, but some of them do.

As we go through our lives, layers upon layers of these emotions accumulate in our minds and shape our thoughts and actions to a large extent. They create imbalances in our system. They hinder us from living out our full potential as human beings. They stop us from giving and receiving love. They neither make us or others around us happy. In acute or chronic cases, they rob us of our health and our peace.

Bach Flower Remedies are prescribed depending on one's state of mind and not on the nature of the malady that may be present in the body. They harmonise and heal, physically, mentally and spiritually. They are non-toxic, not habit-forming and can are harmless, even if wrongly prescribed. They form, perhaps, one of the simplest systems of healing that I know of. They are a gift to humanity from Dr Edward Bach.

Dr Bach was a well-known physician, bacteriologist, homeopath and researcher. He was a well-respected doctor having a lucrative practice at a Harley Street Clinic in London circa 1920.

Final and complete healing will come from within, from the soul itself. - Dr. Edward Bach (1886 -1936)

He had great success with conventional medicine, but was put off by the way doctors were treating only the symptoms or diseases, and ignoring the person who was suffering from them.

He was convinced that it is the mind and emotions that play a vital role in maintaining health (or in recovery). He opined that a physical disease is not (merely) of physical origin, but springs from mental attitude.

He believed that if the mental condition is treated, the physical problem would resolve itself. He considered the true cause of disease to be imbalance in the emotions. Considering that the natural state of the body is to be healthy, he asserted that simply balancing the imbalances would set things right.

Dr Bach wanted to find something that would treat the cause of the malady and not only the effect. He wanted to create a system of remedies that could be used by anyone and everyone to propel themselves towards great health.

To realise this vision, the system had to be as straightforward and easy to use as possible.

It had to be simple and based on the principle, 'Treat the person, not his disease'.

He knew that the remedies couldn't have been found in the

laboratories, hospitals or clinics. He felt they were out there, in the countryside, in the woods and the fields—in nature.

Over a period of about five years, Dr Bach tramped through the English countryside looking for his healing flowers. He found 38 remedies, and rightly felt that these and their 293 million permutations and combinations covered every single state of mind and mood possible. They were complete. There would be never be a need for a 39th.

He authored the book *The 12 Natural Healers*. Short, precise and compact. It was all that was required. He burned all his notes before he died. He likened them to scaffolding, required during construction, but to be removed and discarded once the building was ready.

He wanted his work to be preserved as it was, with no remedy ever to be added or deleted. The Bach Centre in the UK strives to uphold his wishes and his vision and steadfastly guards his wonderful legacy.

The Bach Flower Remedies

For the sake of completeness, here is a very brief description of the Bach Flower Remedies. There are a number of excellent books on the subject and you can find them in the Bibliography.

Making a treatment bottle is quite simple. Rinse and sterilise a 30 ml amber glass bottle. Fill it with clean drinking water and add about half a teaspoon of any good brandy in it. The brandy acts as a preservative for the delicate herbal essences.

The remedies work better when you choose fewer of them. However, if you feel more of them are really relevant, it's fine to have up to seven. From the tincture bottles put two drops of each of your chosen remedies into the treatment bottle. If one of the remedies you have chosen is the Rescue Remedy, you will need to put four drops of that instead of two.

To take the remedy, in about half a glass of water add four drops of the mix from the treatment bottle. Swirl it around a bit and then sip the water. As you sip it, feel some beautiful energy entering your system and cleansing it. Make sure you finish all the water in the glass.

Take your remedy four times a day. First thing in the morning, last thing at night and twice in between.

When Dr Bach was asked how long should one continue to take the remedies, he simply replied, until you forget to take them.

The 38 Remedies

Agrimony: Happy outside, miserable inside, would do anything for peace, minor vices and socialising to avoid persistent worrying thoughts, downplays and jokes when ill.

Aspen: Vague and unknown fears, has nightmares and is afraid to go back to sleep after sudden anxiety attacks.

Beech: Critical, intolerant, arrogant, looks for what is wrong in a situation.

Centaury: Weak-willed, willing slave, easily exploited, can't say no, obedient, subservient, tends to give more than he has.

Cerato: Lack of confidence in own decisions, wants more and more information, hoards knowledge but doesn't use it, is led astray against own better judgement and typically will regret the move because detrimental to self.

Cherry Plum: Fear of losing it, of doing something violent, fear of loss of control, uncontrolled outbreaks of temper.

Chestnut Bud: Repeats the same mistake again and again, doesn't learn, physical illnesses appear at regular intervals for no apparent reason.

Chicory: Motherliness, overbearing, over protective, needy, possessive, interfering, secretly manipulative, resorts to emotional blackmail, clingy, loves to preside, organise, take charge of her brood, feels terrible if not 'needed'. Favourite refrain: 'After all I have done for you....'.

Clematis: Daydreamer, absent-minded, vague dreamy look in eyes, not interested in the present at all, scatter-brained, inattentive, indifference to good or bad news, great for bringing someone back into the body (if they have fainted for example).

Crab Apple: Feels unclean and tainted, infected, disgusted with self, it's the cleansing remedy, nice to give for overcoming addictions.

Elm: Temporarily overwhelmed by responsibilities, doubts his own capabilities.

Gentian: Feels discouraged and despondent when there has been a setback, easily dejected.

Gorse: 'Oh, what's the use?!', given up hope, no longer has the energy to try again, looks pale with dark rings around eyes, possibility of chronic illness for years.

Heather: The talkative hypochondriac, obsessed with his own troubles, lives on other's energies, can't be alone.

Holly: Jealous, distrustful, hateful, envious, revengeful, malicious, suspicious, holly can be given for even small episodes of all these emotions.

Honeysuckle: Longing for the past, wistful, not living in the present.

Hornbeam: Monday morning blues, doesn't have enough energy to start, but once started manages to breeze through.

Impatiens: Impatient, irritable, super quick thinking, in a rush, can't stand dilly-dallying, will take things from others to do himself if he feels they are too slow.

Larch: Feels inferior, expects to fail, lack of self-confidence, totally convinced that he cannot do it, so will not even try.

Mimulus: Known fears, shy, timid, they can name their fears.

Mustard: Deep, heavy, black gloom that suddenly appears and disappears for no apparent reason, cannot be hidden from others, sadness.

Oak: The plodder, the fighter who goes on and on past his limits, and doesn't think of stopping, fights bravely even when brought to his knees.

Olive: Physical and mental exhaustion and fatigue because of a prolonged period of strain, this remedy can give you energy to move on, or make you surrender and fall asleep, great for recovery from jet-lag.

Pine: Self-reproach, guilt, apologises a lot, blames himself, considers himself a coward.

Red Chestnut: Excessive concern and worry about others around him, irrationally fears that things could go wrong.

Rock Rose: Extreme state of fear, terror and panic.

Rock Water: Perfectionist, hard on self, rigid views, suppressed inner needs, sets super high standards for self and pushes and forces self to live up to those ideals, excessive self-discipline, this one can show up in just a few aspects of someone's life as well.

Scleranthus: Indecisive, ever-changing ideas and opinions, jumps from topic to topic in conversation, grasshopper mind, alternating between hunger and loss of appetite, between constipation and diarrhoea.

Star of Bethlehem: Shock, after effects of trauma, considering that trauma and shock can linger for a very long time, sometimes even decades, this is a great remedy to start with if nothing else makes sense.

Sweet Chestnut: Absolute dejection, back to the wall feeling, has reached the limits of endurance, extreme despair but no thoughts of suicide, calls to a higher power for help, still harbours a glimmer of hope.

Vervain: The Evangelist, over enthusiastic about a cause, highly strung, possibly fanatical, impulsive, idealistic, wants to convert others to his side, angered by injustice.

Vine: Dominating, inflexible, power hungry, very capable, ambitious, wants everyone to dance to his tune, feels he is always right, possibly a bully.

Walnut: The delinking remedy, dealing with change, not get influenced by others during the time of change, transitioning from one aspect of life to another, for those who have reached the new place they need to be in, but not quite.

Water Violet: Feels isolated because he comes across as superior, wants to be left alone when unwell, finds it difficult to approach others for help, doesn't permit others to interfere in his life, stiff upper lip.

White Chestnut: Too many persistent and potentially worrying thoughts, constant mental chatter, arguments going round and round in the head.

Wild Oat: Is very good at what he is doing, but knows that there is something bigger out there, but cannot figure out what it is, cannot find direction in life, feels his talents and abilities are not being channelled. He knows he is born for something else than what he is doing, but he doesn't know what that is.

Wild Rose: Apathy, has resigned even though situation is not that bad, no joy or inner motivation, believes he has inherited ill health, accepts fate—unhappy home, relationships, job, chronic illness, etc, has no energy, is always tired and resigned to it.

Willow: Bitterness, poor me, victim, never takes responsibility for bad things that happen in his life, always blames circumstances and others for his fate.

Rescue Remedy: Star of Bethlehem (shock, trauma, numbness), Clematis (grounding, prevents from passing out, brings person back into his body), Cherry Plum (keeping it together, not losing it), Impatiens (irritability, eases coming back into the body), Rock Rose (terror and panic).

Rescue Cream: Rescue Remedy + Crab Apple (feelings of being unclean).

SELECT BIBLIOGRAPHY

Sleep

There are many books on sleep out there. I found these to be the best reads. Matthew Walker is highly recommended for an in-depth knowledge of sleep and dreaming.

1. Walker, Matthew, *Why We Sleep: Unlocking the Power of Sleep and Dreams*, Scribner, 2017
2. Huffington, Arianna, *The Sleep Revolution: Transforming Your Life, One Night at a Time*, Harmony, 2017
3. Winter, W. Chris, *The Sleep Solution: Why Your Sleep Is Broken and How to Fix It*, Berkley, 2018

Learning, Memory and Mind Mapping

Ready, Study, Go! has helped thousands of people to learn and study effectively. It explores the importance of attitude towards studying and has tips and techniques to turn studying into an interesting, enjoyable activity instead of the dull grind that it seems to have become for most people.

The Simon Singh books and *Journey through Genius* are very well-written books on the beauty and elegance of mathematics. They are not leisurely reads though.

Fluent Forever must be read by anyone who wants to learn a new language or is interested in the Spaced Repetition System (SRS).

Brain Rules is a superb lay-person-friendly look at the brain.

1. Batliwala, Khurshed and Ghodke, Dinesh, *Ready, Study, Go!: Smart Ways to Learn*, HarperCollins, 2016
2. Singh, Simon, *The Simpsons and Their Mathematical Secrets*, Bloomsbury, 2014
3. Singh, Simon, *Fermat's Last Theorem*, Fourth Estate, 2002
4. Dunham, William, *Journey through Genius: The Great Theorems of Mathematics*, Jossey Bass, 1990
5. Singhal, Aditi and Sudhir, *How to Memorize Anything: The Ultimate Handbook to Explore and Improve Your Memory*, Ebury Press, 2015
6. Wyner, Gabriel, *Fluent Forever: How to Learn Any Language Fast and Never Forget It*, Harmony, 2014
7. Medina, John, *Brain Rules: 12 Principles for Surviving and Thriving at Work, Home, and School*, Pear Press, 2014
8. Lorayne, Harry and Lucas, Jerry, *The Memory Book: The Classic Guide to Improving Your Memory at Work, at School, and at Play*, Ballantine Books, 1996
9. Oakley, Barbara, *A Mind for Numbers: How to Excel at Math and Science*, TarcherPerigee, 2014

Meditation

Everyone should read all these books again and again throughout their lives. They will enrich you beyond measure.

1. Sri Sri Ravi Shankar, *An Intimate Note to the Sincere Seeker*, Sri Sri Publications, 2010
2. Sri Sri Ravi Shankar, *Commentary on the Yoga Sutras of Patanjali*, Sri Sri Publications, 2016
3. Narasimhan, Bhanumathi, *Gurudev: On the Plateau of the Peak*, Westland Books, 2018
4. Swami Venkatesanada, *Vasishtha's Yoga*, State University of New York Press, 2010
5. *Srimad Bhagawad Gita*, Gita Press

Happiness

Shawn and Emma talk about the science of happiness and positive psychology, giving solid steps to achieve it.

1. Achor, Shawn, *The Happiness Advantage: The Seven Principles That Fuel Success and Performance at Work*, Virgin Digital, 2011
2. Seppala, Emma, *The Happiness Track: How to Apply the Science of Happiness to Accelerate Your Success*, Piatkus, 2016

Food

The first two books are enjoyable reads about why you should eat vegetarian food and what happens to food once you put it in your mouth. Russ Parsons talks about the alchemy of food—quite an interesting read if you want to know the science of what happens when you dice an onion instead of slicing it.

The other books are my favourite recipe books. Some have non-vegetarian recipes in them, but with a little bit of innovation these recipes can be made vegetarian. Vidhu Mittal's book is outstanding for Indian food recipes and Niloufer's passion for food and cooking, especially Parsi recipes, is evident on every page.

I own almost all of Jamie Oliver's books. I enjoy his style and his recipes. His book of Italian recipes is my most favourite.

The Moosewood Cookbook has many interesting recipes to experiment with. *Oh She Glows* is an exclusively vegan cookbook, one of the finest I have seen for vegan recipes.

1. Robbins, John and Ocean, *Voices of the Food Revolution*, Conari Press, 2013
2. Enders, Giulia, *Gut: The inside Story of Our Body's Most Under-rated Organ*, Speaking Tiger, 2015
3. Parsons, Russ, *How to Read a French Fry: And Other Stories of Intriguing Kitchen Science*, Houghton Mifflin Harcourt, 2001

4. Mittal, Vidhu, *Pure & Simple: Homemade Indian Vegetarian Cuisine*, Lustre, 2008
5. King, Niloufer Ichaporia, *My Bombay Kitchen: Traditional and Modern Parsi Home Cooking*, University of California Press, 2007
6. Oliver, Jamie, *Jamie's Italy*, Penguin, 2010
7. Katzen, Mollie, *The New Moosewood Cookbook*, Ten Speed Press, 2000
8. Liddon, Angela, *The Oh She Glows Cookbook*, Penguin, 2014

Exercise

These books are for reference only. Please don't try to learn exercise from a book. Get a good personal trainer, at least to begin with. Or you run the risk of seriously injuring yourself.

1. Campbell, Adam, *The Men's Health Big Book of Exercises*, Rodale, 2010
2. Campbell, Adam, *The Women's Health Big Book of Exercises*, Rodale, 2016
3. Rippetoe, Mark, *Starting Strength: Basic Barbell Training*, The Aasgaard Company, 2011

Bach Flower Remedies

Dr Edward Bach's book, *The 12 Healers*, is available as a free download from the Bach Centre website, www.bachcentre.com, and is a superb introduction to his system. The website has many additional resources for learning about the remedies, as well as details about courses that can certify you to be a Bach practitioner.

Over the years, various practitioners have found it to be very terse and have written books of their own to augment his work. My favourite three among the scores of books I have read on the subject are listed below.

1. Macwhinnie, Lynn, *Emotional Wisdom with Bach Flower Remedies*, eBookPartnership.com, 2014
2. Scheffer, Mechthild, *Bach Flower Therapy: Theory and Practice*, Healing Arts Press, 1986
3. Barnard, Julian and Martine, *The Healing Herbs of Edward Bach*, Ashgrove Publishing, 1995

Others

Surely You're Joking is Richard Feynman's autobiography (the man behind the Technique)—it is superbly written and a joy to read.

The Circadian Code starts really well, but then drags on and on… However, it has a lot of information about the 'when', from exercise to sleeping and everything in-between.

Douglas Adams' book on the dangerous threats that our environment is facing is alarming and funny at the same time. It's a must-read.

No reading list by me would be complete without a few books from P.G. Wodehouse. His hilarious stories from Blandings Caste, involving the ninth Earl of Emsworth, his sister Connie and his beloved pig, the Empress of Blandings, will leave you rolling on the floor with mirth. There are always impostors who need to be exposed and broken hearts that need repairing at Blandings…

1. Feynman, Richard P., *Surely You're Joking Mr. Feynman!*, Vintage, 1992
2. Panda, Satchin, *The Circadian Code*, Rodale, 2018
3. Adams, Douglas and Carwardine, Mark, *Last Chance to See*, Arrow, 2009
4. Om Swami, *The Wellness Sense*, Black Lotus, 2015
5. Wodehouse, P.G., *The Golf Stories*,
6. Wodehouse, P.G., *The Blandings Castle Stories*